The Living Together Kit

by

Attorneys Toni Ihara & Ralph Warner

Edited by
Robin Leonard

Please Read This: We have done our best to give you useful and accurate information concerning living together. But please be aware that laws and procedures are constantly changing, and that you have a responsibility to check the information you read here before relying on it. Of necessity, neither Nolo Press nor the authors make any guarantees concerning the information in this publication or the use to which it is put.

NOLO PRESS • 950 PARKER STREET • BERKELEY CA 94710

IMPORTANT

Nolo Press is committed to keeping its books up-to-date. Each new printing, whether or not it is called a new edition, has been completely revised to reflect the latest law changes. This book was reprinted and updated on the last date indicated below. Before you rely on information in it, you might wish to call Nolo Press (415/549-1976) to check whether a later printing or new edition has been issued.

PRINTING HISTORY

New *Printing* means there have been some minor changes, but usually not enough so that people will need to trade in or discard an earlier printing of the same edition. Obviously, this is a judgment call and any change, no matter how minor, might affect you. New *Edition* means one or more major, or a number of minor, law changes since the previous edition.

First Edition	1974
(Sex, Living Together & the Law)	
Second Printing	1976
Second Edition	1978
Third Edition	1979
Fawcett Editions	1979, 1980
German Edition	1980
Fourth Edition	1984
Third Printing	1986
Fifth Edition	1988
Sixth Edition	1990

Editor	LESLIE IHARA ARMISTEAD
Production Director	JACKIE CLARK
Production Assistant	STEPHANIE HAROLDE
Book Design and Layout	TONI IHARA
Illustrations	LINDA ALLISON
Index	SAYRE VAN YOUNG
Printing	DELTA LITHOGRAPH

Ihara, Toni
    The living together kit / by Toni Ihara & Ralph Warner ; research associate, Robin Leonard.
       p.   cm.
    ISBN 087337-118-6 : $17.95
      1. Unmarried couples--Legal status, laws, etc.--United States.
2. Unmarried couples--Legal status, laws, etc.--United States-
-Forms.   I. Warner, Ralph E.   II. Leonard, Robin.   III. Title.
KF538.I35   1990
346.7301'6--dc20
[347.30616]   89-77596
                                CIP

A LITTLE HISTORY

Carmen Massey and Ralph Warner co-authored the original legal guide for unmarried couples in 1974. It was entitled *Sex, Living Together and the Law* and was a successful and well-received book. In 1976 just as a new edition was being planned, Carmen died. Her death was a severe blow to all who knew her. She was truly a person who gave more than she received, and whose light and good energy made her loved by many.

It wasn't until 1978 that those of us at Nolo Press felt clear enough to go on with revisions for the book. By this time, *Sex, Living Together and the Law* was hopelessly out-of-date and it was necessary to create a new book, *The Living Together Kit*. Some of Carmen's original excellent work was still topical, and an arrangement was made with her estate to include it in *The Living Together Kit*. Even today, over fifteen years later, some of it remains. We feel good that our friend's positive ideas and common sense are still available to help people.

AND A BIG THANK YOU

Many old friends, and a few new ones, helped us make this a better book. We would particularly like to thank Linda Allison, Leslie Armistead, David Brown, Keija Kimura, Robin Leonard, Walter Warner, and Sarah Weisman. Special thanks to Gary Kitajo, Ron Lomax, and Michele Anderson, whose kind assistance has made doing legal research almost a pleasure.

RECYCLE YOUR OUT-OF-DATE BOOKS & GET 25% OFF YOUR NEXT PURCHASE!

Using an old edition can be dangerous if information in it is wrong. Unfortunately, laws and legal procedures change often. To help you keep up to date we extend this offer. If you cut out and deliver to us the title portion of the cover of any old Nolo book we'll give you a 25% discount off the retail price of any new Nolo book. For example, if you have a copy of TENANT'S RIGHTS, 4th edition and want to trade it for the latest CALIFORNIA MARRIAGE AND DIVORCE LAW, send us the TENANT'S RIGHTS cover and a check for the current price of MARRIAGE & DIVORCE, less a 25% discount. Information on current prices and editions is listed in the NOLO NEWS. Generally speaking, any book more than two years old is of questionable value. Books more than four or five years old are a menace. This offer is to individuals only.

OUT OF DATE = DANGEROUS

LTK 1/90

Table of Contents

Chapter 5. Contracts

Chapter 6. Renting and Sharing a Home

Chapter 7. Buying a House

Chapter 8. Starting a Family

Chapter 9. You and Your Prior Family

Chapter 10. Moving On—Dividing Things

Chapter 11. Death

Chapter 12. More Legal Help

Appendix

Introduction

The purpose of this book is to present the legal rules for unmarried couples who live together so that they can deal with essential issues in a spirit of cooperation that allows them to relax and to stay in touch with their love for one another.[1] Our biases are toward simplicity and fairness.

Many people approach the law relating to unmarried couples with hesitation, if not downright revulsion. Perhaps even the thought of introducing "unromantic" legal concepts into a personal relationship based on love and trust raises your hackles. And why not? The American legal system as it now exists is commonly used in an aggressive attempt to screw every last nickel out of an adversary. Lawyers, some of whom have evolved no further than the hired guns of Dodge City, are too often the point people for an adversarial system having little to do with fairness, truth or the resolution of disputes.

Although law in America is seldom used to minimize conflict and paranoia, there' s no reason it can' t be. This book assumes that people of good heart can craft legal rules to sow the seeds of future understanding in personal relationships, and that law, combined with good instincts, can be used to mortar the bricks of a relationship.

Like it or not, however, there are rules and regulations that already apply to unmarried couples. You can ignore them for a while, but they're unlikely to ignore you, at least over the long term. So, your first job is to understand how the law affects your relationship. Once the rules are understood, you and your partner will want to talk, and decide together how to use rules in a positive way. Then you' ll want to record your agreements in writing.

To help you, we provide sample written documents—living together contracts, real property agreements, wills, durable powers of attorney and paternity statements. It's up to you to adapt them to your needs. We advise you to write things down, not because we believe most people are untrustworthy, but because we know that memories tend to blur over time. We ask you to make a small leap of faith and believe us when we say that sensible written agreements can do much to increase trust and harmony. They're best made when you think that you'll never need them, not when storm warnings are flying.

We believe that most unmarried couples can safely and easily master the majority of legal rules that affect them. We confess to our own hostility to what passes for justice in this country and to our bias against lawyers as a group. From time to time, however, we do suggest that certain complicated situations need a lawyer's advice, but understand that doubtless numbers of people would advise you to rely on lawyers far more often.

One point worthy of mention now, concerns the criminal laws in some states that regulate the sexual and living practices of adults. As you'll learn or perhaps already know, law books are full of rules which everyone, including the police, usually ignore. Many of you, as you go about your daily life, are technically law breakers, even though you're conducting your life in an ethical and practical way. Perhaps you'll feel, as we do, that many of these regressive laws need changing, and will realize that the rights of privacy we often take for granted will never exist unless we make our collective voices heard.

---

[1] Nolo Press also publishes *A Legal Guide for Lesbian & Gay Couples* by Hayden Curry and Denis Clifford. This is an extremely useful book, which we heartily recommend. Because of this book, we don't attempt to meet the specific needs of gay and lesbian couples here.

Chapter One

Living Together: Old Wine In a New Glass

WHEN WE WROTE the first edition of this book, we dealt with only the legal and practical problems faced by unmarried couples. Living together itself seemed to be such a sensible, wholesome and easy way to live that we included no material on the emotional side. It never occurred to us that some people still thought unmarried couples were controversial, or that people would care about:

- Why some couples choose to live together rather than get married;

- What you do or say when family members accuse you of "living in sin;"

- How you handle attacks from people who believe that a woman who lives with a man is a prostitute; or

- How you introduce an unmarried couple at a party.

As it turned out, of course, we were wrong. We learned about our narrow vision when we did a publicity tour. We were on national television, ready to recite the legal do's and don't's for unmarried couples when writing a contract, buying a house or having a child. We had ten pounds of legal treatises tucked in our bags, should we be asked a particularly complicated question. But law rarely came up. We were usually asked about our morality (or the assumed lack thereof), lifestyle, sexuality, religion, dishwashing habits, and how we introduced each other at a party. More than once, sincerely outraged people accused us of contributing to the downfall of the moral and ethical standards of America. Although our egos were gratified that anyone would think that we were that influential, we were shocked to learn that many saw us as immoral and depraved.

As we traveled, airports and hotels changed, but the questions were remarkably similar. The few differences were in phrasing, not content. A detached, "professional" interviewer would ask "Why do U.S. Census Bureau statistics show that so many people are living together these days rather than getting married?" while a feisty Mike Wallace or Barbara Walters type would just ask, "Why don't you two get married if you really care for one another?". The fatherly, concerned questioner (usually an ex-newsman with wonderful gray hair, a slightly lecherous twinkle in his eye and big white teeth), would put his hand on Toni's knee and say, "My dear, now tell me honestly, in your heart of hearts wouldn't you really like to be Mrs. Ralph Warner?"

We were unprepared for all of this and didn't respond very well. We'd been close friends and business partners for many years, and had been living together for several. Our relationship had evolved with little thought to our legal status. This may sound strange, but our home was (and still is) in Berkeley, California, where living together as part of a heterosexual couple is considered almost boringly straight. We hadn't gotten married, because, well, we hadn't. Toni was a child of the sixties and never quite wanted to leave the Aquarian age; Ralph, a few years older, had been married twice in his twenties and concluded that he wasn't very good at it.

How did we handle our predicament? We first tried to act lawyerly, that is, we mumbled a lot of complicated words that didn't mean much. But people are too media wise to be impressed by legal gobbledygook and we could feel the TV sets being switched off from Seattle to Scarsdale. So, we looked at each other and talked about our relationship. Surrounded as we were by lights, camera, an ever-smiling host and an occasional live audience, this wasn't easy. But gradually, we began to make sense to ourselves. We weren't experts on why people share a home without license or ceremony, but we had something to say about ourselves. Luckily, we didn't lose it under mock legal profundities and sociological doubletalk. We were living together because we loved each other a whole lot, and it seemed more romantic not to reduce that love to a piece of paper.

Of course, this still ducked the larger question. We had developed some ideas as to why so many people are living together, but they were nothing we could explain in two and a half minutes, between a deodorant commercial and a few words on how to deal with constipation. Instead of trying, we saved them for subsequent editions of this book. So here goes.

To understand why in the last quarter of the twentieth century millions of people find security and self-expression in living together—as opposed to getting marriage, living in a commune, living alone or living in a tree with an orangutan—let's review a little history. The past may not help chart the future, but by looking at our footprints, we can at least learn how we got to where we are.

Let's go back about one-hundred years. Chester Arthur and Grover Cleveland were in the White House, the steam engine and the steel rail were still hot stuff, Victoria of England headed an empire upon which the sun never set, and the census of 1890 showed that the majority of Americans lived on the farm. For our purposes, this last fact is most important. Although the industrial juggernaut that would eventually pull nearly everyone into urban areas had been a growing force for several decades, most of our great-grandparents still followed a plow, pulled by old Dobbin.

Rural America is part of our story because many American values and ideals—especially the notion of "family"—formed there. Farm work was hard—one or two people couldn't do it alone—and farms were often lonely and isolated. Friends, neighbors and hired help were important, but in harvesting the fields, or keeping each other warm on a winter night, nothing substituted for a large family. If you were going to raise corn, you had to raise the corn pickers as well. Thus, an enduring marriage and a stable family made great sense.

This was the also Victorian Age, and so much was said about marriage and the sanctity of family being God's will, but for most, economics, not religion, was the reason to have a big family.

The 1890 family commonly included maiden Aunt Bess, slightly retarded Uncle Charley, Grandmother Elvira, a house full of kids and several hired hands. But as the century turned and the Industrial Revolution hit high gear, things changed fast. The steady flow of people to the city became a flood, and the economics of the family unit changed. Food and space weren't nearly as abundant in the city as they'd been back on the farm, and suddenly Bess, Charley, Elvira and even the kids were in the way.

Within a few decades, mama and papa had new concerns:

Papa: "My, it costs a lot to raise kids these days, to say nothing of fixing their teeth and sending them to college."

Mama: "You're right, dear, perhaps we should only have one or two."

And so it happened that one style of living gave way to another and the family shrank like a wool blanket in a hot wash.

But while people seemed able to change their clothes, jobs, skills, educations and most things necessary to keep up with the twentieth century, they didn't change their relationships. Indeed, in response to the new society cultivated by Henry Ford, Albert Einstein, Tom Edison and Wilbur and Orville Wright, people reached for something "solid" to anchor their lives on. Religion worked for some, and a sense of tradition for others, but for most Americans in the mid-twentieth century, marriage and family were the bricks used to build personal security.

Sadly, however (and now we're reaching the main reason why so many have rejected marriage today), many of the families built in the decades after the second world war were shallow and truncated—almost nonexistent in comparison to the extended family of rural America. Many in the generation held on tight to the myth of the family, but let the substance slip away. But America wallpapered the countryside with single family houses, each one big enough for Mommy, Daddy, Billy, Sue and Spot.

For many, this suburban family life worked successfully. But others found it isolating and stultifying, with little opportunity to deviate from the norm. The different personalities and eccentricities that had been a part of the extended family were filtered out, and everyone was expected to fit in. Perhaps it's an understatement, but living in places such as Lafayette, Larkspur, Larchmont, La Mirada and Lincoln Park during the fifties and early sixties wasn't very sexy.

But then came the late sixties and early seventies, years of reaction and rebellion when, with great love and great fun and great pain, the baby boom generation turned the beliefs and value systems of their parents upside down. Sexual freedom, women's rights, gay rights, LSD and grass, loose work styles—yes, even crooked teeth—were in style and the suburbs were definitely out.

But the youthful—sometimes nutty—energy of the late sixties and early seventies wasn't the stuff of which lives are built. The barricades were fun for a while, but there wasn't much time for home cooking and a job well done. Woodstocks, peace marches, civil rights marches, women's marches, teach-ins, love-ins, and be-ins didn't keep you warm on a cold December night. So the generation learned an old lesson—freedom is the flip side of commitment, and being oneself must be measured against being intimate with others.

Against this background, living together became popular in the mid-seventies. For many, it was a way to pull back from the sexual revolution without going back to Levittown. For others, it was a search for a workable small family at a time when recreating the extended family of the 19th century was unrealistic (communes, an effort to do this, rarely lasted long), and marriage, which came with a heavy load of boredom and divorce, was unpalatable. For others still, it was a trial period before marriage—to see if this was the person you wanted to spend the rest of your life with. If it didn't work, you went separate ways without the mess of divorce.

Living together also provided a way for couples to define their relationship without the state's burdens and restrictions, and without the traditional notions tied to marriage. This was especially important for women seeking to escape the confines of marriage—a historically sexist institution.

But then came Michele and Lee Marvin, who dragged their pain and pride cross our television screens every evening and shocked us out of the idea that living together was simple. My God, there was the naked truth—ending an unmarried relationship could be every bit as nasty and painful as getting a divorce. Much like Mr. McGregor catching Peter Rabbit in the garden, the lawyers had arrived and the fun was over. And right behind the doom-laden esquires came the media, with minicams and portable mikes, begging someone to explain what all the fuss about living together was about. But, sadly,television is never very good at poetry, and although they rolled miles of film and interviewed scores of newly minted experts like us, they completely missed the optimism, joy, freedom and trust that so many people who live together experience.

But what now? Have the muddy legalisms of the *Marvin* case and other big name palimony suits ruined the essence of living together, just as sky-high divorce rates have done so much to tarnish the idea of marriage? Will the average couple conclude that because living together can involve as many legal complications as marriage, they may as well pick up a license?

Not so far.

The number of unmarried couples continues to increase and gives every sign of increasing further in the 1990s. Marriage won't go away, but it's less likely to be automatically adopted by many couples (younger ones, especially) until it becomes more open-ended, or until people have had an opportunity to get to really know the person they marry. Indeed, recent studies show that, for many couples, living together can be a sort of spring training period for a couple to prepare for marriage,[1] while still having the easy option of deciding not to go through with it.

This is where the history lesson ends. Now let's get on with what this book is really about— legal and practical information for unmarried couples, either those who will remain unmarried or those who eventually marry, to cope creatively with the day-to-day problems of how their relationship intersects with the law.

---

[1] See *American Couples*, Blumstein & Schwartz (William Morrow & Co., 1983). The authors studied nearly 10,000 married, cohabiting, gay male and lesbian couples. Although 49% of the married, 16% of the gay male and 8% of the lesbian couples had been together over 10 years, only 1% of the cohabiting couples had been together that long; the authors found that most cohabiting couples eventually married.

Chapter

Two

Sex, Living Together and the Law

TO UNDERSTAND HOW sex, living together and the law are related, it's time for a short vocabulary lesson:

Adultery—voluntary sexual intercourse by a married person and somebody other than a lawful spouse. A single act is called an adulterous act or an act of adultery. When two persons are living together and at least one is married to someone else, this is called adulterous cohabitation.

Bigamy—the crime of intentionally marrying a person while knowing that you're still legally married to someone else. A *bigamist* is a person who commits bigamy. A *bigamous marriage* is a marriage contracted while at least one party was still married to another person.

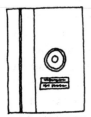

BIGAMY

Chaste—virtuous. A married, widowed or divorced person is described as chaste even though that person is enjoying (if married) or had previously enjoyed (if widowed or divorced), a sexual relationship, as long as the relationship occurred between persons lawfully married to each other.

COHABITATION

Cohabitation—two persons of the opposite sex living together and having a sexual relationship without being married. In a few states, cohabitation includes having regular or occasional sexual relations without living together, but this is unusual.

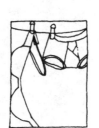

COMMON LAW MARRIAGE

Common Law Marriage—a form of marriage, valid in only 14 jurisdictions (see chart in Section B), in which an opposite sex couple lives together for a long period of time with the intent of being married, and holds itself out to the world as married, though no marriage ceremony ever took place.

Conjugal—relating to marriage. Conjugal rights are a husband and wife's rights to mutual love, affection, comfort, companionship and sex.

Copulation—sexual intercourse; coupling.

Co-respondent—the "other man" or "other woman" named in divorce papers alleging adultery.

FINE

Criminal Conversation—a lawsuit brought by a husband against a man who has sex with the husband's wife. This lawsuit is no longer available in most states.

Felony—a serious crime usually punishable by imprisonment for more than a year.

Fine—a sum of money that must be paid to a court by a person convicted of a crime.

Fornication—generally means voluntary sexual intercourse between unmarried people of the opposite sex. In some states, one of the parties may be married, but most states consider that to be adultery, not fornication.

Incest—sexual intercourse or marriage between close relatives. All states prohibit sexual relations between parent (including step, grand, great-grand, etc.) and child (including step, grand, great-grand, etc.), siblings (including half and step brothers and sisters) and aunt or uncle with niece or nephew. Also, thirty states prohibit marriages between first cousins.

Lewd and Lascivious—a term meaning obscene, inciting to lust, which is used in criminal statutes to describe sexual conduct short of actual sexual intercourse. Exposing oneself in public, for example, is a lewd and lascivious act.

Meretricious Relationship—some states, especially where fornication is illegal, describe cohabitation arrangements as meretricious, meaning of an "unlawful sexual nature."

Misdemeanor—a criminal offense less serious than a felony, usually punishable by a fine and/or a jail sentence of less than one year.

Polygamy—intentionally having more than two spouses at a time. (Intentionally having two spouses at once is called bigamy.) Polygamy is a crime in every state.

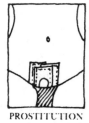

PROSTITUTION

Prostitution—engaging in sexual relations for money. Prostitution is illegal in all states except Nevada, where it is legal in only a few select counties.

Putative marriage—where a couple thinks they are legally married, but for some technical reason (for example, the clergyperson who conducted the marriage had no authority to do so) they are not. The law treats these couples as though they were legally married.

SEDUCE

Putative spouse—a person who reasonably, but erroneously, thinks he or she is married.

Seduce—to induce a person to surrender his or her chastity. The act of seducing is called "seduction." Seduction lawsuits were brought by fathers against men who induced the unmarried daughters into having sex. Most states have eliminated seduction suits.

Sodomy—generally refers to any "unnatural" sexual intercourse (such as anal sex). Some states define it vaguely (unnatural sexual intercourse or crimes against nature), while other states prohibit very specific acts (anal intercourse of a male with another male, anal or vaginal intercourse of a person with an animal, or the touching of the genitals of one person with the mouth of another person).

Spouse—Either member of a married couple; a husband or a wife.

A. If It Feels Good, It May Be Illegal

IT'S ILLEGAL TO HAVE SEX with a porcupine in Florida, to have unnatural sex in Arizona, to make love with someone you're not married to in Utah and to live together (cohabit) in South Carolina. The maximum prison sentences for these heinous crimes vary from six months to 14 years. Pretty silly, huh?

Whether or not it's legal for you to live and have sex with a person of the opposite sex without getting married depends on where you live. Given our country's puritanical roots, it's no surprise that we haven't completely shaken off the sneaking suspicion that pleasure is tantamount to sin. In the past, if it felt good, it was probably illegal no matter where you lived. Today, although law books are still filled with an array of sexual prohibitions, many states have dropped the old sexual taboos, be it in response to the "sexual revolution" or just a pragmatic realization that it's silly to have laws regulating the private areas of people's lives.

Most of this law reform happened when state legislatures decriminalized private consensual acts between adults,[1] doing away with crimes like sodomy, cohabitation and adultery. This trend has gathered momentum over the past decade and seems likely to continue.

States where private sexual acts between consenting adults is legal:[2]

Alaska	Iowa	Oregon
California	Maine	Pennsylvania
Colorado	Nebraska	South Dakota
Connecticut	New Hampshire	Washington
Delaware	New Jersey	West Virginia
Hawaii	New York	Wisconsin
Illinois	North Dakota	Wyoming
Indiana		

Because the law in this area changes, this list may not be up-to-date when you read this. If your state law still concerns itself with how you fit your bodies together, call your state legislator to find out if there are any pending bills to decriminalize consensual sexual acts. If so, send a letter in support. Obsolete laws are dangerous and unfair. Although few of the comic book sex codes are rigorously enforced, occasionally an old statute falls off a shelf and hits somebody on the head. If it happens to be your head—you won't think it's very funny.

Another approach to wiping out-of-date sex laws off the books has been promoted by civil libertarians. Rather than tackling the problem one state at a time, they're hoping for a U.S. Supreme Court decision declaring the laws which regulate private consensual behavior among adults to be an unconstitutional invasion of privacy. The Supreme Court, unfortunately, rejected that argument in 1986,[3] upholding the constitutionality of Georgia's sodomy statute when applied to gay people. (The Court didn't address whether it would be constitutional if enforced against heterosexuals.) Let's hope this case is the only one that goes in that direction.

States are free to offer their citizens more protection than is given by the federal constitution. New Jersey courts have voided that state's fornication and sodomy laws on the grounds that they

---

[1]Much of it happens subtly. State legislatures re-write their criminal codes and just drop the consensual sodomy, fornication and cohabitation laws. The legislators never have to answer to conservative voters, because few voters learn the details of the newly codified criminal laws.

---

[2]In most states, minors within a year or two of the age of majority may live together with parental approval, but will likely face action by juvenile authorities if the parents oppose.

[3]*Bowers v. Hardwick*, 106 S. Ct. 2841 (1986).

violated the right of privacy.[4] In the landmark decision, *State v. Saunders*, the New Jersey Supreme Court said: "We conclude that the conduct statutorily defined as fornication involves, by its very nature, a fundamental personal choice. Thus, the statute infringes upon the right of privacy." The Supreme Court of Florida ruled similarly concerning fornication, as has New York's highest court concerning sodomy.[5] Unfortunately, both the Maryland and Rhode Island courts upheld their state sodomy laws in 1980.[6]

You may wonder how these cases come before state courts in the first place. In *State v. Saunders* (the New Jersey case), the defendant was originally charged with rape. He successfully defended his case, claiming that he and the alleged victim were engaged in consensual intercourse. He was acquitted, but then charged with, and found guilty of, fornication.

[4] *State v. Saunders*, 381 A.2d 333 (N.J. 1977) and *State v. Ciuffini*, 395 A.2d 904 (N.J. 1978).

[5] *Purvis v. State*, 377 So.2d 674 (Fla. 1979) and *People v. Onofre*, 434 N.Y. S.2d 947 (N.Y. 1980).

[6] *Kelly v. State*, 412 A.2d 1274 (Mary. 1980) and *State v. Santos*, 413 A.2d 58 (R.I. 1980).

STATES WHICH PROHIBIT SEX ACTS BETWEEN CONSENTING ADULTS

	Fornication Illegal	Cohabitation Illegal	Sodomy and/or Oral Copulation Between Consenting Adults Illegal
Alabama	No	No	Yes
Arizona	No	Yes	Yes
Arkansas	No	No	Yes
Florida	No	Yes	Yes
Georgia[7]	Yes	No	Yes
Idaho	Yes	Yes	Yes
Kansas[8]	No	No	Yes
Kentucky	No	No	Yes
Louisiana	No	No	Yes
Maryland	No	No	Yes
Massachusetts	Yes	No	Yes
Michigan	No	Yes	Yes
Minnesota	No	No	Yes
Mississippi	Yes	Yes	Yes
Missouri	No	No	Yes
Montana	No	No	Yes
Nevada	No	No	Yes
New Mexico	No	Yes	No
North Carolina	Yes	Yes	Yes
Oklahoma	No	No	Yes
Rhode Island[7]	Yes	No	Yes
South Carolina[9]	Yes	No	Yes
Tennessee	No	No	Yes
Texas[8]	No	No	Yes
Utah[7]	Yes	No	Yes
Virginia	Yes	Yes	Yes
Washington, D.C.	Yes	No	Yes

---

[7] In Georgia, Rhode Island, and Utah, there's no separate statute for cohabitation, but it is probably illegal under the fornication statute.

[8] In Kansas and Texas, the sodomy laws only prohibit homosexual conduct.

[9] South Carolina's fornication statute defines fornication as "living together and carnal knowledge."

As you can see from the table, cohabitation, fornication and sodomy are still crimes in many states. If you're both over 18 and neither of you is married to anyone else, however, you can, for the most part, consider yourself safe from criminal prosecution for your private, hetero-sexual activities. Most sex laws are either never enforced or are used to harass gay people.

Of course, the law is different concerning violent sexual acts, sex with children, prostitution or sexual acts in public. Laws against these activities are enforced, and at least in the first two categories, should be. We're also not concerned with bigamy or incest. Both are illegal in all states, although bigamy is seldom prosecuted.

To find out more about laws (and penalties) regulating fornication, cohabitation, sodomy, oral copulation and assorted "unnatural acts" in your state, see Chapter 12, *More Legal Help*.

B. Common Law Marriage

THERE'S WIDESPREAD BELIEF that if you live with a person for a long time you're automatically married. In most states, including California and New York, this is not true, as any marriage must have a license and ceremony. Fourteen states, however, do recognize these "common law marriages." But even there, merely living together doesn't create a common law marriage—you must intend to be married and hold yourselves out to the world as married. And, despite much belief to the contrary, the length of time you live together doesn't decide whether a common law marriage exists. No state law or court decision says seven years or ten years or whatever is needed for a common law marriage. The length of time you live together would help only determine your intent to have a common law

marriage, should the question ever wind up in court.[10]

There's one little trick in this area, however. A state that doesn't have common law marriage will recognize such a marriage that was properly formed in a state that does have them. For example, Colorado has common law marriages; California does not. If Bob and Carol started living together in Los Angeles in 1967, are still living together and have never moved, they're not legally married, even if they thought they were and they wanted to be. If, however, they started living together in Colorado in 1975 with the intention of forming a common law marriage and moved to California in 1990, both Colorado and California will recognize the marriage as valid.

The chart below shows which states recognize common law marriages. If you have any questions regarding the status of your relationship, do some research as to your state's law. The question of whether there's sufficient "intent" to form a marriage is usually tricky. There are no guidelines; it's normally found from the facts of each situation. Using the same last name and filing joint income tax returns are important.

If you want to protect what you consider a marriage, or prevent yourself from being married against your wish, take steps now—don't wait until you split up. If you do break up and have a common law marriage, you must end your relationship by divorce, and you cannot legally remarry until that time, just like a marriage with a ceremony.

---

[10]This can happen if one common law spouse files for divorce. More commonly, it occurs when a member of an unmarried couple dies without a will or alternate estate plan. In this situation, the survivor will not inherit under intestate succession laws unless he or she can establish a common law marriage.

States Recognizing Common Law Marriage

Alabama	Iowa	Pennsylvania
Colorado	Kansas	Rhode Island
District of Columbia	Montana	South Carolina
Georgia	Ohio	Texas
Idaho	Oklahoma	

States Not Recognizing Common Law Marriage

Alaska	Maryland	North Carolina
Arizona	Massachusetts	North Dakota
Arkansas	Michigan	Oregon
California	Minnesota	South Dakota
Connecticut	Mississippi	Tennessee
Delaware	Missouri	Utah
Florida	Nebraska	Vermont
Hawaii	Nevada	Virgin Islands
Illinois	New Hampshire[11]	Washington
Indiana	New Jersey	West Virginia
Kentucky	New Mexico	Wisconsin
Louisiana	New York	Wyoming
Maine		

If you live together in a state recognizing common law marriages and don't wish to be married, it's a good idea to sign a statement making it clear you don't intend to be married. If you use the same last name and/or mix property together, it's essential that you do this. Here's a sample you may want to use separately or integrate into one of the contracts in Chapter 5, *Contracts*.

SAMPLE AGREEMENT

Wanda Oglethorpe (aka Walters) and Walter Walters agree as follows:

1. That they've been and plan to continue living together as two free, independent beings and that neither has ever intended to enter into any form of marriage, common law or otherwise.

_____   _____
Date   Wanda Oglethorpe

_____   _____
Date   Walter Walters

---

[11]Living together in New Hampshire for at least three years until one partner dies, however, results in a valid marriage for inheritance purposes.

Chapter

Three

Practical Aspects of Living Together

IN CHAPTERS 4, *Living Together Contracts and the Law,* and 5, *Contracts,* we discuss living together contracts, and in the Appendix we provide four basic models (short-form keeping everything separate, short-form pooling income, long-form keeping everything separate and long-form pooling income). Many of this chapter's topics relate to living together contracts.

A. Getting Together

WHEN TWO PEOPLE come together to walk the same path for a while, they bring not only themselves and their love for one another, but also their debts, animals, prior relationships and the like. We'll let you work out the fights over the goldfish, Great Dane and former in-laws, but let us offer our input in other areas.

1. Debts

Even though you live with someone, you take absolutely no responsibility for his or her debts. Your wages cannot be attached and your property cannot be taken to pay for your friend's overdue bills. If your friend's creditors contact you, a good chuckle should handle the problem. Should your friend declare bankruptcy, your property won't be taken, *as long as you've kept it separate.*

Warning: If your friend has debt problems, do not mix property together (called "commingling") in a joint bank account, by jointly owning a car or in any other way. If you do, you'll have problems explaining to your friend's greedy creditors that a portion of the car, bank account or whatever is yours. Also, don't enter into an agreement to pool and share earnings and accumulations. Instead, sign a contract keeping all property separate (see Contract I in

the Appendix) so that your friend's creditors don't come after you.

2. Property Acquired Before Getting Together

Each person retains complete ownership of all property owned before getting together. In the long-form contracts in the Appendix, we provide for each person listing this separate property (see also Chapter 5, *Contracts*). It isn't legally necessary to do this (the property is already separately owned), but it's wise to avoid later confusion. You can, of course, give your friend some of your property, or a part interest in a piece of your property. If you do this, sign and date a note saying something like "I, Sue Jones, give a one-half interest in my boat to Fred Smith." We've seen a lot of problems where people later disagree as to what was or wasn't a gift.

3. Property Acquired After Getting Together

In our opinion, the easiest and cleanest way to handle your economic affairs is to keep them separate. As we noted above, it's imperative to do this if one of you is having debt problems. But even if you both have A+ credit ratings, you can avoid potential complications by maintaining financial independence and keeping your property and debts separate. Here's how:

- Use your own names and don't pass yourselves off as husband and wife.

- Write a simple agreement keeping your income and property separate. Contracts I and III in the Appendix (discussed in Chapter 5, *Contracts*) accomplish this.

- Don't open joint accounts or make joint purchases unless absolutely necessary. Even if you open a joint bank account, keep one in your own name and don't add extra signatures.

- Don't co-sign a loan or credit agreement for your mate unless you're willing to pay it in full if your friend can't or won't.

- If you purchase an expensive item that you intend to jointly own, set out your agreement in writing. Include how the property is being paid for, what happens if you break up, and, if one of you dies, who gets that person's share (see Chapter 5, Section D). Each of you must sign the agreement and attach a copy to your general living together contract. If you jointly purchase a car, you must follow additional registration procedures (see Section D below).

- If you jointly buy a house or other real property, you'll need to prepare a detailed ownership document (see Chapter 7, *Buying a House*).

One Person Supports the Other

If, in your relationship, one of you works outside the home and supports the other, you need a written understanding of your rights and obligations. This is especially true if the one of you who does not work outside the home makes the purchases and pays the bills. If you split up, one person should not say, "I supported him for ten years, he didn't contribute a thing and now the lazy bum has gone and left me." Or, conversely, "I gave up my career to cook and clean for her for ten years, she said she'd support me forever, and here I am, left alone, with no support."

Be sure that your agreement specifies that each person is free and equal in the living arrangement, whether he brings home the bacon, or cooks it and cleans up the mess afterwards. See Chapter 5, Sections F, H and I for sample contracts.

4. Names

Normally, each partner in an unmarried couple keeps his or her own last name. It's easy, legal and creates few, if any, practical problems. Occasionally, however, an unmarried couple wants to use the same last name (his name, her name or a completely new third name). This, too, can be done with little difficulty, as it's legal to change your last name unless by doing so you invade someone's privacy (don't name yourself Elizabeth Taylor or Malcom Forbes) or attempt to defraud someone, such as a creditor.

You can change your name by either using the new name consistently (usage method) or getting a court order (court petition method).[1] The usage method has the obvious advantage of avoiding going to court, but without a court order, it can take years to convince all the private and government agencies that like to know your whereabouts to accept your new name (getting a passport is a particular hassle). While going to court involves an initial bit of trouble, it may be worth it.

Note: If your state recognizes common law marriage (see Chapter 2, Section B) and you use the same last name, you may create an implication that you intend to be married, especially if you hold yourselves out as married. If you want to use the same name, but don't want to be married, sign a brief agreement like the one at the end of Chapter 2, *Sex, Living Together and the Law.*

Also, if your state enforces written, oral and implied living together contracts (more on this in Chapter 4, *Living Together Contracts and the Law*), a court might conclude that by using the

---

[1] *How to Change Your Name* (California Ed.), Loeb & Brown, Nolo Press, gives complete forms and instructions for both types of name change in California.

same last name, combined with other factors (such as a claim that you agreed to pool income), you intended to share your earnings and property. If you wish to keep it all separate, but share your last name, sign an agreement like I or III in the Appendix.

B. Bank Accounts

OUR ADVICE TO ANYONE considering sharing a checking or savings account is: DON'T. If you each have a separate account and pay the agreed-upon expenses, there's no possibility of confusion. Canceled checks serve as receipts. We have seen joint accounts lead to confusion, paranoia and bitterness. Of course, we are prejudiced in this matter. We give the same advice to married couples.

If you insist on having a joint account, you should encounter no problems in opening one. Banks are happy to take care of your money under any names and will assist you in deciding how many signatures you'll need to write a check or make a withdrawal. Whether you decide that only one is needed, or that both of you must sign, you're both responsible for all checks drawn on the account even if your friend empties the account and disappears. And the bank isn't responsible unless two signatures were required for withdrawal.

C. Charge Accounts and Credit Accounts

IF YOU AND YOUR FRIEND want to establish joint charge accounts (where you pay the total bill at once, like American Express) or credit accounts (where you pay a monthly minimum, such as Visa, MasterCard or department stores), we again say DON'T. If you both earn an income, you can

have your own accounts, deal with your creditors on your own terms and not have to worry about the other person's purchases. Of course, some people are determined to share "everything." So if we can't talk you out of it, we might as well give you a hand.

⚠ **Co-Signing is Dangerous.** Even if you have joint bank or credit accounts, be warned: co-signing for a loan—even for an intimate friend—is often a bad idea. A co-signer fully obligates himself to pay the debt if the person taking out the loan fails to do so. The co-signer can be sued for collection, and if he loses, can have his wages and other property garnished if he doesn't pay. No matter how much you care for the person who's asking you to co-sign, most of the time you're asked to co-sign it's, because the other person doesn't have good enough credit to qualify on her own.

1. How to Apply for Credit

Staff members of the Federal Trade Commission are of the opinion that a creditor's refusal to set up a joint account for an unmarried couple is a violation of the Equal Credit Opportunity Act (see Section 2 below). You're unlikely to face such discrimination, however, as most national retail chains will open joint credit accounts for unmarried couples if they have joint accounts at all.[2] After all, they want to have as many people as possible responsible for a debt. If you find a creditor limiting joint accounts to married couples, don't pretend to be married. A little misstatement now can cause big problems later.

---

[2]Some large stores handle the problem by not issuing any joint accounts. If they don't issue joint accounts to married couples, they can't be discriminating by not issuing them to the unmarried. Most stores, however, will let a cardholder authorize additional signatures on his or her account. This allows both people to use the account, but only the person in whose name the account is is legally responsible for the bill.

If you ever file for bankruptcy, the creditor is apt to claim that you fraudulently obtained credit and shouldn't be allowed to get rid of the debt.

If you get a joint account, remember that both of you are legally responsible for all charges made on the account. If Keija lets her cousin Floyd use a card for the account she has with Tomas, and Floyd runs up a $1,000 bill, both Keija and Tomas are legally responsible for the debt, even if Tomas opposed or didn't know about Floyd's use of the card. Or, if Tomas leaves Keija and uses the card on a cross-country spending spree, both he and Keija owe his debts.

To minimize "getting stuck," ask the credit grantor if the account can be structured so that both signatures are required in order to charge. You may find this also cuts down on impulse buying.

If you break up, inform all your joint creditors that you want to close the account immediately. Don't simply divide the accounts and agree that one person can use some of the accounts while the other person uses the others. As long as your name is on an account, you will be liable for all charges. The last thing you'll want to do is paying for your ex-lover's purchases.

Do Joint Accounts Imply a Contract to Share Income?

As we discuss in Chapter 4, *Living Together Contracts and the Law,* in a few states, including California, enforceable contracts between unmarried couples to share earnings and other property can be oral or sometimes even implied from the circumstances of a relationship. Sharing credit and bank accounts might be a factor considered by a court in deciding whether a couple had an implied contract to share income and other property. So if you want to do everything to maximize keeping property ownership separate, it's best not to open joint accounts.

2. Obtaining Credit

A credit grantor needn't extend credit to any particular person. Of course, most normally grant accounts to people considered good financial risks. A person with no apparent source of income, with a history of long periods of unemployment, who regularly pays bills late or misses payments, or who has recently declared bankruptcy obviously isn't a good risk. Also, a person with a low income and many dependents and expenses may not be a good risk. But can a creditor consider factors seemingly unrelated to income or ability to pay?

Federal law prohibits creditors from discriminating on the basis of race, color, religion, national origin, sex, marital status, age or because all or part of a person's income comes from public assistance.[3] Courts have ruled that the

---

[3] The Equal Credit Opportunity Act, 15 U.S.C. 1691.

term "marital status" prevents discrimination against unmarried couples.[4]

This sounds pretty good, especially because the law says that a creditor who discriminates may have to pay the victim $10,000 plus any money that's actually lost as a result of the discrimination. (If the creditor was found to have discriminated against a lot of people, he may have to pay a $500,000 fine.) But—and this is a big but when we try to solve human problems with laws—no one knows what "discrimination" means. For example, asking marital status isn't discrimination if "such inquiry is for the purpose of ascertaining the creditor's rights and remedies applicable to a particular extension of credit, and not to discriminate in a determination of credit-worthiness." This sounds like a pretty fine line. Also, a creditor may consider state property laws in deciding whether to extend credit. This means that a creditor's decision in one state may be okay while it would violate the law in another state.

Specific federal regulations say that a creditor:

- cannot require the use of a married name, but must allow credit to be issued in either your birth-given name or a combined surname.

- can require you to reveal alimony and child support payments you must make, but not payments you receive, unless you rely on them to establish your income for credit purposes.

- may not ignore your income from child support or alimony payments in determining your creditworthiness, but may consider how likely they are to be paid.

- may not ignore income from a part-time job.

- may not ask questions about your birth control practices, or whether you intend to have children.

- cannot terminate your account or require a re-application if you change your name or marital status unless there's evidence you're unwilling or unable to pay your bill.

- must inform you of any reason you are denied credit.

Few cases have tested the Equal Credit Opportunity Act. Since its passage, however, unmarried couples have had fewer obstacles in opening joint accounts. If you feel you were discriminated against, contact the nearest regional office of the Federal Trade Commission (for non-bank related problems) or the Federal Reserve Board (for bank-related problems). Even consider contacting an attorney to bring a lawsuit on your behalf. (See Chapter 12, *More Legal Help.*)

3. Credit Reporting Agencies

Credit reporting agencies (usually referred to as credit bureaus) specialize in keeping credit files on individuals. They are often part of, or have close relationships with, bill collectors. Creditors, landlords, employers and others contribute information to these files; in return, they contact the bureau and, for a small fee, obtain the information contained in your file.

While credit bureaus claim that they keep only information relating to paying bills, this isn't true. Personal data unrelated to financial matters routinely appears in these files. Some files on unmarried persons who live together are cross-indexed (husbands and wives are always filed together); a bad credit rating on the person you live with may show up on your file and prevent you from obtaining credit. Your file will contain every name you've ever gone by. And if Keija ever applied for credit as "Mrs. Tomas Finnegan,"

---

[4]In a case in the federal circuit for the District of Columbia, a court held that a creditor must treat an unmarried couple jointly applying for credit the same way it would treat a married couple in the same situation. *Markham v. Colonial Mortgage Services Co.*, 605 F.2d 566 (D.C. 1979). A California court held similarly regarding rental housing; if a married couple's income would have been combined to see if the couple qualified, so should the unmarried couple's. *Hess v. Fair Employment & Housing Commission*, 187 Cal.Rptr. 712 (1982).

Tomas may find bills in his file he never signed for.

The Fair Credit Reporting Act, a federal law, lets you go to a credit bureau, pay a small fee and see your file. If you dispute any information in your file, the bureau must verify it, correct it or remove it. If they claim it's correct and you disagree, you can place a letter of up to 100 words in your file, explaining your point of view.

If you open a joint account, not only your "sins," but also the "sins" of your partner may haunt you for a long time. If your friend takes off, leaving a large debt behind that you pay, your slow payment record will still remain in your file for up to seven years. (Credit bureaus can keep information for up to seven years, except for bankruptcies, which can stay for ten.)

D. Buying a Motor Vehicle

IF YOU INTEND THAT the vehicle belong to only one of you, but the other advanced part or all of the down payment in the form of a loan, have the borrower sign a written contract to repay (promissory note), such as the one set out below. Register the vehicle in only the borrower's name.

PROMISSORY NOTE[5]

1. For value received, I promise to pay to the order of

_____
(lender's name), the amount of
$_____ on _____
(date) at _____
_____ (address)

2. In the event the holder of this note prevails in a lawsuit to collect on it, I agree to pay the holder's attorneys' fees in an amount the court finds to be just and reasonable.

_____
Date

_____
Location (City or County)

_____
Name of Borrower

_____
Address of Borrower

_____
Signature of Borrower

If you intend to own the vehicle jointly, you need an agreement outlining the details, especially if only one of you signed the loan but both of you are contributing funds toward its purchase. (See Chapter 5, *Contracts,* Section D.) When you

---

[5]This is a simple promissory note. The borrower fills out the lender's name and address and the amount borrowed, and then signs and dates the form. For a promissory note that provides for installment payments (so much per month), interest or both, see *Simple Contracts for Personal Use,* Elias (Nolo Press).

register the vehicle with the state, put it in both names. You have three choices:

1. "Tomas Finnegan *or* Keija Adams." This creates a joint tenancy in many states; if one person dies, the other automatically inherits the car without going through probate. (See Chapter 11, *Death.*). Without specifically stating joint tenancy, however (see option 3 below), the *"or"* ownership lets either party sell the vehicle without the knowledge or consent of the other.

2. "Tomas Finnegan *and* Keija Adams." This establishes a tenancy in common; both signatures are required to transfer title of the vehicle. At death, however, each person can leave her share to anyone she wishes. If no estate plan is made, the nearest blood relative inherits by intestate succession. If you want your friend to inherit your share (think of how silly it would be to have your mother and your lover co-own a car), see Chapter 11, *Death*.

3. "Tomas Finnegan *and* Keija Adams, as JTRS" (joint tenants with right of survivorship). Not only does this let the survivor automatically inherit without going through probate in the event one of you dies, but also it requires both signatures to transfer title while you're both alive.

Check Your State's Rules: Before relying on this information, check with your state's motor vehicle department. Your state's rules may vary slightly.

E.   Travelling

LOOKING OVER THE NEXT HILL, across an ocean or perhaps for the end of a rainbow seems to be one of our great national joys (some would say diseases). How you'll travel, whether strapped into a great silver bird or wandering slowly down a country road, is less important than the fact that, almost certainly, you'll travel. When you move about together, you may experience those funny (sometimes scary) moments when, with pen poised in hand over motel register, you freeze—and don't know what to write. You may not want to claim to be married if you aren't, but you also don't want to be hassled, and you especially don't want the poetry of your trip ripped off by an obnoxious desk clerk.

Here are some tips. Many places require only one name and signature on the register, though you'll have to state the number of people that will be occupying the room. Start by registering this way and let the clerk ask for more specifics if he wants them. If you both must register, some places prefer that you do it under one last name ("Keija and Tomas Finnegan"), regardless of whether you are married. A few places may hassle you if you register under both names ("Tomas Finnegan and Keija Adams"), and if the issue is forced and you say you're unmarried, refuse to give you lodging.

These days, however, it's unlikely you'll be challenged, as many married women retain their own last names. We talked to a number of hotel chains, including Hilton and Hyatt, and found that they have official policies of "not inquiring" into the status of a couple, even if they register using separate last names.

Sometimes travel discount rates are available to only married couples. Most are extended to any two adults traveling together, but you may still have a chance to save money by saying you're married. Do you run any legal risk by doing this? Probably not. For purposes of tours, tickets and the like, you're pretty safe in claiming the status that will get you the cheapest rate. Because many married couples use different last names these days, no one is apt to ask for proof that you've said "till death do us part."

⚠️ **Warning:** What happens if a hotel or motel discriminates against you because of your marital status? Do you have any legal recourse? Absent a local ordinance prohibiting discrimination in public accommodations on the basis of marital status, which do exist in many major cities and some university towns, the answer is usually NO.

F.   Discrimination in Employment

UNLESS YOU'RE IN AN EXTREMELY important or sensitive position, it's unlikely that a private employer will be aware of, never mind care about, your marital status. If your employer does care, and threatens to fire or demote (or not hire) you when she discovers you live with someone, consider talking to an attorney about whether you can do anything to protect yourself (see Chapter 12, *More Legal Help*). In most cases, little can be done unless you live in an area where it's illegal to discriminate on the basis of one's marital status.[6]

Your only other protection may come from your employer itself. Although private employers are free to fire workers just as an employee is free to resign and move on, some national corporations have recently announced policies of not discriminating on the basis of marital status. If your employer has announced such a policy, you have a legal right to rely on it.

Jobs with local government (state, county or city) or requiring a state license, however, are another story. While police departments, school boards and public libraries are subject to the U.S. Constitution's Fourteenth Amendment requiring "equal protection of the laws," a Supreme Court decision in this area is horrible. The Court, over Justice Marshall's eloquent dissent, refused to hear the case of Rebecca Hollenbaugh and Fred Philburn, who were fired from their jobs at the Carnegie Free Library in Connellsville, Pennsylvania, for living together.[7] The lower courts held that, while there needed to be some relationship between the reason for the firing and job performance, this legal test was met because the couple lived in a state of "open adultery."

Other courts have made wiser decisions. The Virginia Supreme Court, for example, upheld the right of a woman with a live-in-lover to become an attorney.[8] Also, federal district courts in Michigan and Arkansas have upheld police officers' rights to cohabit.[9]

Court decisions involving federal employees have usually given cohabitors more protection. A postal clerk in California was fired because his living with a woman he wasn't married to constituted "immoral conduct." He appealed and the Federal District Court of Northern California decided that his dismissal was unconstitutional because the post office failed to show the connection between his private sex life and his job responsibilities.

---

[6]This is especially true when jobs are considered "sensitive." For example, an unmarried pregnant North Carolina woman who lived with her lover was fired from her job at the YWCA because she was "setting a bad example." *Harvey v. YWCA*, 533 F.Supp. 949 (N.C. 1982).

---

[7]436 F. Supp 1328 (1976); aff'd 578 F.2d 1374 (1977), aff'd (with a dissent by Justice Marshall) 439 U.S. 1052 (1978).

[8]*Cord v. Gibb*, 254 S.E. 2d 71 (Va. 1979).

[9]*Briggs v. North Muskegon Police Dept.*, 563 F. Supp 585 (Mich. 1983); *Swope v. Bratton*, 541 F.Supp. 99 (Ark. 1982).

G. Paying Income Taxes

THIS ISN'T A HANDBOOK on income taxes. It's important that we point out, however, that many unmarried couples who live together pay less in Federal income tax—sometimes substantially less—than do their married counterparts.

1. Comparing Tax Rates for Married and Unmarried Couples

The American tax system is very complicated and illogical. Many people are so confused and intimidated by tax forms and regulations that they hire someone to prepare their returns. Part of the confusion arises in classifying income, taking deductions and claiming exemptions or credits. Part of it arises from the fact that different people pay different rates of tax, depending on their marital or family status.

A person completing a 1040A short form who earned $25,000 income for tax year 1988 (tax due April 15, 1989), for example, paid $4,687 if single, $3,900 if an unmarried head of household, $5,073 if married and filing separately and $3,754 if married filing jointly with a spouse who had no income. Of course, one can't file any way one wants. The filing must correspond to actual family status.

Let's take an example. Tomas and Keija live together and each earn $20,000. For tax year 1988, they each file a 1040A short form and neither itemizes deductions. Each paid $3,287 (filing as a single person), or $6,574 together. Were they married (filing jointly), they'd pay tax on their joint income of $40,000. For tax year 1988, that was $7,447, $873 more than if they paid as single people.

What if Tomas makes $45,000 and Keija $60,000? As single people in tax year 1988, he'd pay $10,380 and she'd pay $14,479.50, or $24,859.50 altogether. Were they married, they'd pay $27,187.50 on their $105,000. They save $2,328 by remaining unmarried.

Of course, this will vary greatly with the individual or couple, especially as we haven't considered dependents or other variables. But as a general rule, working couples with fairly similar incomes will find a tax advantage in not marrying. Couples with only one income, or with widely disparate incomes, will find a tax advantage to being married. For example, if Tomas made $60,000 and Keija $10,000, as single people he'd pay $17,064 in taxes and she'd pay $1,432, totaling $18,496. If they were married, they'd pay $17,590, a savings of $906.

Despite the tax differences, don't make your marriage-or-living-together decision solely on the basis of tax tables. After all, tax rates shift from time to time (and so, probably, will your income). It is legal to divorce and continue living together to qualify for lower tax rates, as long as you don't marry and divorce every year or so to try to get the benefits of both marriage and living together. If you do this, the IRS will take the position that your divorce is a sham and prosecute you for tax evasion.

2. Dependents and Taxes

May you claim your mate or his children as your dependents, even if they aren't related to you?

Internal Revenue Code 152 defines dependents as close relatives or unrelated persons who live in the taxpayer's household as the principal place of abode and are supported by the taxpayer. IRS regulations say, however, that "an individual isn't a member of taxpayer's household if at any time during the taxable year the relationship between such individual and taxpayer is in violation of local law."[10]

One court held this regulation to prohibit a North Carolina man from claiming the woman he lived with as his dependent, as cohabitation is illegal in North Carolina.[11] In states where living together is legal (see Chapter 2), you can claim the dependency deduction if your mate and his children have their "principal abode" in your household, you provide more than one-half their support, they haven't earned more than $1,000 each, they haven't filed a joint return with anyone else and they meet certain residency requirements. For details, see the IRS guidelines.

H. Public Benefits

WELFARE REGULATIONS ARE much like quicksand. What looks safe, solid and reliable one minute can gobble you up the next. Changing rules seem to be part of a system that has never found a comfortable place in the American consciousness. So before you rely on what we say here, check with your local social services agency.

---

[10]IRS Regs. 1.151-1-(b).

[11]*Ensminger v. Commissioner of Internal Revenue*, 610 F.2d 189 (N.C. 1979). In *In re Shackelford*, 3 BR 42 (W.D. Mo. 1980), however, a court held that a Missouri woman could claim her living together partner as a dependent because they didn't violate the state law that prohibited "open, gross lewdness or lascivious behavior."

1. AFDC

A person (usually a woman) receiving welfare under the Aid to Dependent Children (AFDC) Program who starts living with a man (not her children's father) can usually continue to receive her monthly check. As long as the man doesn't actually contribute to her support or the support of her children, welfare won't be cut off or reduced. Some welfare departments require considerable proof that money is being kept separate, others aren't so tight. The welfare department isn't supposed to care about the physical relationship between the mother and the man, only about what he contributes. It's wise, though, to call and find out the exact local procedures so you can adjust your situation to fit any technicalities.

Both the AFDC mother and the unrelated man will have to sign a welfare department statement stating, under penalty of perjury, the amount of money, if any, he pays. Most welfare departments require a man who has income to contribute at least the fair cost of his monthly expenses. If you do this, be sure that your contributions are kept separate and are only used for your own expenses. You have no legal duty to contribute to the support of either the AFDC mother or her children, and the welfare department can't force you to. If they subtract money from the mother's grant because you're living in the house, the mother should appeal (called a "fair hearing"). See your nearest legal aid or welfare rights group for help.

Hint: Find out what the minimum monthly contribution for a man for his own expenses is in your state. Document that the man pays this much and no more and doesn't contribute to the expenses of the woman or her children. This will result in the AFDC mother keeping most or all of her grant. If you report that the man pays more than the minimum, the benefits will be reduced.

Example: Tara and her child receive a monthly AFDC grant. Ben, who makes $1,500 per month, moves in and contributes $120 per month for his rent and household expenses (This is the minimum in Tara's state). Tara can keep the majority of her grant as long as Ben doesn't provide additional money for her or the child. Tara should keep neat and sensible records of her income and expenses to prove she's taking no more from Ben.

2. Food Stamps

Food stamp rules are a little tighter. Tara and Ben will be assumed to eat together because they live together. Because Ben has a substantial income, food stamps will be cut off. If Tara can prove that she buys and stores her food separately, however, she may be able to keep her food stamps.

Hint: The money you receive from AFDC is quite large when compared to your food stamps. You may be wise not to be "too greedy" and press for food stamps too. If you do, you risk the authorities taking a closer look at your situation—something many people on welfare find that it's wise not to encourage.

3. Medical Benefits

Medical benefits for older Americans are figured in much the same way that AFDC benefits are. You can live with someone and qualify faor medical care for you and your children as long as the person who you're living with doesn't contribute to your support.

Older Couples Liability for Medical Care of a Mate

Generally, one member of a married couple is legally liable to pay for health and nursing home care for the other, over and above what is reimbursed by Medi-care and private insurance. Fortunately, the opposite is true for unmarried couples—if one moves to a nursing home, the other's property is not at risk. If the institutionalized person exhausts his property and his half of jointly owned property, Medi-care pays the rest and the other member of the couple need not exhaust her savings.

This is a complicated topic. For more information, see *Elder Care: A Consumer's Guide to Choosing and Financing Long-Term Care,* Joeseph Matthews, Nolo Press.

I. Social Security

THE SOCIAL SECURITY PROGRAM discriminates against unmarried couples. If you're married to a wage earner covered by Social Security, you're eligible to receive retirement benefits. If you're the widow, widower or divorced spouse of a wage earner, you can get benefits.[12] If you've been living together, however, you're not entitled to benefits, except for those earned individually by the wage earner.[13] Is this fair? Of course not, but it's the law. If the trend away from marriage continues, changes may happen, but for now, a non-wage earner is better off financially if married to a wage earner rather than living with one.

---

[12]Basic Social Security questions are answered in the pamphlet "Your Social Security." To get a copy, call a Social Security office. For more details, see *Social Security, Medicare & Pensions: A Sourcebook for Older Americans* (Nolo Press), Matthews and Berman.

[13]Children of deceased or disabled unmarried parents are eligible for benefits if paternity can be proven. See Chapter 8, *Starting a Family,* Section J.

Common Law Marriage Note: If you live with someone covered by Social Security in a state that recognizes common law marriage (see Chapter 2) and your mate has recently died or become disabled, you may be able to claim that you were married and that you thus qualify for benefits. A common law marriage is just as valid as a formal marriage for Social Security.

If you're a divorced wife, 62 years of age or older, you can get benefits on your ex-spouse's Social Security account if he's getting payments and your marriage lasted at least ten years (the old law required 20 years). If you a qualify for benefits as a divorced spouse and your ex has died, you can receive survivor's benefits as early as age 60 (50 if you're disabled).

J. Insurance

GENERALLY SPEAKING, IT'S now possible for unmarried couples to purchase most types of insurance at competitive rates. It's still possible, however, to encounter some discrimination.

1. Life Insurance

Obtaining life insurance used to be a particular problem for unmarried couples because insurance companies required that a person purchasing life insurance and naming himself as beneficiary to have an "insurable interest" in the insured's life. This meant that the beneficiary and the insured must have a relationship that makes it unlikely that the beneficiary will take the insured on an early trip to the happy hunting ground in order to collect on the policy.

As an extreme example, no insurance company would sell Joe Gunslinger a policy (naming himself as beneficiary) on the life of Harry Sheriff. Children, spouses, parents and other close relatives have long been held to have an "insurable interest" in one another, but unmarried mates have not. Apparently, insurance companies believed that people living together were more likely to slip a little arsenic into the rice pudding than were the married.

The result was that many unmarried couples lied—pretended they were married—in order to purchase insurance on the other's life. This played right into the insurance companies' sweaty palms. When one partner died, the insurance companies often refused to pay on the grounds that they'd been misled on the application. And many courts ruled that the insurance companies could do this.

Today, some insurance companies realize that people who live together do have an "insurable interest" in one another and will let unmarried partners buy insurance on each other. If you can't find a company that will do this, however, you can buy insurance on your own life and name your friend as the beneficiary.

If you really want to insure your friend's life and not yours, however, list your friend as your fiance. This usually works, as insurance companies never seem to be interested in the length of an engagement. But let us repeat— don't claim to be married if you aren't. If you have a policy in which you've said (wrongly) that you were married, change it.

⚠️ **Warning.** Some insurance companies try to charge higher rates to unmarried couples. Call a few companies and compare rates before you buy.

2. Insurance on Your Home

Homeowners insurance used to be difficult for unmarried couples to buy, but this is no longer true. Many companies now write policies for unmarried couples at the same rates that married couples get. To find these companies, ask any home-owning unmarried couple you know, or call a broker in a part of town where a lot of unmarried couples live. She should know who to approach.

3. Renters Insurance

Renter's insurance is rather easy for an unmarried couple to obtain together. Insurance companies insure the property—not the owners of the property—and the rates are related to the age (and security) of your building, the neighborhood you live in and whether your landlord maintains the building well. Shop around. You should easily be able to find one policy for both of you.

4. Automobile Insurance

Purchasing automobile insurance can be a problem for unmarried couples, but not to the extent it was a few years ago. Before issuing a policy, many companies want a complete list of who lives in the house with the insured, their license numbers and their car ownership status. Insurance companies often run checks to be sure that people with bad driving records won't be driving your car. If you live in a large group, insurance companies may balk at writing you a policy.

Unmarried couples who jointly own one car will want to get one policy. It's cheaper than each person getting her or his own policy. But you may have to shop around. We know one unmarried couple who were happily sold a joint policy and another who were refused a month later, by a different agent of the same company.

If you each own a car, you should have no trouble getting separate insurance. If you together own two or more cars, however, you may find that companies won't insure both people and cars on one policy. Rather, they'll insist on writing two policies, listing you each as the primary driver of one car and the other as secondary driver on the other car. This may sound okay, but it isn't A married couple owning two cars would qualify for a second car discount; with two policies, you wouldn't.

One way around this is to list both cars in one person's name, and list the other person as a secondary driver of both. But better yet, find a sympathetic insurance salesperson, explore the angles and compare prices. Some companies will give unmarried couples the same privileges and rates as if they were married.

5. Health Insurance

Unmarried couples face serious discrimination in qualifying for employer-paid health insurance family coverage. Many employers cover a worker's spouse and children, but rarely the person you live with. If you and your friend are each covered by your own employer-paid health insurance, you haven't a problem. If one of you doesn't have employer-paid insurance, however, and you can't qualify because of your unmarried status, you face very serious (but very legal) discrimination.

One way to remedy this is by providing health coverage to the registered domestic partners of employees. In a few areas of the country, cities governments have begun doing this. We believe this type of legislation is way past due.

K. Serious Illness—Durable Powers of Attorney

IF ONE MEMBER of an unmarried couple becomes seriously ill or disabled and medical authorities need someone to okay a treatment decision, they turn to spouses, parents, adult children and siblings for the go ahead. Except in those few cities where domestic partners legislation gives living together couples rights akin to those enjoyed by married couples, you're out in the cold.

But you need not be. You can make sure that your partner will make medical decisions for you—and vice versa—if you each prepare a Durable Power of Attorney. Unlike its cousin, the traditional Power of Attorney, which automatically terminates if its creator becomes unconscious or otherwise mentally incapacitated, a Durable Power of Attorney remains in effect (or, in some instances, takes effect) should its creator become unable to make decisions.

Durable powers of attorney cover two areas— health care (including turning off life support systems after a diagnosis of a terminal illness) and financial management. You can create them to take effect now (if you face a major operation or immediate health problem) or take effect when you become incapacitated.[14] The latter is called a "springing durable power of attorney." In that document, you can specify that the deter-

mination of your incapacity be made by your doctor.

Durable powers of attorney are valid in virtually every state. Specific rules, however, vary tremendously from state to state. Some states require specific language, typeface or warnings, or the separation of health care from financial management. We cannot include all the variations here. Fortunately, *The Power of Attorney Book,* by Denis Clifford (Nolo Press), contains all the necessary forms and instructions, and explains how to customize the forms to fit your situation. For example, you can give your partner full power to manage your finances should you become incapacitated, but prohibit him from selling your vacation cabin, which you inherited from your grandfather.

Warning. If you don't prepare a durable power of attorney and you become ill or incapacitated, a court hearing will be necessary to appoint someone to make health care and asset management decisions for you. It's possible that the court will appoint your parents, siblings, adult child or other blood relative instead of your friend.

If the appointed relative disapproves of your relationship, your friend may be excluded from all decision-making. If you jointly own assets (such as your house) with your friend, she may now have to cope with a new hostile partner.

L. Miscellaneous Rights and Responsibilities

INCREASINGLY IN THE LAST several years, unmarried couples have sought rights and privileges traditionally associated with marriage. Unmarrieds have tried to qualify for health insurance and travel benefits through their

---

[14]Even if you create one to take effect now but are not currently incapacitated, in most states medical personnel listen to your wishes and only turn to the person named in your durable power of attorney when you become incapacitated.

friend's job and have brought unlawful death actions (claiming loss of consortium) when their partner has been killed.[15] They've also sought unemployment benefits when they left a job and moved to be with their living together partner.

To date, few of these efforts have been successful, except to the limited extent that a few cities have adopted domestic partner legislation. Generally, when courts are asked to extend marital rights to unmarried couples, they refuse, allowing businesses and governments to continue to treat married and unmarried couples differently. A recent decision by New York's highest court, however, may mark the beginning of a counter trend. The Court interpreted New York City's rent control law to allow a homosexual couple in a long term, committed relationship to qualify as a family.[16] The New York court wrote "a more realistic and certainly equally valid view of a family includes two lifetime partners."

---

[15]One California court granted damages for loss of consortium, *Butcher v. Superior Court of Orange Co.* 188 Cal.Rptr. 503 (1983), but that case was overruled in *Elden v. Sheldon,* 250 Cal.Rptr. 254 (1988).

---

[16]*Braschi v. Stahl Associates Co.,* 74 N.Y.2d 201 (1989).

Chapter

Four

Living Together Contracts and the Law

IN THE OLD DAYS, couples who lived together without getting married existed pretty much in a legal vacuum *vis a vis* each other. The little law there was established that money and property belonged to the person who earned it or originally owned it. Contracts to share earnings or property usually weren't enforced by courts on the ground that the agreements were based on "meretricious consideration." Consideration is the price paid in a contract; meretricious means "resembling a prostitute."

What the courts were saying was that living together contracts were actually contracts for sex outside of marriage, which was illegal in all states until about 1970, and illegal contracts cannot be enforced. This essentially left unmarried couples unable to enforce their agreements to share or divide property. But in 1976, *Marvin* v. *Marvin* gave unmarried couples in California the right to make contracts. Below, we discuss the *Marvin* case and its interpretation in the other states. Then we address the effect a subsequent marriage has on a couple's living together agreement.

A. The Marvin Case and Others: Changes in the Law

WITH THE *MARVIN* CASE, the California Supreme Court put living together contracts in the public eye, partly because of the litigants' fame, and partly because of the sweeping nature of the decision. The case involved the late actor Lee Marvin, and Michelle Triola Marvin, the woman he lived with. After they broke up, he supported her for a while, but then stopped. She sued him, claiming that in exchange for giving up her career to be a full-time homemaker and companion, he had orally promised to support her for the rest of her life.

The trial court ruled against Michelle, stating that any contract between living together couples was illegal and unenforceable. Michelle appealed to the California Supreme Court, which handed down the well-known "Marvin decision,"[1] making several significant new laws for unmarried couples in California. Because the case was so widely reported in the press, many have assumed it's the law everywhere. But it's not—the California Supreme Court has no authority outside the state, except by way of example. Indeed, several aspects of the *Marvin* case have been rejected in other states.

Here's what Marvin decided for Californians, and how other states have responded:

1. Unmarried couples aren't covered by the rules affecting the married (you're either married or you're not). The Court held that California divorce laws—alimony and the division of property—don't affect unmarried couples. You can't back into the legal rules of marriage by living together. This doesn't mean that a court can't divide property when unmarried couples split up, but only that the specific divorce laws don't apply. This rule has been widely adopted in other states.

---

[1] *Marvin v. Marvin*, 557 P.2d 106 (1976).

2. Unmarried couples may enter into contracts. The second part of the *Marvin* decision simply states that unmarried couples may make *express* contracts concerning their property. An express contract is one made in words, oral or written. This was a significant change; contracts between people living together in a sexual relationship were no longer illegal. The court added a caveat, however: if the contract is explicitly based on the performance of sexual services by one partner, the contract is invalid.[2]

Most states have adopted this part of *Marvin* and now enforce written contracts between unmarried partners. The major exceptions are Georgia[3] and Illinois,[4] where the courts still hold that the "immoral" nature of living together prevents a couple from forming a contract.

In addition, most states recognize oral contracts if they can be proved. (Proving them is extremely difficult.) A few states, however, require that living together contracts be in writing to be enforced.[5] So, if you've had an oral contract, and your relationship has disintegrated and you can't get it into writing, you have legal recourse in many, but not all, states. But if you and your partner are still happily involved, be warned that oral contracts are almost impossible to prove (one word against another), so get it in writing.

3. A court may imply a contract from the circumstances. The was a groundbreaking aspect of *Marvin:* that "implied contract" and "unjust enrichment" legal theories could be applied to unmarried couples. Implied contract means just what it says—a contract is implied from your actions, not words. Unjust enrichment means that one person contributes something (usually labor) to the other's project, with the expectation of a benefit in return.

Some states have adopted this portion of *Marvin* and will look at the circumstances of a relationship to see if a contract can be implied or should be imposed because one person has unfairly profited from the labors of the other. A few recent cases are summarized in the accompanying box.

Cases Based on Implied Contracts and Unjust Enrichment

- **Wisconsin**—*Watts v. Watts,* 137 Wis.2d 506, 405 N.W. 2d 303 (1987). Here, one partner gave up a career to move in with the other and become a full-time homemaker and mother; the court said she could sue claiming any theory available to non-cohabitants,

[2]See, for example, *Jones v. Daly,* 176 Cal.Rptr. 130 (1981). Daly died without a will and Jones sued the estate for a share of the accumulated property, alleging that he gave up his career as a model to be Daly's "lover, companion, homemaker, travelling companion, housekeeper and cook" in exchange for a share of the property. The court applied *Marvin* principles and rejected the argument, saying the word "lover" showed that sexual services were an inseparable part of the agreement. But see also, *Whorton v. Dillingham,* 202 Cal.App.3d 447 (1988), where the court ruled that the word "lover" could be cut off from the contract and the rest of the agreement enforced.

[3]*Rebak v. Mathis,* 238 S.E. 2d 81 (1977). In fact, Georgia doesn't recognize any contract between unmarried partners. See *Samples v. Monroe,* 358 S.E. 2d 273 (1987).

[4]*Hewitt v. Hewitt,* 394 N.E. 2d 1204 (1979). But in *Spafford v. Coutts,* 118 Ill. App. 566 (1983), the court suggested that contracts not based entirely on living together, and not resembling marriage claims, may be enforced.

[5]For example, Minnesota statute 513.075 says that if sexual relations are contemplated, any living together contract concerning property and finances is enforceable only if it's in writing, signed by both parties and sought to be enforced after the relationship ends. In *Estate of Eriksen,* 337 N.W. 2d 671 (1983), the court said that this statute applies only when living together is a part of the contract—that is, an agreement to live with another person in exchange for support, property, or whatever must be in writing. An agreement to buy a house together or divide property need not be written.

including implied contract (they had an unspoken agreement that she'd be paid for her services), unjust enrichment (although there was no agreement, he has benefitted from her efforts and should compensate her) or partition of the jointly-held property.

- **North Carolina**—*Suggs v. Norris,* 364 S.E. 2d 159 (1988). Like in *Watts,* the court allowed one partner to sue the other's estate under any legal theory available to non-cohabitants. She chose unjustly enrichment, claiming that they had a joint business, all the proceeds went to him, and she should be paid her for her work.

- **Massachusetts**—*Hatton v. Meade,* 23 Mass. App 356, 502 N.E. 2d 552 (1987). In this case, Meade gave a gift of a house to Hatton, but never put her name on the deed. When he died, she sued his estate; the court imposed a constructive trust on the house, saying that his estate must keep the house for her use. This is another traditional contract theory, previously not applied to unmarried couples.

- **Connecticut**—Boland v. Catalano, 202 Conn 333, 521 A.2d 142 (1987). This couple lived together for nine years, pooling assets and earnings. The court found an implied contract to share income and the "fruits of joint labor."

    Example: *Janet works to improve Todd's boat for nine months, expecting a share of the resulting increased value. They split up, and Todd refuses to give her a cent. She doesn't want to sue him, and convinces him that the courts in their state would likely hold that he has been unjustly enriched by her work, and that she should be paid for the labor expended.*

Although unjust enrichment and other "equitable" theories have been recognized by many states,[6] some states, including New York,

won't recognize implied contracts.[7] Even in states that do, the practical problems inherent in suing on an equitable theory are not worth the trouble unless large amounts of money are at stake. If you contributed economically to your partnership and feel you should be compensated, see a lawyer (Chapter 12, *More Legal Help*). If it's not too late, however, write down your understanding.

Does Registering As Domestic Partners Create an Implied Contract to Share Property?

A few cities allow unmarried couples to register as domestic partners. The benefits given those partners vary among cities, but include the right to visit each other in public hospitals, the right of city employees to bereavement leave if their partner dies and the right to family health coverage for city employees.

Registering as domestic partners raises the question of whether the couple has created an implied contract for other purposes, such as sharing income and property. In states that don't recognize implied contracts between unmarried couples, the answer is clearly no. In other states, however, it is possible that courts will hold that registering as domestic partners implies a contract to share property. This is especially likely to occur when one partner dies without an estate plan (see Chapter 11, *Death*) and the survivor claims to own part of the decedent's property.

If you want to register as domestic partners, but don't to share property or income beyond sharing day-to-day expenses, simply use one of

---

[6]Unfortunately, proving an "equitable" theory takes a lot of time and money.

[7]See *Morone v. Morone,* 50 N.Y.2d 481 (1980) and *Bower v. Weisman,* 650 F.Supp. 1415 (N.Y. 1986), which cites Morone in denying an implied contract. Other cases denying implied contracts include *Hill v. Ames,* 606 P.2d 388 (Alaska 1980); *Poe v. Levy,* 411 So.2d 253 (Fla. 1982); *Carnes v. Sheldon,* 311 N.W.2d 747 (Mich. 1981); *Tapley v. Tapley,* 449 A.2d 1218 (N.H. 1982) and *Merrill v. Davis,* 673 P.2d 1285 (N.M. 1983).

contracts (found in the Appendix) designed to keep property separate.

B. To Be Safe, Write It Down!

BY NOW, OUR THEME is clear: reduce your living together agreement to writing. A written contract is the only way to truly protect your rights. Putting your contract in writing needn't be time-consuming or dreary (and it's certainly better than having a court write one for you). If you approach the task in the spirit of preserving the shared memory of two fair-minded people, it may even be fun. The details are in the next chapter.

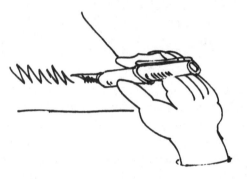

C. What Happens to Your Written Living Together Agreement if You Get Married?

LET'S SUPPOSE YOU TAKE our advice and write down your living together agreement. Several years later, you're feeling blissful and secure, and you decide, "Hey, why not just tie the knot?" Is your living together contract carried into your marriage, and, if necessary, enforceable after the big day? Generally, no. Although a few states might treat it as a pre-nuptial (pre-marriage) contract, most will disregard it and apply only

your state's marriage and divorce laws to your relationship.

But all states allow couples contemplating marriage to enter into a pre-nuptial agreement, so, if you want the terms of your living together agreement to apply during your marriage, you can convert your living together agreement to a pre-nuptial agreement. There's little difference between the two, but because pre-nuptial agreements state that they are made in contemplation of marriage and don't take effect unless you actually marry (unlike living together contracts, which state neither), courts let pre-nuptial agreements preempt state marital property laws.

To convert your living together contract into a pre-nuptial agreement, follow these steps:

1. Use your upcoming marriage as an opportunity to take another look at your agreement; make any agreed-upon updates and changes.

2. Rewrite your agreement. Call it a pre-nuptial agreement, and state that it is made in contemplation of marriage and does not take effect until you marry.

3. If you have any doubts about your state's laws governing this area, have your new agreement looked at by an expert (see Chapter 12, *More Legal Help*).

Pre-nuptial Laws

Eleven states[8] have adopted the Uniform Pre-Marital Agreement Act, which lets couples make written contracts prior to marriage concerning ownership, management and control of property; disposition of property at separation, divorce and death; alimony; wills; and life insurance beneficiaries. The states that haven't adopted the Act have other pre-marital agreement laws, which

---

[8]Alaska, California, Hawaii, Maine, Montana, North Carolina, North Dakota, Oregon, Rhode Island, Texas and Virginia.

differ in only minor ways from the Act.[9] In every state, couples are prohibited from making binding provisions about child support in the event they divorce.

Here are the main provisions of the Act:

§3. Content

(a) Parties to a premarital agreement may contract with respect to:

(1) the rights and obligations of each of the parties in any of the property of either or both of them whenever and wherever acquired or located;

(2) the right to buy, sell, use, transfer, exchange, abandon, lease, consume, expend, assign, create a security interest in, mortgage, encumber, dispose of, or otherwise manage and control property;

(3) the disposition of property upon separation, marital dissolution, death, or the occurrence or nonoccurrence of any other event;

(4) the modification or elimination of spousal support;

(5) the making of a will, trust, or other arrangement to carry out the provisions of the agreement;

(6) the ownership rights in, and disposition of, the death benefit from a life insurance policy;

(7) the choice of law governing the construction of the agreement; and

(8) any other matter, including their personal right and obligations, not in violation of public policy or a statute imposing a criminal penalty.

(b) The right of a child to support may not be adversely affected by a premarital agreement.

---

[9]One important difference is that a few states, including California, do not allow pre-nuptial agreements to modify or eliminate the right of a spouse to receive court-ordered alimony at divorce.

Chapter

Five

Contracts

THE WONDERFUL THING about living together contracts is that, unlike marital property laws which seem to fit no one particularly well, you can custom tailor yours to meet your specific needs and have it fit like a glove, not a handcuff. You can cover items as small as a teapot or as large as a lifestyle. The only real no-no is sex. Even if it's your favorite pastime, pretend you're a good puritan and don't mention the subject in your agreement. If you do, and wind up in court, you contract will likely be torn to little pieces.

Legally, a contract is no more than a promise (or promises) to do something in exchange for someone else's promise (or promises) to do something else. Pretty simple. Anything more complex relates to lawyers and their love for mumbo jumbo and obfuscation, not with the nature of a contract itself.

Don't become intimidated by visions of your prior, powerless experiences with contracts— leases, insurance policies, bank loans or major installment purchases. Then, you wanted or needed what the seller was offering and had to accept the one-sided contract that went with it. No one called Henry Ford and got him to add a few months to a warranty.

Fortunately, living together contracts needn't be written like these standard form monsters. You can design one to say exactly what you want, and should do it in English, not lawyer talk. Refer to your partner by his name, not the "party of the second part." Make sure that the meaning of your agreement does not escape somewhere between the second "wherefore" and the third "pursuant."

Step 1. Reach an Understanding

Writing down your understanding is basic, but even more important is arriving at the understanding of what you want to write down. With courts increasingly recognizing property rights and obligations of unmarried couples,

people must agree on how to relate to each other economically. This is especially true if one of you makes sacrifices in order to live with the other, such as moving a long distance or giving up a job to care for small children.

We have no magic advice about how to reach a good understanding. It's up to you. We arrived at ours informally rather than in a structured business meeting. But we don't set ourselves up as models, and we're as capable of arriving at misunderstandings as the next couple. We do suggest, however, that before trying to reach an agreement, carefully read the rest of this book so you understand your options. And one more thing—don't put off making your contract until you have a fight—the best time to agree is when you're feeling relaxed and no agreement seems necessary.

Step 2. Put It in Writing

We cannot emphasize this enough. By writing down your understanding, the complicated "equitable" remedies discussed in Chapter 4, *Living Together Contracts and the Law,* can be avoided[1] and you're extremely unlikely to end up fighting in court. And if you do, the judge will be interested in interpreting your written agreement, not in inferring from your behavior.

From a down-to-earth, practical perspective, little gets resolved in court. Those of you who've been through a divorce already know this—those of you who haven't are lucky. Any money or property that exists at the start of a court dispute almost always gets consumed by the lawyers. Add to that the time, emotional pain and bitterness that are a part of our adversary process, and we hope we've convinced you. A written agreement as to who owns what and how property is

---

[1]No one has put it better than the French legal scholar Beaumanoir in his *Coutumes de Beauvasis,* written in 1283. "For the memory of men slips and flows away, and the life of man is short, and that which is not written is soon forgotten."

to be divided if you separate, may avoid all of this.

Step 3. Design Your Contract

Living together contracts can include a wide variety of economic arrangements. This flexibility, free from the constraint of institutional marriage rules, is one reason living together has become so popular. Your agreement can be carefully designed to meet your needs. You can keep all property separate, or agree that what belongs to one belongs to both. Of perhaps your agreement will be somewhere in between—such as keeping earnings separate, but compensating one person for services that benefit the other.

Living together contracts can also include anything relevant to your living together, such as the division of housework, whether or not to have children, the name to be used, property division at separation and even who takes the dog out for his nightly piddle. If you wind up in court, however, contracts are normally enforceable as they relate to property, and to a lesser extent, children. A court will enforce child support and custody provisions if they are in the best interest of the children (see Chapters 8, *Starting a Family* and 9, *You and Your Prior Family*). Terms involving your personal conduct, including the cocker spaniel's ablutions, are not enforced. Judge Jones simply will not tell your friend to put the cap back on the toothpaste or watch less football.

Contracts for Houses and Other Real Property

We cover buying houses and other real property in Chapter 7, *Buying a House*. Real property has its own specialized rules and is usually, but not always, handled in a separate agreement. Several samples are included in Chapter 7.

Note: Can a person married to someone (other than her living together partner) make a living together contact? We are often asked by people living together while one of them is married to someone else if they can create a valid living together contract. In many states, property accumulated after a married couple permanently separates (being divorced is usually not the crucial point) is the property of the spouse acquiring it. Thus, a still married person living with someone other than his spouse should be able to create a valid living together contract.

Unfortunately, however, little is certain during a contested divorce. Therefore, if one of you is still married to someone else, agree in writing to keep all your property separate until the divorce is final. Then you can write a new agreement, pooling your property if so desired.

Special Problems of Artists, Writers and Inventors

Creative people often work on inventions, software programs, art work or books for a long time. While the work is in progress—and even when it's done—it's often unclear how much value, if any, the finished product will have. If you keep all your property and income separate, valuing creative works won't be a problem. Each person owns what he or she has created.

If you agree to pool the property you accumulate after living together, however, valuing creative work—in the event of separation—can be a real problem. Suppose, for example, you're a successful writer who's been working on a slightly esoteric but exciting book for two years. If you split up, who knows whether this yet-to-be-published book will sell five thousand copies, a million copies, or some number in between. Even if you happily agree to divide your property when you split up, it may be difficult to do.

One solution is to not pool your property in the first place. But if you're determined to do this, your contract will need a scheme for valuing unsold works and works in progress at separation. If you're both creators, you can simply say what's yours is yours and what's mine is mine. Another possibility is to set a date after separation at which time all creative work will be sold with the proceeds divided. Works that aren't sold go back to their creator. Other arrangements are possible, including having works in progress appraised. We give a sample contract in Section H below; if the work in question is likely to be valuable, check your contract with a lawyer (see Chapter 12, *More Legal Help*).

A. The Basic Living Together Contract

WE INCLUDE FOUR TEAR-OUT contracts in the Appendix. Two (one each for keeping earnings separate and sharing them) are thorough and attempt to cover most areas of concern to unmarried couples. The other two (again, one for pooling assets and one for keeping them separate) are short and cover the essentials only. Sections D through J below present specialized contracts.

Please read (or at least skim) all the contracts below before deciding on which one to use. You may copy one verbatim, or create your own by adding material from one or more of the specialized ones.

1. Deleting Material

If you use one of the agreements in the Appendix but want to delete some clauses, simply cross out and initial the offending provisions. If you make many changes, you'll want to re-type the whole contract. Just use regular 8 1/2" x 11" typing paper.

2. Adding Material

Additions are a bit more complicated—you have to write or type out the new provision and add it to the contract. We left space before the signatures in the contracts in the Appendix for additions. If you don't use this space, cross it out with a large "X." If you use one of the sample contracts from Sections D-J, add whatever clauses fit your situation and then renumber the clauses as necessary. Retype and proofread your new draft.

If your deletions and additions eat up the original, consider having your finished product checked by a lawyer. This is a particularly good idea if you have a lot of money or property. But be careful in choosing lawyers—many charge outrageous prices and have little experience with the problems faced by unmarried couples. Investigate before you see someone. and be sure to get the fee set in advance. Because you've already done most of the work and you're only asking a lawyer to check it, a consultation of an hour or two should be adequate unless you have unusual problems (see Chapter 12).

3. Signing the Contract

When you have the final draft of your contract, photocopy it. Both of you should sign and date both copies. Notarization is optional—unless your contract involves real property and you plan to record it at the County Recorder's office—then notarization is required. Notarization doesn't make your contract legal; it proves that your signatures are not forged, in the unlikely event anyone later questions their validity.

4. Property Division at Death

It's legal (but not required) to include a clause stating that if one partner dies, the survivor keeps the jointly-owned property. We include a provision dealing with death in some, but not all, of our contracts, depending (in our view) on how likely an average couple will want such a provision in a given contract. If you disagree with us (and by all means, please do), modify your agreement accordingly.

If death is omitted from a living together agreement that covers jointly-owned property, each person's portion can be left in a will or other estate plan, unless the property is held in joint tenancy. Then, the surviving joint tenant(s) automatically inherit. If there's no estate plan, the property passes under your state's intestate succession laws, which means it goes to your parents, children, other relatives or the state, not to your friend. (See Chapter 11, *Death,* on how to avoid this.)

5. Relax

One last word. Many people find that filling out or creating a contract forces them to deal with the very guts of their relationship. This is usually a healthy thing to do, but it can also be trying. Take your time; don't expect to finish in an evening. A good contract involves compromise and accommodation. If you both feel you've given up a little more than you've received, you're probably on the right track. Preparing your contract should be an affirmative act, but it's up to you to make it so. If you get bogged down in trading this for that and wonder why you're dealing with all of this legal bullshit, write each other a poem.

B. Basic Short Form Property Agreements

IF YOU WANT TO RECORD your broad understanding but are turned off by a long document, we include two simple, one-page contracts. One keeps property separate, the other shares most property acquired after you live together. The rest of the chapter contains longer and more specialized contracts designed to fit a variety of circumstances.

BASIC PROPERTY AGREEMENT (SHARING MOST PROPERTY)

Phillip Mendocino and Ruth Alameda agree as follows:

1. That they plan to live together beginning March 1, 19__ and to continue to live together indefinitely;

2. That while they live together, all income earned by either Phillip or Ruth and all property, whether real or personal, accumulated with those earnings belong equally to both; should they separate, all accumulated property shall be divided equally;

3. That all real and personal property earned or accumulated by either Phillip or Ruth prior to their getting together and any income produced from this property belongs absolutely to the person earning or accumulating it [an itemized list of the property should be attached];

4. Should either Phillip or Ruth inherit or be given property, it belongs absolutely to the person receiving the inheritance or gift;

5. That the separate property of either Phillip or Ruth covered in paragraphs 3 and 4 of this agreement can become the separate property of the other, or the joint property of both, only under the terms of a written agreement;

6. That should Ruth and Phillip separate, neither has any claim for money or property except as set out in paragraph 2.

7. That this agreement represents Phillip and Ruth's complete understanding regarding their living together and replaces all prior agreements, written or oral. It can be amended, but only in writing, and must be signed by both;.

8. That if the court finds any portion of this contract to be illegal or otherwise unenforceable, that the remainder of the contract is still in full force and effect;

9. [Insert mediation/arbitration clause from Section L]

_____   _____
Date   Phillip Mendocino

_____   _____
Date   Ruth Alameda

BASIC AGREEMENT (KEEPING PROPERTY SEPARATE)

Keija Adams and Tomas Finnegan agree as follows:

1. That they have been living together and plan to do so indefinitely;

2. That all property, whether real or personal, owned by either Keija or Tomas as of the date of this agreement shall remain the separate property of its owner [an itemized list of valuable items should be attached];

3. That Keija and Tomas will share their love and good energy, but agree that the income of each, and any property traceable to that income, belong absolutely to the person who earns the money. Any joint purchases shall be made only under the terms of paragraph 7 below;

4. That in the event of separation, neither Tomas nor Keija has a claim upon the other for any money or property for any reason unless there's a subsequent written agreement to the contrary under paragraph 7 or 8;[2]

5. That Tomas and Keija shall each use his/her own name and will maintain his/her own bank, credit, credit cards, investment and other accounts;

6. That the monthly expenses for rent, food, household utilities and upkeep, and joint recreation shall be shared equally;

7. That if, in the future, Keija and Tomas purchase any item jointly, the joint ownership shall be reflected on the title slip to the property, or by use of a separate written agreement dated and signed by both. Any agreement to purchase or own property joint shall cover only the property set out in that agreement and shall not create an implication that other property is jointly owned;

8. That property owned now, or acquired in the future, as the separate property of either Tomas or Keija, can become the separate property of the other, or Tomas and Keija's joint property only under the terms of a written agreement signed and dated by the person whose property is to be re-classified;

---

[2]One area where problems can develop is if one partner does work on property belonging to the other (e.g., puts a roof on a house). If this applies to you, prepare a written agreement like the one in Chapter 7, Section E(3) or in Section E below.

9. That this agreement replaces any and all prior agreements, whether written or oral, and can be added to or changed only by a subsequent written agreement;

10. That if a court finds any portion of this contract to be illegal or otherwise unenforceable, the remainder of the contract is still in full force;

11. [Insert mediation/arbitration clause in Section L]

_____	_____
Date	Keija Adams
_____	_____
Date	Tomas Finnegan

C. Basic Long Form Property Agreements

IN THE APPENDIX, we include two long form agreements. These cover the same topics as the short forms, and provide space to list all separately-owned property. They also include children-related provisions and a thorough mediation-arbitration clause. To save space, we don't print them here; they're in the Appendix at Contract III (long form keeping everything separate) and Contract IV (long form sharing income and property).

D. Agreement Covering Jointly Acquired Items

MANY PEOPLE WANT a basic keeping-things-separate approach. Often, however, they will want to own a major item, or several major items, together. Paragraph 7 in both the short and long keeping-things-separate contracts allow you to do this with a separate agreement. Here's a sample:

AGREEMENT COVERING A JOINT PURCHASE

Emiko Takahashi and Sam Armistead agree as follows:

1. That they'll jointly acquire and own a stereo system including a compact disk player, for approximately $1,400;

2. That should they separate and both want the system, they'll agree on the fair resale value of the system and then flip a coin, with the winner keeping the system after paying the loser one-half of the agreed-upon price;

3. That if on separation neither person wants the system, or if they can't agree on a fair price, they shall advertise it to the public, sell it to the highest bidder and divide the money equally;

4. That should either person die while they are living together, the system shall belong absolutely to the survivor. If either Emiko or Sam makes an estate plan, this provision shall be reflected in that document.[3]

5. That this agreement can be amended, but only in writing, and signed by both Sam and Emiko.

6. That if a court finds any portion of this contract to be illegal or otherwise unenforceable, that the remainder of the contract is still in full force and effect.

7. [Insert mediation/arbitration clause from Section L]

_____   _____
Date   Emiko Takahashi

_____   _____
Date   Sam Armistead

Sometimes, a couple will want to purchase and own an item jointly, but only one person will actually make the purchase. This can occur if one person uses her credit card or separate checking account to buy an item. Even though only one name is on the contract with the seller, you'll want an arrangement showing you own the property together. Here's an example:

---

[3]If they didn't want the survivor to own the entire stereo system, they would delete this clause. Then, the survivor and the deceased's estate would own the system in the same proportions as Emiko or Sam did before the death.

AGREEMENT

Joseph Benner and Josephine Clark hereby agree that:

1. Joseph has entered into an agreement with Racafrax Company to purchase a bedroom set consisting of one king-size bed, one double dresser, two nightstands and two lamps at a total cost of $2,500.

2. Joseph has agreed to pay to Racafrax that sum in monthly installments of $240, including interest, for 12 months, due on the first of every month beginning January 1, 19___.

3. Joseph and Josephine intend that this bedroom set shall be jointly owned (50-50) and that each shall pay one-half the cost.

4. Each shall make one-half of the payments on the furniture. Josephine shall pay Joseph $120 per month at least one week before the payment is due. Joseph shall pay the entire installment due to Racafrax in a timely manner.

5. Should either Joseph or Josephine fail to make his or her share of the payment, the other shall have the right to do so, and the ownership percentage of this person shall be proportionately increased.[4]

6. Each person shall keep a record of his or her payments made. All payments shall be made by check.

7. If Joseph and Josephine stop living together, either person may buy the bedroom set from the other by paying the other one-half of the bedroom set's current resale value; Consideration will be made of any money still owing.

8. If Joseph and Josephine cannot agree as provided in paragraph 7, the furniture shall be sold. Any balance owed Racafrax shall be paid, and the remaining money shall be divided equally unless either Joseph or Josephine has made extra payments under paragraph 5 of this agreement, in which case he or she shall be entitled to the percentage of the payments he or she made.

9. Should either Joseph or Josephine die while they are living together, the furniture shall belong absolutely to the other. If either Joseph or Josephine makes an estate

---

[4]If, for example, Josephine made eight payments (all of hers and two of Joseph's), she'd own 8/12 or 2/3 of the furniture.

plan, this provision shall be incorporated in that document.[5]

10. This agreement can be amended, but only in writing, and must be signed by both Joseph and Josephine.

11. Joseph and Josephine agree if a court finds any portion of this contract to be illegal or otherwise unenforceable, that the remainder of the contract is still in full force and effect.

12. [Insert mediation/arbitration clause from Section L]

_____   _____
Date   Joseph Benner

_____   _____
Date   Josephine Clark

Note: If only one of you signs a credit agreement to purchase an item, only that person is legally obligated to pay the creditor. This is true even if you and your friend sign an agreement to share ownership and payments. The creditor will accept money from anyone and properly credit the account, but if a payment isn't made, the creditor will pursue only the person whose name is on the account.

E. Agreement Covering Joint Projects

JOHN AND MARSHA LIVE together. They have no property to speak of, but they have a dream—to build a boat and sail around the world. They know it will take a lot of time, energy and cooperation, and want to protect their vision should any of life's disappointments affect their relationship.

AGREEMENT

John and Marsha agree as follows:

1. That they both want to construct a 30-foot sailboat to be jointly owned upon completion.

2. That each will contribute $12,000 for the purchase of necessary supplies.

---

[5] If they didn't want the survivor to own the entire bedroom set, they would delete this clause. Then, the survivor and the deceased's estate would own the set in the same proportions as Joseph and Josephine did before the death.

3. That each person will work diligently on the boat (this means at least 20 hours per month).

4. That should they separate, Marsha shall have the opportunity to buy out John's share for an amount of money equal to John's actual cash investment plus $10 per hour for each hour he has worked on the boat.[6]

5. That if they separate and Marsha decide not to buy out John's share under the terms of paragraph 4, John shall have the opportunity to buy out Marsha's share on the same terms.

6. That should neither John nor Marsha elect to purchase the other's share of the boat at separation, they shall sell the boat and divide the proceeds equally.

7. That if either fails to work on the boat at least 20 hours per month for three consecutive months, the other may buy out non-worker's share under the terms of paragraph 4.

8. That should either John or Marsha die while this agreement is still in effect, the other becomes sole owner of the boat. If either John or Marsha makes an estate plan, this provision will be incorporated in that document.[7]

9. That this agreement can be amended, but only in writing, and must be signed by both John and Marsha.

10. That if the court finds any portion of this contract to be illegal or otherwise unenforceable, that the remainder of the contract is still in full force and effect.

11. [Insert mediation/arbitration clause from Section L]

_____   _____
Date   John Mason

_____   _____
Date   Marsha Deere

---

[6]There are, of course, other ways to handle a break-up— selling the unfinished boat to the highest bidder and then dividing the proceeds, or flipping a coin to decide who gets first right to buy it. If you use the method we set out above, calculate the value of each person's work realistically. If, because of experience or training, the work of one of you is more valuable than the other's work, modify the agreement.

[7]If they didn't want the survivor to own the entire boat, they would delete this clause. Then, the survivor and the deceased's estate would own the boat in the same proportions as John and Marsha did before the death.

F. Agreement Covering Homemaker Services

TED IS 45, DIVORCED and has custody of his two children. He's a physician with an annual net income in excess of $100,000. Joanne is 38, also divorced with custody of her child. Her ex-husband never pays child support. Ted and Joanne decide to live together and agree that Ted will earn the money and Joanne will take care of the children and of the household full time.

They want a contract that will provide Joanne with fair compensation for housework and child care, but not give her any rights to Ted's property should they separate.

AGREEMENT

Ted Corbett and Joanne Lewis agree that they plan to live together and hope theirs will be a committed, long-term relationship that will provide love and nurturing for both themselves and their children. In a spirit of fairness, and to help this come about, they agree that:

1. Ted shall continue to work as a physician. He and Joanne expect that he'll work 40-50 hours a week and will have little time or energy to care for the home.

2. Joanne will work in the home raising the children and doing all the domestic chores including the cleaning, laundry, cooking and gardening. Ted will pay Joanne $300 a week for her services, over and above the costs of running the home as set out in paragraph 7. These payments shall be adjusted from time to time to reflect changes in the cost of living.

3. Ted will make Social Security and other legally-required employer payments for Joanne as his employee and will pay for medical insurance coverage for her and her son, Tim.

4. All real and personal property owned by either Ted or Joanne prior to the date of this agreement shall remain the separate property of its owner. (They should attach an itemized list.)

5. As of the date of this agreement, all property owned, earned or accumulated by Ted or Joanne shall belong solely to the person earning or accumulating it. The home and furnishings will be provided by Ted and owned solely by him. All property purchased by Joanne with her earnings will belong to her.

6. The separate property of either Ted or Joanne, owned now, or acquired in the future can become the separate property of the other, or their joint property only under the terms of a written agreement signed by the person whose separate property is to be re-classified.

7. Ted will provide reasonable amounts of money each month to provide food, clothing, shelter and recreation for the entire family as long as they live together. [By doing this, Ted assumes no obligation to support Joanne or her son upon termination of this agreement]. (Delete this bracketed material if you include bracketed material in paragraph 8).

8. Either Ted or Joanne can end this agreement by giving the other two months' written notice. No reason is necessary. [Joanne will be entitled to severance pay at her then current weekly rate of pay for two months for every year this agreement has been in effect. This shall be paid by Ted in a lump sum at the time of separation. Neither Ted nor Joanne shall have any other financial obligation to the other upon separation.] (Delete this bracketed material if you include bracketed material in paragraph 7.)[8]

9. [Insert mediation/arbitration clause from Section L.]

10. This agreement represents Ted and Joanne's complete understanding regarding their living together and replaces any and all prior agreements, written oral. It can be amended, but only in writing, and must be signed by both parties.

11. If a court finds any portion of this contract to be illegal or otherwise unenforceable, that the remainder of the contract is still in force and effect.

_____	_____
Date	Ted Corbett
_____	_____
Date	Joanne Lewis

---

[8]See Chapter 10 for more information on separation agreements.

Note—One Person's Promise to Raise the Children of the Other: When members of an unmarried couple have minor children from a prior marriage, they often want to agree by contract that, should one of them die, the other will raise the children. This type of contractual provision isn't legally enforceable. To nominate your friend as personal guardian of your children, you must do so in your will. If your children's other legal parent (who usually has first claim of custody) is deceased, has abandoned the children, or isn't a fit parent, a court will likely honor your wishes and appoint your friend as guardian should you die before the children reach age 18.

G. Agreement Covering Household Expenses and Personal Idiosyncrasies

ANNIE AND CLEM HAVE been seeing each other for over two years and have decided to live together. Annie is a fashion model and Clem is a private detective. They want to keep their earnings and property separate, and want to spell out their general understandings and agreements.

AGREEMENT

Annie Auburn and Clem Black agree that:

1. They plan to live together for the indefinite future.

2. Each will use his or her own name.

3. Neither will use the credit of the other and both will maintain separate bank and credit accounts.

4. They shall keep their earnings and other assets separate, that all real and personal property, whenever accumulated, shall be kept separate and that each shall be responsible for his or her personal expenses including clothing, medical and dental bills, long-distance telephone calls, car, entertainment and the like, unless otherwise agreed to in writing. If they acquire any property jointly, they shall make a separate written agreement to cover this property and what happens to it if they separate.

5. Financial management of the joint household bills, which include rent, utilities, food, cleaning supplies, laundry and dry cleaning shall be payable using a "joint funds" system that shall work as follows:

    a. Each year on January 1, Clem and Annie will tell one another the amount of their current annual income after taxes (minus any alimony or child support paid for prior family obligations).

b. The two income figures shall then be totaled and a ratio arrived at by dividing the total into Annie's net income and then into Clem's net income.

c. Household expenses shall be paid according to the ratios. For example, if Annie clears $60,000 and Clem $45,000, the total—$105,000—would be divided into $60,000 and $45,000 respectively. Annie would pay 57% of the total household expenses and Clem 43%.

6. Annie and Clem's separate property, whether owned now or acquired in the future, can become the separate property of the other, or Clem and Annie's joint property, only under the terms of a written agreement signed by the person whose property is to be re-classified.

7. Each shall be responsible for domestic tasks.[9] Certain daily tasks, however, will be assigned based on the following reality: Annie has no love for shopping and cooking, while Clem isn't too neat and doesn't require as high a standard of order and cleanliness as does Annie.

a. Clem will do food shopping and cooking and will take care of all the plants.

b. Annie will wash dishes and do the cleaning, including general straightening, sweeping, dusting and keeping the bathroom in order.

8. Neither Clem nor Annie wants children at this point. Because the most effective mutually acceptable birth control methods on the market today are female contraceptives, Annie will take responsibility for birth control. If, however, a safe and effective oral male contraceptive becomes available, Clem agrees to use it.[10]

9. Either Clem or Annie can terminate this agreement by giving the other a 30-day written notice. Upon separation, each shall take possession of his or her separate property and any jointly held property will be divided according to their written joint ownership agreements.

10. Neither Clem nor Annie will have any financial responsibility to support the other after separation.

---

[9]Agreements to perform domestic tasks are expressions of intent, not enforceable contracts.

[10]Agreements to have or not to have children are only expressions of intent and not legally enforceable contracts. See Chapter 8, *Starting a Family.*

11. This agreement represents Clem's and Annie's complete understanding regarding their living together and replaces any and all prior agreements, written or oral. It can be amended, but only in writing, and must be signed by both people.

12. That if a court finds any portion of this contract to be illegal or otherwise unenforceable, that the remainder of the contract is still in full force and effect.

13. [Insert mediation/arbitration clause in Section L]

_____   _____
Date   Annie Auburn

_____   _____
Date   Clem Black

H. Agreement for Struggling Artists

TERRI AND CHRIS HAVE lived together on and off for three years. They decide to enter into a living together agreement that would give each time to pursue his or her own interests. Terri is a potter

and Chris is a musician, but both have taken part-time jobs in order to make ends meet. Now they plan to take turns supporting each other, so that the person being supported can pursue his or her personal muse full-time.

AGREEMENT

Terri McGraw and Chris Macklin agree as follows:

1. Each of us will keep as our separate property, all property (and income earned by that property in the future) held as of the date of this agreement. Any property or income, including salaries or financial returns from artistic pursuits, which either of us earns or acquires from this date forward, belong equally to us as long as we live

together. All joint funds will be kept in joint savings and checking accounts.

2. We agree to take turns working at regular full-time jobs in order to earn enough money for us to live on. While one person works, the other will be free to pursue his or her creative endeavors. Terri will work for the first six months of this agreement, Chris the next six months and then we will alternate six-month periods for the duration of this agreement.

3. All our household expenses and personal and medical expenses will be assumed by the one who's employed at the time the expense is incurred.

4. If we have children, we agree to participate in at least three conciliation sessions before we cease to live together;[11]

5. If one of us wants to end the relationship and the other doesn't, before splitting up, we agree to participate in conciliation sessions with a mutually acceptable third party. If, after a minimum of three sessions, one of us still wants to end the relationship, it will be.

Each of us will take our separate property (property we owned prior to living together). All jointly-owned property (property acquired or created while we lived together) will be evenly divided, except for our unsold artwork, including works in progress more than half complete, which will belong to both of us for three years. During the three years, we will actively try to sell this artwork at a reasonable price. All proceeds received (including periodic payments such as royalties) during this period will be equally divided. Any work that cannot with reasonable diligence be sold during this period belongs to its creator. No other financial responsibilities will continue between us after separation.

6. Chris and Terri's separate property (property owned before signing this agreement, or income from that property) cannot become the separate property of the other or the

---

[11]We include an agreement to try to work out problems that threaten a relationship with a third party because many people want it. We don't routinely include this language in agreements because conciliation and other problem-solving techniques are effective only if both people are fully committed to the process when the problems arise,; thus, it's not normally effective to try to make this commitment in advance.

joint property of both without a written agreement signed by the person whose separate property is to be re-classified.

7. This agreement represents our complete understanding regarding our living together and replaces any and all prior agreements, written or oral. It can be amended, but only in writing, and must be signed by both of us.

8. If a court finds any portion of this contract to be illegal or otherwise unenforceable, the remainder of the contract is still in full force and effect.

9. [Insert mediation/arbitration clause from Section L]

_____   _____
Date   Terri McGraw

_____   _____
Date   Chris Macklin

I. Agreement for People in School

AGREEMENTS FOR UNMARRIED couples where one will help support the other, a student, can take many different forms. Here, Carol plans to become a veterinarian and Bill is an aspiring dentist. To maximize both career opportunities and their personal relationship, they use the following contract. You'll need to modify it to fit your situation.

AGREEMENT

Carol Thayer and Bill Fujimoto agree as follows:

1. That they're living together and plan to continue to do so indefinitely.

2. That all property owned by either person prior to the date of this agreement (including all future income earned

from this property) shall be the separate property of its owner.

3. That they'll take turns going to school so that the one not in school can support the other until he/she gets a degree. They'll flip a coin to decide who goes first. The loser will be responsible for the winner's educational expenses and support, to $12,000 per year, for three years. At the end of three years, the winner will assume these responsibilities for the loser, for three years, to $14,000 per year.

If they split up during the first two years, the student shall pay the other $1,000 per month for each month he/she has been in school. If the relationship lasts more than two years, their financial obligations shall not be affected by subsequent separation. Thus, if dissolution occurs during the third year, the non-student still must pay the other's tuition and living expenses to $12,000 for that year. If dissolution occurs in year four, five or six, the then student shall be supported by the other to $14,000 per year. All tuition is to be paid when due, and all living expenses in 12 equal monthly payments.

4. During the first six years they live together, all income and property of either person, excluding gifts and inheritances, shall be jointly owned. The income-producing person will manage and control the funds. After six years, they will inventory their accumulated property and divide it equally. Thereafter, each person's earnings shall be his or her separate property and neither will have any interest in the present or future property of the other.

If Carol and Bill separate before the end of six years, all accumulated property shall be divided according to the fraction of time each has provided the support (if Carol supports Bill for three years and Bill support her for two, Carol is entitled to three-fifths of the property). After separation, neither shall have any financial obligations to the other except as set out in paragraph 3.

5. Carol and Bill will retain their own surnames.

6. If they have children, Carol and Bill agree to participate in at least three conciliation sessions before separating.

7. Any change in the ownership status of any property (from separate to joint, or from separate one person to the

separate of the other) shall be made in writing and signed by the person making the transfer.

8. This agreement is Bill and Carol's complete understanding regarding their living together and replaces any and all prior agreements, written or oral. It can be amended, but only in writing, and must be signed by both.

9. If a court finds any portion of this contract to be illegal or otherwise unenforceable, that the remainder of the contract is still in full force and effect.

10.[Insert mediation/arbitration clause in Section L]

_____   _____
Date   Bill Fujimoto

_____   _____
Date   Carol Thayer

J. Agreement to Protect Person Who Moves a Long Distance or Gives Up a Job

OCCASIONALLY, ONE PARTNER moves a considerable distance to be with the other. Sometimes it's no particular hardship and in fact, a welcomed adventure. Other times, however, it's traumatic, and may involve giving up a good job and a supportive network of family and friends. And there's always the fear that the relationship won't work out and the person who moved will have to go back, or be alone in a new town. This can compounded if the mover has small children.

To deal with this potential problem, some couples agree that the person who moved or gave up a job will be compensated if the relationship dissolves within a relatively short time. Here are two slightly different clauses that can be included in any living together contract in this book:

As a condition of Sarah giving up her job and moving with John to _____ _____(place)_____, John agrees

that if, for any reason, they cease living together before _____(date)_____, John shall immediately pay Sarah _____(amount)_____ to help her establish a separate household.

or

John and Sarah agree that as a condition of John giving up his present employment and moving to _____ _____(location)_____ to live with Sarah, she will immediately pay him the sum of _____(amount_____.

K. Enforceability of Contracts

AS WE'VE STATED, agreements between unmarried partners are generally enforceable to the extent they cover property, payment for services or payment in exchange for a person giving something up. To the extent they cover nonmonetary issues, they're unlikely enforceable. So, your agreement to pay your friend $500 a month for two years in exchange for putting you through school should be enforced by a court; a contract to feed Nectarine, the pet turtle, however, on the days your friend gets up early to make coffee, won't be.

In addition, a living together contract won't be enforced if a judge concludes that one person has taken advantage of the other. As an extreme example, a court won't uphold a one-sided living together contract made by a lawyer with an unsophisticated nineteen-year-old who just moved to America and speaks little English. If one of you is more savvy in business than the other, and a lot of property or income is involved, the less business-wise person should briefly consult with a lawyer before signing.

Georgia and Illinois Note: As we discussed in Chapter 4, *Living Together Contracts and the Law,* in Georgia and Illinois it's unlikely that any living together contract is enforceable. Courts in those states still think that living together is sinful and that living together contracts somehow encourage the "nasty practice." It's possible that a few traditionally-minded judges in other parts of the country would follow these states, but the trend is the other way. If you're worried about the state of the law in your area, see a lawyer before signing on the dotted line.

L. Solving Problems Without Going to Court

UNTIL FAIRLY RECENTLY, most lawyers, and a surprising number of others, believed that people bickering—at the near lawsuit level—should have a lawyer and do battle in court. Now, many people (even some lawyers) prefer alternatives to court, especially mediation and arbitration.

In mediation, the disputing parties meet with a neutral person—the mediator—who draws out the issues and helps the parties to settle their own dispute. With arbitration, an agreed-upon person or persons—the arbitrators—decide a dispute that has been presented to them by the parties (or their lawyers) in an adversarial context.

1. Mediation

The great attraction of mediation is that no one has the power to impose a solution on the disputing couple; rather, the parties to the dispute must voluntarily agree. Unlike a lawsuit (or even arbitration), the mediator's role is to help the disputants find common ground. When this happens, both parties usually feel like winners (or at least, not defeated) and a good foundation is laid for future dealings. This is especially important if the couple has children.

2. Arbitration

In many ways, arbitration resembles litigation—the arbitrator acts like a judge and the rules that govern often resemble court procedures. There are, however, important differences. Arbitration takes place without a long delay, is less costly, is private and usually, the disputing parties decide what rules govern the procedure (including, for example, prohibiting lawyers). In a sense, you and the other party hire a neutral person to solve your dispute reasonably, quickly and efficiently.

3. Which is Better?

We believe that mediation is the better dispute resolution for unmarried couples. It works particularly well when you lay all the facts on the table, and confidently assert your point of view. If one of you is far more powerful or informed than the other, however, mediation may be too one-sided. In that case, the weaker person will probably want to hire a lawyer, and have the issues resolved in arbitration, or as a last resort, in court.

Mediation's Advantages

- Mediation is always less costly than litigation and almost always cheaper than arbitration.

- Mediation allows the disputing people to solve their problem themselves.

- Mediation is faster and less stressful than arbitration or litigation

- Mediation is private.

If mediation fails to resolve a dispute, arbitration is the next best choice. Thus, we recommend that you include a mediation/arbitration clause in any agreement you write. What follows is one mediation/arbitration provision. If you don't like ours, you can find other mediation/arbitration provisions at your local law library.

MEDIATION & ARBITRATION CLAUSE

Any dispute arising out of this agreement shall be mediated by a third person mutually acceptable to both of us.[12] The mediator's role shall be to help us arrive at a solution, not to impose one on us. If good faith efforts to arrive at our own solution with the help of a mediator prove to be fruitless, either may make a written request to the other that the dispute be arbitrated.

Our dispute will be submitted to arbitration under the rules of the American Arbitration Association. One arbitrator will hear our dispute.[13] The decision of the arbitrator shall be binding on us and shall be enforceable in any court which has jurisdiction over the controversy.

---

[12]If you both trust someone you think might work well, consider naming that person in the contract as your mediator. Of course, make sure he or she is willing to serve before you do this. If you can't find a mutually acceptable mediator, the American Arbitration Association will, for a fee, make a referral.

[13]Under the American Arbitration Association's rules, you can have your case heard by one arbitrator or three arbitrators. If you prefer three, replace "one arbitrator" with "three arbitrators." The more arbitrators you hire, however, the more expensive and complicated the arbitration will be.

4. If You Do Have a Dispute

If you and your partner are disputing and want outside help, your first step is to find a mediator. If you named someone in your living together agreement, great. If not, finding a mediator shouldn't be too hard—mediation services for domestic disputes are widely available. Key is finding someone with good human relations skills and a basic knowledge of the law relating to unmarried couples. Getting a personal referral from a friend, co-worker, lawyer, therapist or clergyperson is best. Failing that, look in the yellow pages. Call a local mediation organization for a referral.

If mediation fails, arbitration is your next best bet. We recommend working with the American Arbitration Association (AAA), an established,non-profit leader in the field. AAA has a detailed

system of arbitration rules, and a large network of arbitrators.

You can use AAA in two ways. First, you can submit your dispute directly to AAA. They'll appoint an arbitrator(s), set the places and dates of your hearings and charge you for the service. Their fees run from $300 to $1,250 or more, depending on how much you're arguing over.

If you don't want to submit your dispute to AAA, ask AAA to send you its rules, and apply them yourself. You would choose your own arbitrator—the person named as mediator in your living together agreement, a mutually-acceptable person chosen when the dispute arose, or a professional arbitrator (look in the yellow pages under Mediation Services or Alternative Dispute Resolution).

Briefly, AAA's basic rules are as follows:

- either of you may request arbitration.
- both of you may have lawyers.
- both of you may submit evidence and call witnesses.

- if your dispute involves financial matters, you both must make full financial disclosures.
- if your dispute involves child custody, the arbitrator can interview the child, but cannot force the child to choose between his or her parents.
- hearings are private. Anyone other than the disputing people (and their lawyers) must have the arbitrator's permission to attend.
- the arbitrator must make a decision within 30 days after the hearing.
- arbitration can proceed even if one person doesn't show up, if that person was notified. The other person still must submit evidence; the arbitrator's decision will be binding on both people.

M. A Living Together Certificate

IF YOU VISIT A COUNTY CLERK and fill out the papers necessary to get married, you're basically paying the government a tax for permission to live together. There's nothing wrong with this. If you ever want the permission slip to end the marriage, however, the fees will be vastly higher.

Of course, to live with your lover, you need no permission slip and you pay no tax. But many of us love certificates. The good news is you don't have to get married to get one—you can make your own. Paper and ink are cheap, and a printer can doubtless help you make up a wonderful official-looking (or kooky) certificate for less than the county clerk will charge. And isn't being independent and creative what living together is all about? In the event neither of you is a budding artist, we include a living together certificate in the Appendix. Ours hangs over the stove—half as a joke and half as a reminder that we're serious about our relationship.

Chapter

Six

Renting and Sharing a Home

IT'S TIME FOR YOUR SECOND vocabulary lesson. (The first one came in Chapter 2, *Sex, Living Together and the Law*.)

Assignment—an assignment of a lease is when one tenant moves out, another moves in in her place, and the second tenant takes over the remainder of the first tenant's lease.

Evict—to legally force someone to move out of an apartment or house. The landlord must sue the tenant and obtain a court order that the tenant remove himself from the premises.

Landlord (Male), **Landlady** (Female), **Landperson** (Gender Neutral)—the person who owns property rented to a tenant.

LEASE

Lease (noun)—a written agreement in which a landlord agrees to rent certain property for a specified period (such as one or two years) in exchange for a certain amount of money; the lease may contain many other agreements or restrictions. (verb)—to enter into such an agreement.

Lessee—the person who has the right to possess (live in) property under a lease; another term for tenant.

Lessor—the person (usually the owner) who leases the property to the tenant.

Liable—legally obligated; a tenant is liable to pay rent, a landlord to keep the premises habitable. If a tenant damages the property, a court can order her liable to pay for the repairs.

RENTAL AGREEMENT

Rental Agreement—A contract between a landlord and a tenant where the tenant agrees to make periodic (usually monthly) rental payments in exchange for the right to possess certain property. The agreement may be ended by either party or the rent raised on very short written notice (usually 30 days).[1] A rental agreement usually contains other agreements and restrictions, and may be written or oral.

Sublessee or subtenant—a person who leases from a tenant rather than a landlord. Most leases require the tenant to get permission from the landlord before subleasing. In many states, permission can be withheld only if the landlord has a good reason for not wanting the proposed subtenant to occupy the property.

Tenant—a person who rents property.

A. Renting a Home

THIS IS THE NITTY GRITTY, isn't it? If you're going to live with someone, you have to get a place. We can't help you find a beautiful, cheap flat across from a rose garden, but we can give you

---

[1] A few cities in California, New York, New Jersey and other states have ordinances requiring a landlord to have "just cause" to end a month-to-month tenancy. Just cause always includes a failure to pay rent and usually lets a landlord terminate a tenancy so he (or his close relatives) can occupy the unit or substantially rehabilitate it.

some hints about dealing with the landlord and each other if you do find it. We cover many of the special legal problems encountered by unmarried couples renting together, not all aspects of landlord-tenant law.

There are all sorts of landlords. A little old man who raises African violets and doesn't add well may own a house right next to a six-story building owned by an investment corporation. Their attitudes toward life (including yours) will differ vastly. We can give you information about your legal rights, but you're on your own in arriving at a good human understanding of the owner or manager.

Most landlords are interested in your money, not your morals. As long as you pay rent on time, keep the apartment clean and don't fight with the neighbors, they don't care which beds you sleep in. There are, of course, exceptions—people who still refuse to rent to unmarried couples. Some (despite the divorce statistics) believe that unmarried couples are inherently less stable than married ones. Others refuse on religious grounds.[2] Others simply won't rent to unmarried couples because they don't like them.

Do you have a legal right, as an unmarried couple, to rent a place? Although no federal law bars private housing discrimination against unmarried couples, Department of Housing and Urban Development regulations ban marital status discrimination in public housing. Otherwise, it depends on your state, city or county. Few have laws barring landlords from discriminating because you can't produce a marriage license. In the backward states where it's a crime to live together (see Chapter 2, *Sex, Living Together and the Law*), you have little recourse.

---

[2]In recent cases in Minnesota, Massachusetts and California, property owners have refused to rent to unmarried couples. The California owner refused because she feared not joining her husband in heaven if she rented to an unmarried couple. She lost at a fair housing hearing, but she has vowed to continue fighting on the ground of First Amendment religious freedom.

In more progressive states, such as Wisconsin and California, and in many cities, including New York, Washington,D.C., Seattle, Minneapolis, Philadelphia, and some university towns, laws ban sexual orientation discrimination in housing. While these laws were passed primarily to protect lesbian and gay couples, they usually protect heterosexual couples as well.

For up-to-date information for your area, call your local District Attorney's office or go to the library and get a copy of your state laws and your county and city ordinances (see Chapter 12, *More Legal Help*). Check under "Housing Discrimination."

If your area has no anti-discrimination law to protect you, you'll have to decide how open you want to be with your landlord. Here are some helpful suggestions:

- Act responsible and respectable. Present financial and personal references, especially from former landlords. If you convince a landlord that you'll be excellent tenants, other factors, such as your marital status, will be less important.

- Don't flaunt the fact that you're not married. Many landlords will assume you are and won't ask. Many won't care. And it's not illegal to wear a ring that looks like a wedding ring on the ring finger of your left hand.

- It may help to go with the flow. In every city, and most large towns, there are neighborhoods with lots of unmarried people. This tends to be especially true near universities. Ask around.

- Don't rent from someone who obviously disapproves of unmarried couples living together, even if she thinks you're married. This is especially true if she lives nearby. Life is too short for all the hassles you're inviting.

If a landlord asks if you're married, and saying no means losing the apartment, what happens if you say yes? Probably nothing, if you're otherwise good tenants. Legally, however, if you have a lease and the landlord later discovers the truth, he might have a just cause to evict you in a state where cohabitation is a crime, but not elsewhere. If you have only a month-to-month agreement, a determined bigot will easily give you 30 days notice to move out.[3] There's no realistic chance that claiming to be married when you're not will result in criminal prosecution.

How does a woman sign a lease or rental agreement when you'd just as soon have the landlord think you're married? If you use the same last name, no problem. If you use different names, there may be legal implications, but few practical ones. In most states, you can use any name you want, as long as you're not defrauding someone and you use the new name consistently. But if Clem Lawrence and Julie Renoir sign a lease as Clem Lawrence and Julie Lawrence and Julie doesn't usually use Lawrence, can she get into trouble? There's little law on the point, but it shouldn't be a problem. If they pay their rent, the landlord has suffered no financial loss and has no reason to complain.

---

[3]A few cities in California, New York, New Jersey and other states have rent control ordinances which require "just cause" to terminate a tenancy—even a month-to-month one. Many of these cities also prohibit housing discrimination against unmarried couples. So if you rent in a city with a rent control law prohibiting evictions without just cause, living together probably won't provide that cause.

Worrying about how to sign your name is pretty dismal, isn't it? As society tolerates more lifestyles, however, the problem should be less frequent. In the end, good business will probably win over good morals and landlords will rent to those who pay on the first of the month, without regard to their participation, or non-participation, in civil ceremonies. We hope that day is almost here.

B. Leases and Rental Agreements

BEFORE SIGNING, CAREFULLY EXAMINE the fine print rules and regulations (called covenants). Many are extremely restrictive and some are downright illegal, but landlords use pre-printed, and often out-of-date, forms. For example, the form may purport to give the landlord the right to evict you without getting a court order (or posting a bond) if you fail to pay the rent. This is illegal—only a judge can order that you be moved out.

We don't have the room to list all illegal lease provisions, but if something rubs you the wrong way, check it out; look particularly for a clause prohibiting "immoral behavior." If living together is legal in your state, this clause can't be used to evict you, but if cohabitation is still illegal where you live, a landlord may attempt to evict you. Consider asking the landlord to cross out any "immoral behavior" language. If she refuses, it's probably a good sign that you'd be happier renting elsewhere.

Important: Keep copies of all leases, rental agreements and correspondence with your landlord in a safe place in case a misunderstanding develops. In general, it's best to act in a friendly, courteous manner and hope for the same in return; but be prepared for the worst.

C. Moving in Together

WHEN YOU RENT TOGETHER, you create legal obligations vis-a-vis the landlord and each other. Let's consider each of these separately.

1. Legal Obligations to the Landlord

If both of you enter into a lease or rental agreement with the landlord, you're each on the hook for *all* rent and *all* damages to your place. It doesn't matter if the woman used the man's last name when she signed; she's still liable

> Example 1: *Clem and Julie sign a month-to-month rental agreement for $700 a month. They agree between themselves to each pay one-half of the rent. After three months, Clem moves out with no notice to Julie or the landlord. Julie is liable for all the rent. Clem, of course, is equally liable, but if he's unreachable, the landlord will come after Julie for all of it. Julie can cut her losses by giving her landlord written notice of her intention to move, and when she moves out, her liability ends.*

> Example 2: *This time, Clem just lies about the place, refusing to pay or leave. Even if Julie gives written notice and moves out, she may still be liable for Clem's rent. Her best bet is to cajole (or even bribe) Clem to get out. If he refuses and Julie leaves, the landlord will evict Clem and possibly try to collect any unpaid rent from Julie.*

> Example 3: *The same facts as Example 1, but they have a one year lease. Again, Clem and Julie are both liable for all the rent. If one won't pay, the other must unless someone new is found to take over the lease. This may be easy if Julie and Clem live where there's a rental housing shortage. The landlord must limit his lost rent (called "mitigation of damages") by renting to a suitable new tenant. If the landlord doesn't, he loses the right to collect lost rent from Julie and Clem.*

If either Clem or Julie pays the landlord more than his or her fair share of the rent, the person who paid too much can recover from the other. If payment isn't made voluntarily, try Small Claims Court.[4]

2. Legal Obligations of the Tenants to Each Other

People renting together usually have certain expectations of each other. Sometimes it helps to write them down. After all, you sign an agreement with a landlord almost as a matter of course—why not do the same with each other? It helps refresh memories if the relationship gets rocky. Below we give you a sample agreement to cover rented living space. This can stand alone, or be incorporated into a more comprehensive living together contract, such as the ones discussed in Chapter 5, *Contracts.*

---

[4]See *Everybody's Guide to Small Claims Court,* Warner, Nolo Press.

AGREEMENT

Julie Renoir and Clem Lawrence agree that:

1. They will jointly rent apartment number 4 at 1500 Peanut Street, Falfurrias, Texas.

2. Each of them will pay one-half of the rent and one-half of the utilities, including the basic monthly telephone charge. Each person will keep track of and pay for his or her long distance calls. Rent shall be paid on the first of each month and utilities within ten days of when the bill is received.

3. If either wants to move out, the one moving will give the other and the landlord 30 days' written notice and will pay his/her share of the rent for the entire 30-day period even if he/she moves out sooner.

4. No third person will be invited to stay in the apartment without the agreement of both.

5. If one person no longer wishes to live with the other, but both want to keep the apartment, they will ask a third person to flip a coin to see who gets to stay. The loser shall move out within 30 days and shall, within 10 days of moving out, pay all of his/her obligations for rent, utilities and any damage to the apartment.

　　or

5. If one person no longer wishes to live with the other, but both want to keep the apartment, the person who needs the apartment most shall retain it. Need shall be determined by a third party who Julie and Clem agree is objective, within two weeks of when one informs the other that he/she wishes to separate. Consideration shall be given to each other's relative financial condition, proximity to work, the needs of any minor children and [list any other important factors]. The person who is to leave shall do so within two weeks of when that decision is made, and shall have an additional 10 days to pay his/her obligations for rent, utilities and any damage to the apartment.

6. [Insert mediation/arbitration clause from Chapter 5, Section L]

_____   _____
Date   Julie Renoir

_____   _____
Date   Clem Lawrence

D. Moving Into a Friend's Home

PERHAPS JUST AS COMMON as two people looking for a home together is one person moving in with the other. This can be simple and smooth where the landlord is relaxed and sensible, but can raise tricky problems and isn't recommended if the landlord is a Neanderthal idiot who despises unmarried couples. When it comes to arguing with idiots, our best advice is don't. Use the time and energy to look for a place where the landlord is pleasant.

Sometimes, especially if the landlord lives far away or isn't likely to make waves, it seems sensible to have the second person move in and worry about the consequences later. But isn't a tenant required to tell the landlord when a second person moves in? It depends on the lease or rental agreement. Read it carefully. If it doesn't mention the number of people allowed in the apartment (most do), use your discretion and knowledge of your landlord. Some don't care or (like parents) would prefer not to know.

Remember, though, that a written rental agreement can be terminated on short notice (30 days in most states) without any reason given. A landlord can easily get rid of you unless you have a lease or live in a city with rent control requiring "just cause" for eviction. In our experience, however, if you have a good payment record and are cooperative, a landlord won't bother putting you out even if he prefers people who've mumbled "until death do us part."

If your town or state prohibits marital status discrimination in housing, your landlord can't legally put you out because you're living together. If he tries, file a complaint with the local or state agency charged with enforcing the anti-discrimination law. Of course, the landlord can evict you for violating another term of the rental agreement (e.g., only one person may live in the house) or may make up a phony reason. If you suspect the latter, file your complaint and let the landlord explain why he found you to be an adequate tenant while you lived alone but wants to evict you now that you live with someone. If the landlord files an eviction action in court, you'll have to make your case to the judge.

If you have a lease, you may be in a better bargaining position if your friend moves in. To evict you before the lease expires, the landlord must establish that you violated a lease term. If your lease allows occupancy by only one person, your landlord probably wins if your friend moved in without the landlord's permission. If the landlord accepts rent from him, however, the landlord probably waived his right to enforce that clause.

If the lease simply says that the premises shall not be used for "immoral or illegal purposes," it's highly questionable whether the landlord can terminate the lease, unless your state still makes cohabitation illegal. If it doesn't, and your landlord tried to evict and you defended in court, your success would probably depend on the biases of the judge. In any case, the landlord wouldn't be sure of winning and would probably hesitate to incur the time and expense of an eviction if you're a good tenant. Of course, the landlord can refuse to renew your lease when it runs out. Again, unless your town has rent control or prohibits marital status discrimination, this refusal would probably be legal.

If one of you plans to move into the other's rented space, here's our advice:

- Read the lease or rental agreement to see how many people may live on the premises. Typically, additional people are for a slight rent increase. As long as the extra rent isn't excessive under the circumstances, the landlord's position is reasonable, and you should offer to pay the extra.

- Contact the landlord as far in advance as possible to explain your plans. If you can't do it in person, send a letter like the one below:

1500 Peanut Street, #4
Falfurrias, Texas
June 2, 19__

Smith Realty
10 Jones Street
Falfurrias, Texas

Dear Smith Realty:

I live at the above address and regularly pay rent to your office. As of July 1, 19__, a second person will be living in my apartment. As set forth in my lease, I enclose the increased rent due that now comes to a total of $700. I will continue making payments in this amount as long as two people occupy the apartment. If you want us to sign a new lease, please let us know. My friend, Julie Renoir, is regularly employed and has an excellent credit rating.

Very truly yours,

Clem Lawrence

1. The Legal Relationship Between the Person Moving In and Landlord

If Julie moves into Clem's apartment, what is her legal relationship with the landlord? Must she pay rent if Clem doesn't? If Clem ruins or breaks the windows, must Julie pay for the damage? And if Clem dies or moves out, can Julie remain?

Julie begins with no obligation to pay the rent or for damage, and no right to live in the apartment, as she has no contract with the landlord.[5] Clem, who has a lease, remains completely liable for the rent and any damage he causes. If Clem leaves or dies, Julie has no right to take over his lease without the landlord's consent.[6]

Julie can, of course, gain the rights and responsibilities of a tenant by:

- Signing a new lease or rental agreement that named both Clem and Julie as tenants. Clem would have to agree with this, and he might not if he wants to be in a better position to keep the apartment if he and Julie break up. This can be particularly important if the apartment qualifies for rent control and the rent is low (see Section 2 for more).

If Things Get Ugly

Terri and Joe had been dating for a year when Joe moved into her apartment, with the landlord's permission, for a small rent increase. Terri had a month-to-month rental agreement, which Joe didn't sign. He agreed, however, to pay Terri half of the rent.

---

[5]If she damages the property, she'd be liable just like a visitor, a trespasser or a thief who caused damage.

[6]Unless they live in New York City in a rent-controlled or rent-stabilized apartment where *Braschi v. Stahl Associates Co.* 74 N.Y.2d 201 (1989) and regulations enacted after that case prohibit landlords from evicting an unrelated tenant if the people lived together no less than two years and can show "an emotional and financial commitment and interdependence."

Things were fine for two months, and then Joe lost his job and became depressed. He stopped paying rent, and he and Terri argued constantly. Terri wanted him out, but Joe said he was just as much a tenant as she was, and that she'd be the one who'd have to leave. Terri enlisted the help of mutual friends and a city mediation service, but Joe was stubborn, unreasonable and uncooperative.

Terri liked her apartment and wasn't going to move, so she had Joe served with a three-day notice to move or pay the rent.[7]. She stayed with a friend, and when the three days ran out, she served Joe with eviction notice. Joe moved out before the court hearing, but Terri went to court and got a money judgment for Joe's share of the unpaid rent. Fortunately for Terri, Joe got a job and became less depressed. He eventually paid her what he owed.

- Making an oral rental agreement with the landlord. An oral agreement can be no more than a conversation between Julie and the landlord in which she says she'll pay the rent and keep the place clean and he says okay. If Clem and the landlord have a written agreement and Julie and the landlord have an oral one, the landlord may claim that there's no agreement with Julie, but most judges will give Julie the rights and responsibilities of a tenant if she has obviously been one.

- Julie paying rent to the landlord and the landlord accepting it, especially if it's done on a regular basis. This would set up a month-to-month tenancy between Julie and the landlord, and would require written notice (by either one) of an intent to end the tenancy.

If Clem ever wants to move out and Julie remain, Julie and the landlord's legal relationship needs to be clear. Clem should give written notice of his leaving at least 30 days before he leaves. If he has a rental agreement, he owes no rent after the 30 days. If he has a lease and leaves before it expires, he's still okay because the landlord must limit his loss by finding a new tenant. Because Julie, a reasonably solvent and non-destructive person, wants to stay, there's no loss. If the landlord refuses Julie without good reason, Clem still owes no money, and any loss is the landlord's problem for refusing to let Julie remain.

---

[7]A short notice period (often three days) is allowed to evict when a tenant hasn't paid the rent. This is usually a landlord's remedy, but a tenant may be able to use it against a sub-tenant. It's not clear in every state, and Terri may be better off by simply giving the landlord 30 days notice that she plans to move, and leave the landlord to evict Joe.

(For use if you have a rental agreement)

> 1500 Peanut Street, #4
> Falfurrias, Texas
> June 27, 19__
>
> Smith Realty
> 10 Jones Street
> Falfurrias, Texas
>
> Dear Smith Realty:
>
> I live at the above address and regularly pay rent to your office. On July 31, 19__ I'll be moving out. As you know, my friend Julie Renoir also resides here. She wishes to remain and will continue to pay rent to your office on the first of each month.
>
> We'll be contacting you soon to arrange for the return of my damage deposit of $300, at which time Julie will give you a similar deposit. If you have any questions, or if there's anything we can do to make the transition easier, please let us know.
>
> Very truly yours,
>
> Clem Lawrence

(For use if you have a rental agreement)

> 1500 Peanut Street, #4
> Falfurrias, Texas
> June 27, 19__
>
> Smith Realty
> 10 Jones Street
> Falfurrias, Texas
>
> Dear Smith Realty:
>
> I live at the above address under a lease that expires on October 30, 19__. A change in my job makes it necessary that I leave on the last day of August. As you know, for the last six months my friend, Julie Renoir, has been sharing this apartment. Julie wishes to either take over my lease or enter into a new one with you for the remainder of my lease term. She's employed, has a stable income and will, of course, be a responsible tenant.
>
> We will soon be contacting your office to work out the details of the transfer. If you have any concerns, please give us a call.
>
> Very truly yours,
>
> Clem Lawrence

What if Clem was evicted (for a reason other than Julie's moving in) or died, or the building is slated for conversion to a condominium? Does Julie have any rights?

If Clem was evicted, Julie has no legal rights until she enters into an agreement with the landlord or until the landlord consents to Julie's being on the premises. If Clem is evicted (for not paying rent, or for being noisy, dirty or rude to other tenants), chances are the landlord will want Julie out too.

If Clem dies, the landlord will probably let Julie stay if the landlord had a good relationship with Clem, and if Julie can show she'll be able to pay the rent.[8]

If the building converts to a co-op or condominium, Clem has whatever rights his state law or local ordinances give tenants (usually the right to buy their unit and sometimes to remain as a tenant for a reasonable period after conversion); Julie has no rights unless she has legal status as a tenant. If Clem lives in a co-op or condo when Julie moves in, and Clem wants Julie to have the property should he die, he must name Julie as his "successor in interest" on the ownership document and leave the unit to Julie in his estate plan

---

Important: Rental agreements, leases, evictions and general landlord-tenant law can get confusing. If you have a problem, you'll need to find some tenants' rights information particular to your state. Also, consider consulting a tenant's organization, or a lawyer who specializes in the field, for a one-time consultation. This needn't be expensive and you'll then know your rights (see Chapter 12, *More Legal Help*).

---

[8]In New York City, Julie will be allowed to stay if she was in a rent-controlled or rent-stabilized apartment, had been there at lease two years and she and Clem had an "emotional and financial commitment and interdependence." See footnote 6.

2. The Legal Relationship Between the Person Moving In and the Person Already There

Alas, it seems all too common that big-brained monkeys go through violent changes in emotional feelings. A relationship that's all sunshine and roses one minute may be more like a skunk cabbage in a hurricane the next. Sometimes, when feelings change, memories blur and questions such as "whose apartment is this, anyway?" turn into serious disputes. When you're feeling relaxed (preferably when you first move in together), write down your understanding, either as part of a comprehensive living together agreement or in a separate agreement.

If it's done to aid the all too fallible human memory, not to promote paranoia, it should be a positive experience. Below is an example you can change to fit your circumstances. This sort of agreement is particularly wise if the right to occupy the rental unit is uniquely valuable, as is often the case if it's covered by rent control.

===

AGREEMENT

Julie Renoir and Clem Lawrence make the following agreement:

1. Clem will move into Julie's apartment and will give Julie one-half of the $700 monthly rent on the first of each month. Julie will continue paying the landlord under her lease and Clem will have no obligation under the lease.

2. Clem will pay one-half of the electric, gas, water, garbage and monthly telephone service charges to Julie on the first of each month. Julie will pay the bills.

3. If Clem wants to move, he'll give Julie as much written notice as is possible and will pay one-half of the rent for 30 days from the time he gives Julie written notice. If Julie wants Clem to move, she'll give him as much written notice as possible, in no case fewer than 30 days.[9] If a serious dispute arises, Julie has first choice to remain in the apartment and Clem must leave on her request.

4. [Insert mediation/arbitration clause from Chapter 5, Section L]

5. This agreement represents Clem's and Julie's complete understanding regarding their living together and replaces any prior agreements, written or oral. It can be amended, but only in writing, and must be signed by both.

6. If a court finds any portion of this contract to be illegal or otherwise unenforceable, the remainder of the contract is still in full force and effect.

_____	_____
Date	Julie Renoir
_____	_____
Date	Clem Lawrence

---

[9]In many states, a person must be given the same number of day's notice to move out as the interval between rent payments. Thus, if you pay rent once a month, you're entitled to 30 day's notice.

If you get into a serious dispute involving your shared home, you'll have to do the best you can to muddle through to a fair solution. Here are a few suggestions:

- In a few cities with rent control, such as New York and San Francisco, a "master tenant" provision often governs the legal relationship between tenants, especially if only one name is on the lease. Normally, a "master tenant" provision allows the original tenant first preference to stay. If your city has no such ordinance, however, consider having the new tenant sign an agreement giving the original tenant the first option to keep the apartment.

- In the absence of an master tenant provision or agreement, if you lived there first, are the only one to sign an agreement with the landlord and send in the monthly rent, you probably have first claim on the apartment. Give your friend a reasonable period of time to move out (30 days is often required) and find another place, especially if she's been contributing to the rent and/or living there for any considerable period of time.

- If you've both signed an agreement and/or both regularly pay rent, your rights to the apartment are probably equal (unless theres a local ordinance or written contract to the contrary), even if one of you got there first. Talk out your situation and let the person who needs the place the most stay. Mediation (see Chapter 5) may help, but make sure the mediator isn't a close friend, as a person who loses the apartment is likely to have hard feelings. Be overly fair about the last month's rent and damage deposits. Allow the person moving out reasonable time to find another place. *We've found that the best compromises are made when both people feel they've gone more than half way.*

- Each person has the right to all his personal belongings, even if he's behind in his share of the rent. Never lock up the other person's property.

- Don't deny a person access to his home except in extreme circumstances. If you're going to lock a person out, be ready to sign a police complaint, because it may come to that if your former friend uses force to try and get in. Except where a person has no legal right to live on the premises (hasn't signed a rental agreement or lease, hasn't been living with you long and hasn't paid rent), locking a person out is illegal and you can be sued for damages.

E. Deposits

GETTING CLEANING AND security deposits returned can be a problem for all tenants—not just the unmarried. To avoid trouble, and to handle it when unavoidable, prepare good documentation in advance. Make a written and photographic record of what the place looks like when you move in and when you move out. Witnesses—people you know who will examine your place and speak out if necessary—are also extremely valuable.

Let's assume that Clem and Julie move into a rented flat and pay $400 ($200 each) for cleaning and security deposits. How can they ensure that they'll get those deposits back?

Step 1:

Document any problems that exist when they move in. Dirty conditions, damaged rugs or appliances, and scratched, chipped and cracked walls or floors should be noted. We include a landlord-tenant checklist in the Appendix to help. If the landlord won't do it or drags her feet, Julie and Clem should note that self-protection is essential. They should have friend(s) check the place over and take pictures of offending conditions. The photographer should write his name and the date on the back.

Step 2:

Before Clem and Julie move out, they should ask the landlord over to discuss any conditions that might lead to deduction in their deposit. Clem and Julie don't have to leave the place exactly as they found it—part of their rent covers normal wear and tear. If there's a problem above what might be considered normal—say Julie burned a counter top with an iron or Clem cracked the bathtub—they should get their deposits back less the cost of repairs. If the object damaged was already in poor shape, they should argue that it

needed replacement anyway and they should not pay to repair it. When Clem, Julie and the landlord come to an agreement, they should write it down and sign it.

Now and then, a tenant gets advance warning —from a former tenant or from a direct conversation with the landlord herself—that she doesn't return deposits voluntarily. If you face this situation, you can take affirmative steps to protect yourself. You especially want to do this if you plan to move out of town so that suing in the local Small Claims Court would be difficult.[10] The simplest way to protect yourself is to withhold last month's rent, or the portion of that rent equal to the deposits. If you do this, notify the landlord in writing (see letter below) of what you're doing, and leave the place clean and undamaged.

---

[10]Some small claims courts allow people (especially tenants) who no longer live in the area to sue in small claims court by mail and present testimony in court by way of a written declaration under penalty of perjury. In California, military personnel who've moved out of state may designate someone else to present their testimony in small claims court.

1500 Peanut Street, #4
Falfurrias, Texas
June 1, 19__

Smith Realty
10 Jones Street
Falfurrias, Texas

Dear Smith Realty:

    As you know, we occupy apartment #4 at 1500 Peanut Street, Falfurrias, Texas, and regularly pay rent to your office. As we notified you previously, we will be moving out on July 15, 19__.

    In speaking to other tenants in the building, we've learned that the return of cleaning and damage deposits has been the subject of disputes between your office and departing tenants. Accordingly, we've decided on the following course of action: Instead of sending you the normal $700 rent check for June, we're sending you a check for $1000 to cover rent for both June and July and request that you apply our cleaning and damage deposit of $400 to cover the rest of the rent owed for this period.

    We'll leave the apartment spotless. We've no intention of causing you any loss or other problems. If you should doubt this, or want to discuss this matter further, please give us a call so that we can make an appointment to check the apartment over. We think you'll be satisfied that we're dealing with you honestly and in good faith and that the apartment, which is clean now, will be spotless when we leave.

        Very truly yours,

        Julie Renoir

        Clem Lawrence

Step 3:

If Clem and Julie move out and have no understanding with the landlord, they should carefully document the condition of the premises. After they clean up, they should get friends to inspect the place and take pictures. It's also wise to keep copies of receipts for cleaning materials.

Clem and Julie should receive their deposits back within of two weeks after moving out. If they don't, they should write a letter (see below) and then sue in Small Claims Court.

800 Walnut St.
Pampa, Texas
August 1, 19__

Smith Realty Co.
10 Jones Street
Falfurrias, Texas

Dear Mr. Smith:

On July 15, 19__, we vacated the apartment at 1500 Peanut Street, #4. As of today, we haven't received our $400 cleaning and security deposits.

We left our apartment clean and undamaged, paid all of our rent and gave you proper notice of our intention to move. In these circumstances, it's difficult to understand your oversight in not promptly returning our money.

Perhaps your check is in the mail. If not, please put it there promptly. Should we fail to hear from you in one week, we'll take this matter to court.

Very truly yours,

Julie Renoir

Clem Lawrence

If this doesn't work, the next step is going to Small Claims Court. In most states, you can sue for at least $2,000, which should cover most deposit cases. But Clem and Julie shouldn't assume that they'll win automatically. The landlord may show up claiming they left the place a mess. To counter this, they'll need their pictures, witnesses and cleaning receipts. Julie and Clem might present their case in the court something like this:[11]

JULIE: Good morning, your Honor, my name is Julie Renoir and this is Clem Lawrence. From May 15, 19__ to July 15, 19__, we lived at 1500 Peanut Street, #4 here in Falfurrias. When we moved out, the Smith Realty Company refused to refund our $400 cleaning and damage deposits even though we left the place spotless. We cleaned the rugs, washed and waxed the kitchen and bathroom floors, and washed the insides of the cupboards and the windows. Our friend Sandra Kimura helped us.

CLEM: Your Honor, I can testify that everything Julie said is true. We worked a full day to get that place really clean. I have some pictures that were taken of the apartment by our neighbor, Mrs. Edna Jackson, the day we moved out. Also, I have receipts for a rented rug shampooer and waxer, plus receipts for other cleaning supplies totaling $22.00. I have nothing else to add except that Mrs. Jackson and Ms. Kimura are here to testify.

After the witnesses are sworn in and give their names and addresses, their testimony should be brief and to the point.

MRS. JACKSON: Julie and Clem asked me to check their place on Peanut Street on July 15, the day they moved. It was very clean and neat. I took the pictures that you looked at, your Honor; I wrote my name and the date on the back. I would have been happy to move into a place as clean as that.

MS. KIMURA: Your Honor, I didn't take any pictures, but I did help Clem and Julie clean up and move out and I can say the place was spotless. I know because I did a lot of the work, including helping with the windows, cleaning the bathroom, and applying the smelly oven cleaner.

Assuming you get a judgment, you'll need to collect it. If the other party won't pay voluntarily, contact the local sheriff, marshal, or constable's office about a wage garnishment or bank account attachment.

---

[11]In most states, no one occupies the witness box in small claims court. Testimony is given from a table which faces the judge. See *Everybody's Guide to Small Claims Court*, Warner (Nolo Press).

Buying a House

BEAR WITH US as we present your third vocabulary lesson.

Closing Costs—the costs associated with buying a house; paid by the buyer, the seller or both, these costs include realtor commissions, recording fees, notary fees, penalties for paying off a loan early, lender fees (points) and past due taxes.

Conventional Loan—a loan normally made by a bank or savings and loan company, not guaranteed by the Federal Housing Administration (FHA), Veterans' Administration (VA) or other government agency.

Deed—a legal document by which an owner of property transfers title (recorded ownership) to another person. If the transfer is by a grant deed, the owner makes certain guarantees regarding the title. If the transfer is by quitclaim deed, the owner makes no guarantees, but simply transfers to the other person all the interest he has in the real property.

DEED

Deed of Trust—a security interest in property similar to a mortgage, which allows a lender to recover the property if the purchaser fails to repay the loan. While a mortgage typically involves only the borrower and lender, a deed of trust brings in a third party—the trustee (often a title company) who holds security interest in the property for the lender. In some states, such as California, a deed of trust is routinely used instead of a mortgage because it allows the property to be sold without a court hearing if the borrower defaults.

DOWN PAYMENT

Down Payment—a percentage of the total purchase price that is paid before title is transferred. With a conventional loan, the down payment is usually 10-25%. If the loan is guaranteed under a government program, such as the FHA or the VA, or the buyer agrees to buy private mortgage insurance (PMI), the down payment may be less than 10%.

FHA—Federal Housing Authority.

Mortgage—Because buyers rarely have all the cash needed to pay for a home, they borrow most of it in the form of a promissory note, which is secured by a mortgage or deed of trust. This allows the lender to sell the property and recover the amount the borrower owes if the borrower defaults.

Mortgage Broker—an independent real estate broker who matches house buyers with appropriate mortgage lenders. Their fees are often paid by the lender, not the buyer. Also known as a "loan broker."

Note—a written document spelling out the terms of a loan (such as the amount loaned, interest rate, length and amount to be paid each month). Normally, the note is secured by a deed of trust or mortgage in which the buyer makes the house itself collateral for repayment of the note.

VA—Veterans Administration.

Points—Often called a loan discount fee, one point equals 1% of a mortgage. To obtain a mortgage, buyers must often pay lenders points, but there's usually a trade-off between points and the mortgage interest rate. If you'll pay more points, the lender will offer you a slightly lower interest rate, and vice versa. If you plan to occupy the house for many years, and don't plan on refinancing, paying more points in exchange for a lower rate of interest is advantageous.

There may come a time when you and your friend decide to purchase a home. Sadly, however, as urban America has become more crowded and building supplies scarcer and more expensive, few decent living spaces are available in many areas. The past few generations have seen the death of America's founding dream— each family with a good home on good land and room to grow. Now, many of us rent, or buy a cooperative apartment or condominium. Yet, in America more than in most parts of the world, owning a home is a possibility, despite high land, construction and interest costs—and exorbitant property taxes.

This chapter provides a general overview of several important aspects of buying a house. While of interest to all prospective purchasers, our main focus is the specific needs of unmarried couples.

A. Do You Need a Lawyer or Broker?

IN MANY STATES, the sale of real estate is handled by, or in close consultation with, an attorney. In others, real estate brokers handle the transactions and attorneys aren't normally involved. In all states, you have the right to handle the purchase yourself. With a good deal of study, effort and care, a buyer and seller working together (without a real estate broker) can save at least 10% of the value of the property.

But because the financial community (banks, real estate brokers, title companies and lawyers) is interrelated, one or more may pressure you to patronize them. If you want to go it alone, hold your own, and if you're interested, check your bookstore or library for helpful materials. Several paperback books on buying and selling a house without a real estate broker are available. Look for a book on your state, not one with a national scope. Nolo Press publishes *How to Buy a Home in California: Strategies for Beating the Affordability Gap,* by Ralph Warner, Ira Serkes and George Devine, which contains all the forms and contracts necessary to purchase a California house without a broker.

B. Finding a House

FOR AN UNMARRIED COUPLE, buying a house generally involves four distinct steps:

- Finding the house.
- Financing the purchase.
- Transferring ownership (taking title to the house).
- Working out a sensible ownership agreement between the buyers.

Finding a house is normally no different for an unmarried couple than a married couple. Few sellers will care about your marital status. But if, despite good business and common sense, a seller refuses to sell to you because you aren't married, there's not much you can do in most places. In a few states, such as California, Wisconsin and Oregon, and some cities, including Washington, D.C., however, discrimination on the basis of marital status in the sale of real property is illegal.[1] Check your state and municipal codes under "Housing Discrimination" or "Real Estate Practices."

Note: In Chapter 2, Sex, Living Together and the Law, we point out that cohabitation (living together in a relationship that includes sex) is a crime in some states. Will you have difficulty buying a house in these states? No. As noted, these laws aren't enforced, and it's no more difficult for an unmarried couple to buy property in these states than in the others.

You may face another obstacle: zoning ordinances. Some local communities have zoning ordinances preventing more than a specified number (usually two, three or four) of unrelated adults from living together in an attempt to bar group living. While some legal scholars feel these ordinances are an unconstitutional denial of equal protection, the U.S. Supreme Court doesn't agree. In *Village of Belle Terre v. Boraas,* 416 U.S. 1 (1974), the Court upheld an ordinance prohibiting more than two unrelated adults in the same house.[2] But *Belle Terre* upheld a zoning ordinance that prohibited *more* than two unrelated people from living together, not two. To date, the Court has not ruled on an ordinance barring two unrelated people from living together.

Nonetheless, a few communities prevent unmarried couples from living together. One Missouri court evicted an unmarried couple, with their children, from a neighborhood zoned for single family residences, stating that "there is no state policy which commands that groups of people may live under the same roof in any section of a municipality they choose."[3] And a Maryland court allowed a co-op to restrict residents to the immediate family of the co-op member, stating that it would provide "a more stable community."[4] Because these laws are upheld, be sure no zoning ordinance bars unmarried couples from living in the neighborhood where you want to buy.

---

[1] Several other cities and counties, including Los Angeles and Philadelphia have enacted ordinances which prohibit discrimination in housing on the basis of sexual orientation. Most of these ordinances are broad enough to protect both straight and gay couples.

[2] Several state courts have interpreted their own constitutions to prohibit local communities from discriminating against unrelated adults. For example, the New Jersey Supreme Court declared that a zoning ordinance prohibiting more than four unrelated adults from sharing a house violated the New Jersey Constitution, *State v. Baker,* 405 A.2d 368 (1979). California ruled similarly in *City of Santa Barbara v. Adamson,* 164 Cal. Rptr. 539 (1980), and more recently held that any restriction on how many people may live together must be tied to objective standards related to crowding. *Park Redlands Covenant Control v. Simon,* 226 Cal.Rptr. 199 (1986).

[3] *City of Ladue v. Horn,* 720 S.W.2d 795 (1986).

[4] *Maryland Commission on Human Relations v. Greenbelt,* 475 A.2d 1192 (1984).

C. Financing Your House

SHOPPING FOR A MORTGAGE can be very confusing. Literally thousands of real estate lenders offer a variety of very similar products under different (sometimes bizarre) names. Given the number of lenders, borrowers and mortgage possibilities, no magic formula can help you determine what mortgage is best. But by reading this section, you'll know how to shop wisely and how to make an informed choice. In addition, we recommend you read *The Common Sense Mortgage*, Miller (Harper & Row).

1. Financing: What's Involved?

Very few people pay cash for a house. Most have to borrow money and accept the conditions imposed by the lender. Here are the basic steps to financing your house:

- *Determine how much house you can afford.* A general principle (for all house buyers) is that the purchase price should not exceed three to four times your family's annual gross income —unless relatives or friends will help with a gift or loan which needn't be paid back immediately. Also add the cost of any required structural repairs,[5] the closing costs and at least one-half of the redecorating expenses you plan to incur the first year. You'll typically need to make a down payment of 10-20% of the purchase price.

- *Get a general sense of interest rates and market conditions before making an offer to buy a house (a discussion on fixed and adjustable rate mortgages follows).* Your offer to buy should include contingencies relating to the physical inspection of the house and your ability to find satisfactory financing—usually 80-90% of the sales price at a (specified)

affordable interest rate, for a set number of years. If you can't secure a loan at an interest rate you can afford, this contingency lets you get out of (or renegotiate) the purchase contract.

- *Shop around for interest rates and mortgage terms.* For most people, a house is the most expensive purchase they'll ever make; it should not be financed without a careful attention to details. Sometimes a realtor will offer to arrange financing. This can help, as a realtor may convince a lender to loan you money when you wouldn't otherwise qualify. But don't rely only on a realtor's recommendation—she may favor a particular lender out of habit or she may know only the practices of banks she usually deals with. These may not be the best interest rates and mortgage terms.

Before accepting an offer of help, compare mortgage terms, points and interest rates of different lending institutions, which can vary considerably within a small geographical area. To get an overview, check the mortgage rate interest tables published in real estate sections of most Sunday newspapers. Consider subscribing to a computerized mortgage rate comparison service for your area. Also, a mortgage broker can help find the best deal. Before meeting with a lender or mortgage broker, however, read the sections below on fixed and adjustable rate mortgages so you'll have a broad idea of the pros and cons of each.

- *Make sure you can qualify for the mortgage you need to buy a particular house.* With conventional loans, lenders typically qualify buyers on the following criteria:

  Δ the value of the property as determined by the lender's appraisal. A lender normally loans 80-90% of this appraised value.

  Δ the amount of the down payment. Lenders usually require 10-20% down to insure

---

[5]Some lending institutions require repairs to be made before the loan is granted. Sometimes, the seller makes these repairs and the cost is reflected in the purchase price.

resale of the home and recoupment of the investment if you default on the mortgage. If your credit history, current income or future prospects convince the lender you may have difficulty making the payments, they may demand 25% or more.

Δ the borrower's financial situation. Most lenders require that the monthly costs of mortgage principal, interest, taxes and insurance (called PITI in the real estate business) total less than 28-36% of gross monthly income. The exact ratio of debt to income involves many factors including the amount of your down payment, your other long-term debts, your credit history, the lender's policies, and in some cases, your future earning potential. You may need to make a higher down payment to meet the qualifications for a loan.

Different lenders place emphasis differently and you'll need to find a lender that best fits your situation. For example, some banks place high importance on the value of the property, feeling that their investment is well-protected even if you default, as long as the property is worth substantially more than half their loan. These banks allow lower down payments, but charge slightly higher interest rates and points, and may require you to purchase Private Mortgage Insurance (PMI) which will reimburse them if you default and the house is sold at a loss. Other lenders emphasize the borrower's financial status and lend only to people in excellent financial shape. They often charge a slightly lower than average "preferred customer" interest rate.

Years ago, unmarried couples had difficulty getting mortgage loans. Fortunately, hostile attitudes of lending institutions toward unmarried couples all but disappeared in most areas of the country as unmarried couples began buying together. Additional help came with the passage of the Federal Equal Credit Opportunity Act, which forbids credit discrimination based on marital status, meaning that a lender must consider an unmarried couple's income jointly, to the extent it would consider a married couple's income jointly.[6]

Even with the Equal Credit Opportunity Act, a few lenders still ask unmarried couples for information about their relationship, claiming that they similarly query all business partners who purchase property together. We're not sure of a non-discriminatory intent, but suggest you simply reply in writing that your relationship consists of wanting to jointly purchase and live in a good house and that you plan to live in it and improve it over the years to maximize your joint investment.

An unmarried couple's (for convenience, let's again call them Tomas and Keija) liability to pay a mortgage comes in two ways—the house itself is liable (can be foreclosed on), and Tomas and Keija are liable. If the loan is made to Tomas and Keija together, both owe the entire amount. Tomas can't excuse his failure to pay by claiming that Keija hasn't made her share of the payments. Let's say it again, because it's important: Tomas and Keija are independently liable to repay the whole mortgage. Even if the house is destroyed by fire, Tomas and Keija must pay it back. (Of course, banks know that people don't like to pay for things that no longer exist and therefore require owners to buy insurance.)

---

[6]The Act also prohibits sex discrimination. Women who believe they've been discriminated against should contact the nearest regional Federal Reserve Board office (for bank-related problems) or the nearest regional Federal Trade Commission office (for non-bank related problems).

2. The Fixed Rate Mortgage

A generation ago, mortgage rules were simple—interest rates were fixed in advance and repayable in equal monthly installments over a term of 15 to 30 years, depending on the mortgage. The lender, usually a bank or savings and loan on a main corner, downtown, required a down payment of 20% or more, steady income and a good credit rating.

Take Bill and Sue, for example. They borrow $100,000 on a fixed rate mortgage at 10% interest for 30 years. Their monthly payments are approximately $878. Over the 30 years their total obligation will be $315,929, paying over twice as much in interest as in principal. Regardless of what the economy does, they'll pay $878 a month.[7]

Today there are more options, including adjustable rate mortgages (ARMs), discussed below. If your budget is very tight, and you can barely afford the house you like, you probably can't afford a traditional fixed rate mortgage. An adjustable rate mortgage, which carries a lower initial interest rate and lower monthly payments, and is therefore easier to qualify for, may be your only choice. This is true, paradoxically, even though a fixed rate mortgage will almost always be a better deal over the long run. If you're truly stumped for cash and have very little money for a down payment, even an ARM may be impossible; a low cost house that qualifies for a government subsidized fixed rate mortgage may be your only reasonable alternative.

The following chart shows monthly payments on a $100,000 mortgage at different interest rates over 15 and 30 years. As you can see, a 1% interest rate change can result in a large difference in the total amount of money you end up paying. If Bill and Sue had a 9% interest rate (not

---

[7]If their mortgage had no pre-payment penalty, Bill and Sue could achieve substantial savings by pre-paying the principal.

10%), they'd save $73 per month, or $26,280 over 30 years.

MONTHLY PAYMENTS ON A $100,000 MORTGAGE

Int Rate (%)	15-Year Period ($)	Total Payments ($)	30-Year Period ($)	Total Payments ($)
7.0	898.83	161,789	665.31	239,512
8.0	955.66	172,019	733.77	264,157
8.5	984.74	177,253	768.92	276,811
9.0	1,014.27	182,569	804.63	298,669
9.5	1,044.23	187,961	840.86	302,710
10.0	1,074.61	193,430	877.58	315,929
10.5	1,105.40	198,972	914.74	329,306
11.0	1,136.60	204,588	952.33	342,839
11.5	1,168.19	210,274	990.30	356,508
12.0	1,200.17	216,031	1,028.62	370,303
12.5	1,232.53	221,855	1,067.26	384,214
13.0	1,265.25	227,745	1,106.20	398,232
14.0	1,331.75	239,715	1,184.88	426,557

You would also pay substantially less with a 15-year (not 30-year) mortgage. At 10%, a 30-year mortgage will cost $315,929 total; a 15-year mortgage at 10% will cost $193,430 total, for a savings of $122,499.

You'll also have to pay monthly insurance and property taxes. Normally, it's cheaper for a homeowner to find and pay these costs directly, rather than have the lender purchase the insurance and pay the taxes for her.

3. More Affordable Fixed Rate Mortgages: Graduated Payment and Equal Mortgages

A Graduated Payment Mortgage (GPM) is an option for upwardly mobile purchasers who want a fixed rate mortgage but don't qualify because their income isn't high enough. GPM payments are set artificially low in the first years (making it easier to meet the debt to income ratio) then increase at set amounts at pre-established intervals. The idea is that your payments increase as your income does.

Initial interest rates, and therefore loan payments, of a typical 30-year GPM are about 60% of the current fixed rate loan rate. Payments then increase a set amount for a period of years, (for example, 5% each year for five years), and remain at that level for the remaining 25 years. GPMs are offered with slightly different features by lenders and are a good way to avoid the uncertainty of ARMs. The table below compares the payments on a GPM and a fixed rate mortgage for a 30-year loan of $136,900 at 10%.

	GPM—5% YEAR INCREASE FOR 5 YEARS		FIXED PAYMENT	
Year	Payment	Balance at Year End	Payment	Balance at Year End
0		$136,900		$136,900
1	$1,000	138,670	$1,201	136,139
2	1,050	139,996	1,201	135,298
3	1,103	140,796	1,201	134,369
4	1,158	140,988	1,201	133,343
5	1,216	140,472	1,201	132,210

One negative feature of GPMs is that in the early years payments don't cover the interest due, which means the amount you owe increases (called negative amortization, which is discussed in ARMS below) until your payments go up enough to reverse the process.

Some buyers find it unpalatable to owe more for even a few years and thus the Equal (for easy qualifying) Mortgage was created. An Equal Mortgage is essentially a GPM with a one-time up-front payment (3%-6% of the cost of the house) large enough to prevent negative amortization. If you are strapped for the up-front cash and are buying a new house, the builder may put it up

for you. If you're buying an existing housing, you'll have to come up with the money yourself. A friend, relative or employer may help. Or consider making a smaller down payment and contributing the money yourself.

Other variations of fixed rate mortgages are available. Ask your lender for more information.

FHA and VA Financed Housing

The Federal Housing Authority (FHA) guarantees loans on moderate-priced houses, typically tract homes built after World War II. The guarantee allows a low down payment (5% or less) for first-time buyers. Under some programs, the FHA loans money to low-income people. For more information, contact the nearest FHA office.

At one time, it was difficult for unmarried couples to qualify for FHA loans—the FHA would make the loan but count only the man's income in determining whether the couple qualified. Because most people who turn to the FHA don't qualify for conventional financing, this was like saying to a starving person, "I'll give you a terrific meal as soon as you fatten up a little." The FHA no longer does this and now counts the man and woman's incomes, for both married and unmarried couples, when determining financial ability.

The Veteran's Administration (VA), like the FHA, guarantees loans. VA loans are available to most veterans who served a required minimum time. The loans are an excellent value—probably the best in today's market for moderate priced housing. Most guarantees are on fixed rate mortgages with no down payment and interest rates usually slightly below the current market rate.

If one member of an unmarried couple is a qualifying veteran and the other isn't, the VA will guarantee only the veteran's share, which probably means the non-veteran will have to make a larger down payment. VA loans discriminate against unmarried couples, as a married veteran whose spouse does not qualify can have the entire loan guaranteed. For details, contact a local VA Office.

State and/or municipal-assisted mortgage programs may also be available in your area.

4. The Adjustable Rate Mortgage

In looking around for the money to finance a house, you'll find many lenders who will loan you money at a fluctuating rate of interest using an adjustable rate mortgage (ARM). Most of the time, the ARM rate goes up gradually for the first three to five years of the mortgage. Then it rises and falls, roughly tracing interest rate fluctuations in the economy generally. If societal interest rates move quickly, however, most adjustable rate mortgages adjust a bit more slowly.

The idea behind these loans is that the lender profits because its money is loaned out close to the market interest rate, and the borrower benefits because the initial rate is considerably lower (often 20-30% less) than available fixed rate mortgages. This lower interest rate (which is in part possible because the lender need not build in a cushion against the possibility of future interest rate increases, as they must do with fixed rate mortgages) means that the buyer can qualify to buy a more expensive house.

ARMs are no consumer bargain, however. Built in mathematical formulas mean most mortgages will carry a higher interest rate than comparable fixed rate loans in three to five years. In addition, if interest rates go up (and they always do sooner or later), you will find your monthly payments increasing even further; and, if rates go up enough, you may even be priced out of your own homes. To prevent this as much as possible, we recommend that if you are attracted to the lower interest rates of ARMs, insist on the following mortgage provisions:

Caps—The amount your monthly mortgage payment can rise should be limited to a certain percentage per year. Annual or periodic caps are on either monthly payments (look for an ARM with payments that can go up or down a maximum of 7.5% per year) or interest rates (look for an interest rate cap of 2.5 percentage points or less per year). In addition, the maximum interest rate that can be charged during the life of the loan should be capped at no more than five interest points over the initial rate. When comparing loans, look at the interest rate to which the caps are tied (often called the designated initial interest rate), as well as the maximum amount the interest rate can increase and how fast. This is important because lenders often offer initial low "teaser" rates for a few months, that have to relationship to caps.

Convertibility—Some ARMs can be converted (usually for a fee) to a fixed rate mortgage after a certain period of time, such as two years. The advantages of convertible mortgages, however, are often oversold. Only if ARM interest rates drop precipitously is there an advantage in converting. (And then, you could refinance your ARM with a fixed rate mortgage, regardless of whether it's convertible.) In the meantime, you often pay more interest to get convertibility. While it's a nice feature, it's not worth much extra. If you want a convertible mortgage, find one that has a low conversion fee and can be converted at any time.

Index and Margin—ARM interest rates periodically fluctuate, based on interest rate changes in inflation-sensitive financial indexes, such as one-year Treasury Bills. As a general rule, your ARM should be tied to a financial index that will fluctuate slowly. An index computed over an average of the previous 26 to 52 weeks moves much more slowly than one tied to daily or weekly rates. Your ARM should also have a low margin (the number of interest points, usually 2-2.5, which the lender adds to the index) to arrive at your interest rate. For example, if your index is at 8% and your margin is 2%, you'll be paying 10% before long.) A small difference in the margin can mean a substantially higher cost for you.

Negative Amortization—Negative amortization means that if interest rates increase faster than your yearly payment cap, the amount you pay won't cover what you owe. The overage will be added to your loan balance. Thus, with negative amortization, if interest rates go up fast you can make all required mortgage payments and still owe more. It's best to avoid mortgages with negative amortization and insist on an ARM with a true periodic cap (one that limits what you owe as well as what you pay) even if it means paying a slightly higher rate of interest.

Prepayment—Insist on an ARM that can be prepaid in whole or part without penalty. This allows you to raise money elsewhere and reduce or eliminate the loan if interest rates soar. (Prepayment is a good feature in all loans; it can result in substantial interest savings.)

Do You Want a Fixed or Adjustable Rate Mortgage?

Many people choose an ARM because they can't qualify for a fixed rate mortgage. If you have a choice, however, consider an ARM only if you plan to own your home for just a few years. As a general rule, if interest rates in society are flat or increasing, payments on an ARM will be lower than on a fixed rate mortgage for three or four years. After that, you'll pay more than with a fixed rate mortgage.

5. Alternative Financing

If you don't have enough savings to make a substantial down payment, find a seller who'll finance a portion of the purchase. (This is often called "carrying paper " or "taking a second.")

Rather than requiring you to make a down payment and borrow the balance from a lender, the seller lets you pay some of the sale in the form of a promissory note. (You may have to find a creditworthy person to co-sign the note) The seller receives the balance (from the note) over time, not at the sale.

If the seller needs all of her cash at once, she won't be willing to carry your paper. But many sellers aren't pressed for cash and will work out a flexible payment plan (especially if it's the only way to sell the house or the seller wants to spread out receipt of the money for tax reasons). For example, if the seller's plan is to put the money in a bank, lending it to you instead makes great sense if you offer to pay an interest rate higher than the bank. The loan to you is secured by a note on the house in return and the seller can foreclose if you fall behind in your payments.

Assume for a moment that you want to buy a house selling for $180,000. Your savings, coupled with borrowing from some friends and getting a loan on your car, you can raise $60,000. You need $120,000 more (plus $9,000 for closing costs). The seller has owned the home for seven years and has $90,000 remaining on the mortgage at 9% interest. Here are several different possible methods of financing your purchase over a 30-year term.

Plan A

Offer to purchase the home for $180,000 cash as follows:

- $50,000 down payment
- $9,000 closing costs (and $1,000 for pocket money);
- $130,000 mortgage at current bank interest rates; 10% rate will cost $1,140.86 per month or $410,710 for 30 years.
- The total cost for the house is $460.,710 plus closing costs.

Plan B

Pay the sales price of $180,000 as follows:

- $36,000 down payment;
- $9,000 closing costs (and $1,000 for pocket money);
- $90,000 by assuming[8] the seller's old mortgage at 9%; payments are $724.16 per month or $199,868 for the remaining 23 years.
- $54,000 second mortgage loan from the seller for seven years at 11% interest, with monthly payments of $500; the total payments would come to $42,000. At the end of seven years, you'd owe a a final (balloon) payment of $53,372.
- The total cost for the home this way is $331,240 plus closing costs.

Plan C

Same as Plan B, except you offer $186,000, not $180,000 to give the seller an incentive to accommodate your financing needs.

To summarize: The sales price is only one consideration in any home purchase. The down payment, interest rates, repayment schedule and the like can be equally as important.

---

6. Escrow and Closing Costs

In buying a house, paperwork and money must eventually change hands. The buyer delivers the money and seller delivers the house deed to a third person, called the escrow holder (often a title or escrow company or, in some states, an attorney). The escrow holder holds everything until the papers are signed and financing is arranged. Then, "escrow closes," the deed,

showing the buyer as the owner, is given to the buyer and recorded with the county, and the seller gets the money. In some states, the parties are represented by lawyers, which adds to the cost. In other states, such as California, lawyers are normally not involved.

Closing costs, not surprisingly, are the costs that have to be paid when escrow closes. The buyer's closing costs often include recording fees, pest control and structural inspections, a pro rata share of the year's taxes, bank charges (including a month's prepaid interest, points and often a "loan origination fee"[9]), title search and title insurance and, in many states, attorney's fees. Closing costs always mount up, often totalling 2-4% of the purchase price.

7. Your House as Investment and Tax Shelter

Now the good news! There are financial benefits to owning a house, especially in times of rapid inflation. Not only does your home provide a place to live, but with any luck, its value will increase. And, federal tax laws provide significant tax advantages for homeowners—you can deduct the interest and taxes paid from your taxable income. If you're in the 28% federal tax bracket, that means you can reduce your taxes by 28% of the interest and property taxes you pay. (You'll also save on state taxes.) You get no such deduction if you rent—even if your rent helps pay the landlord's taxes and mortgage interest payments.

Homeowners also qualify for another tax advantage. (Now you know why tax accountants say that people with good incomes can't afford not to own a home.) If you sell a house and buy another within 24 months, and you put the profits from the first into the second, you can postpone paying taxes on the capital gains until

---

[8]Some existing mortgages are freely assumable by a new buyer; others aren't. Before you plan on adopting this strategy, be sure the mortgage is assumable.

[9]This fee commonly runs $150-$200.

you sell the second home. If you sell the second and buy a third, you get the same postponement, as long as you only use this rollover provision once every two years. This means you can keep trading up and postpone paying taxes on your accumulated profits while doing so. That is, you can invest money that would otherwise have been taxed.

Finally, there is a tax rule that helps older folks whose houses have skyrocketed in value. It lets anyone 55 years and older sell a home and not pay any taxes on the first $125,000 profit. You can do it only once. As with all the tax rules we discuss, be sure to check the current status of this tax regulation before acting.

Older Couples: Sell Your House Before You Marry

Unmarried older couples who plan to eventually marry face a big potential problem with this over 55 rule if both own a house when they meet and they plan to sell one or both houses. If one mate has already claimed the benefits of the over 55 rule, after the couple marries, the other spouse can't get the same tax savings on selling his or her house. The over 55 exemption can be claimed only once by a married couple, or either member. So stay unmarried at least until the person who hasn't previously claimed the exemption sells his or her house.

D. Taking Title to the House

WHEN YOU PURCHASE A HOUSE together (or any other property, for that matter), use your correct names—those by which you're generally known and which appear on your identification documents, such as your driver's licenses, passports and credit cards. This needn't be the name that appears on your birth certificates. Keija should take title as Keija Adams if she uses "Keija" on all identification documents, even though her birth certificate says "Carolyn."

What is Title?

Title is written proof of ownership of real property. It is evidenced by a deed recorded at the County Recorder's office which gives the seller'(s) and buyer'(s) name(s), and indicates how the buyer(s) take ownership.

When you purchase your home, you'll have to decide how to "legally" take title. In most states these are your choices:

- one person's name
- joint tenants
- tenants in common

1. In One Person's Name[10]

This means that absent a contract to the contrary, only the person named in the deed owns the house. Don't put only one name on the deed unless only one of you owns the home. If you're tempted to put only one name to save on taxes, avoid creditors or befuddle welfare or food stamp administrators, this is a poor strategy, even if you fool your creditors. The danger is that the person named in the deed (the presumed sole owner) will sell the house and pocket the money, die

---

[10]The deed often states the name of the buyer and adds "a single man/woman." Our friend Alice put down "a singular woman" but it never made it past the escrow officer.

and leave it to someone other than the other owner or die without a will, in which case it will be inherited by a passel of money-hungry relatives under the laws of intestate succession.

To protect your interest if you invest in a house, but your name isn't on the deed, insist on a written contract recorded at the county deed recording office which makes the true ownership clear. Absent a contract, the best you can do to recover your portion of the property (assuming there's a serious problem) is sue. But most states have a legal presumption that the person whose name appears on the deed is the owner; a lawsuit to recover your share is likely to be difficult, or even impossible.

2. As Joint Tenants

If you take title as joint tenants, it means you share property ownership equally and that each of you has the right to use the entire property. It also means that if one joint tenant dies, the other (or others) automatically takes the deceased person's share, even if there's a will to the contrary.[11] And at death, joint tenancy property passes to the surviving joint tenant without probate proceedings. Another feature of joint tenancy is that if one joint tenant sells his share, the joint tenancy ends (even if the other joint tenant is unaware of the sale). The new owner and the other original owner become tenants-in-common (see below).

---

[11]This is called the right of survivorship. Some states require that you add the words "with right of survivorship" to qualify for this. If in doubt, add them. Some unmarried people who own homes on their own are tempted to put the house in joint tenancy with their lover so that the lover will get it if the original owner dies. Think before you do this. As we discuss in Chapter 11, by putting the house in joint tenancy, you make a gift of one-half of it to your lover. If you split up, you have no right to get that half back. If you want your lover to get the house on your death, make a will or living trust leaving her the house. If circumstances change, you can change the will or trust.

Warning! Joint tenancy cannot be used if a house is owned unequally. It's appropriate only when each joint tenant owns the same portion. You and your lover can take title to a house you own 50-50 in joint tenancy, or three people can be joint tenants, with each owning one-third. If you own 60% of a house, however, and your lover owns 40%, joint tenancy won't work.

3. As Tenants In Common

The major difference between joint tenancy and tenancy in common is that tenancy in common has no right of survivorship. When a tenant in common dies, her share of property is left to whomever she specified in her will or living trust. If there is no such document, her share goes to a relative by "intestate succession" (see Chapter 11). Also, and of particular importance for many unmarried couples, tenants in common can own property unequally—one person can own 80% and the other 20%. Both are listed on the deed as tenants in common. You can specify the precise percentages on the deed, or you can list the owners' names on the deed and set out the shares in a separate written agreement. Especially if shares are unequal, prepare a contract.

If you take title in one form and want to change it after the purchase, you simply record a new deed. If for instance, you start as tenants in common and later change to joint tenants, make and record a deed granting the property "from Andrew West and Joanne Yu as Tenants In Common, to Andrew West and Joanne Yu as Joint Tenants with Right of Survivorship." If you add a new person, the IRS will consider it either a sale or a gift and tax you accordingly.

E. Contracts for Couples Owning a Home Together

A HOUSE IS A MAJOR economic asset. It's foolish to avoid or postpone clearly defining your expectations and obligations. In this section, we discuss ways to handle joint ownership problems and provide a number of sample contracts to cover the most common.

A Last Note for People Who Hate Contracts. Earlier in the book, we suggested that you prepare a living-together contract if you live together for an extended period. Even if you haven't followed this advice, you absolutely should have a contract if you plan to jointly own a house. It's plain nuts to try and wing it with pillow talk when it comes to an investment of this size. Most of the samples we give are simple and uncomplicated. Incidentally, we have found that many people who resist preparing a contract do so because they don't have a mutual understanding in the first place. If this is you, sit down immediately and have a long, honest talk.

Keep it Simple! We can't over-emphasize that the best contracts are the simplest. Round ownership interests off (25% and 75%, not 23.328% and 76.672%). Trying to achieve absolute accuracy—even if it were possible—is usually more trouble than it's worth. If one person puts up a little extra cash or labor, or forks out a bit more money in an emergency, consider the extra contribution a loan to be paid back either when the house is sold or by the other owner making a similar extra contribution, rather than redrafting the basic agreement. As long as any promissory notes are paid off before the house is sold, this approach is safe and simple.

If, however, despite your best efforts your ownership arrangement is complex, and so is your proposed contract, you may want to have it checked by a lawyer familiar with real estate. This doesn't mean you should take a full wallet and a basketful of problems to the lawyer. Do as much work as possible yourself and have the lawyer help you with particular problem areas or check the entire agreement when you're finished.

---

1. Equal Ownership

The first agreement is for two people who contribute equal amounts of money toward the down payment and intend to share all costs (and eventual profits) equally. In this contract, Michael and Helen take title as tenants in common, so if either dies, his or her inheritors—not the other person—will get half of the property. Tenancy in common is a cautious approach. It allows each owner to leave his or her share to the other by a will or living trust, but does not require him or her to do so.

CONTRACT FOR EQUAL OWNERSHIP

Michael Angelo and Helen Rifkin make the following agreement to jointly purchase a house where both of them will live:

1. They'll purchase a house at 423 Bliss Street, Chicago, Illinois for $180,000.

2. They'll take title as tenants in common.

3. They'll each contribute $18,000 to the down payment and closing costs and will each pay one-half of the monthly mortgage and insurance costs, as well as one-half of the property taxes and costs for repairs that both agree are needed.

4. Should either decide to end the relationship and cease living with the other, and should both want to keep the house, a friend will be asked to flip a coin within 60 days of the decision to separate.[12]

The winner of the coin toss is entitled to buy the house from the loser, provided that the winner pays the loser the fair market value (see clause 5) of his or her share within 90 days. When payment is made, Michael and Helen will deed the house to the person retaining it in his or her name alone. If payment isn't made within 90 days, or if neither person wants to buy the house, it will be sold and the profits divided.

5. If Michael and Helen cannot agree on the fair market value of the house, the value will be determined by an appraisal as follows: Michael and Helen will designate in writing one appraiser to do the job. If either doesn't agree with the result, he or she may hire a second appraiser. If the parties still cannot agree on a fair price, the two appraisers will be asked to jointly choose a third appraiser. The fair market value of the house will be the average of the three appraisals. The fees of the three appraisers will be divided equally between Michael and Helen.

---

[12]Your contract could provide that one person gets first choice to remain in the house if the couple breaks up. Or, the decision could be made with the help of a mediator, rather than the caprice of a coin, relying on a coin flip only if mediation fails. Or, you could simply sell the house on the open market and split the proceeds.

6. If either Michael or Helen dies, the survivor, if he or she hasn't been left the deceased person's share, has the right to purchase that share from its inheritor(s) by paying its fair market value (to be arrived at under the terms of Paragraph 5) to the inheritors within 200 days of the date of death.

7. If either Michael or Helen is unable or unwilling to pay his or her share of the mortgage, tax or insurance payments in a timely manner, the other may make those payments. The extra payments will be treated as a personal loan to be paid back by the person on whose behalf they are made within six months, including 10% interest per annum (or the highest interest rate permitted under the state law, whichever is lower).

8. This contract is binding on our heirs and our estates.

9. [Insert mediation/arbitration clause from Chapter 5, Section L.]

Dated:_____   Signature:_____
                                          Michael Angelo

Dated:_____   Signature:_____
                                          Helen Rifkin

(Notarize and Record)

After they signed the contract, Michael and Helen discussed what they wanted to happen if one of them died. Michael wanted to leave his mother the original $18,000 down payment, but otherwise wanted Helen to get the house. Both were worried that the other wouldn't be able to afford to buy the deceased person's entire share if the house went way up in value. Helen would have left her entire share to Michael, but decided that if he was going to reduce his share by $18,000, she would too. They came up with the following, and rewrote clause 6:

6. If Michael or Helen dies, the survivor, if he or she hasn't been left the deceased person's entire share, has the right to purchase that share by paying the sum of $18,000 to the estate or heirs of the deceased, either in cash, or with a note for $18,000, plus 10% interest per year, payable in 36 equal monthly installments.

What if the couple wants to own the home equally, but only one can come up with the initial cash? Andrew and Alice, were in that situation. Andrew, a successful artist, sold a few paintings and came up with the full $50,000 down payment for a little cottage with a mansard roof. Alice can't contribute to the down payment, but can pay one-half the monthly mortgage, insurance and maintenance costs. They want to equally own the home, but also want to account for Andrew's down payment.

Our suggestion is that Andrew call one-half of the down payment a *loan* to Alice that can be either paid back in monthly installments or deferred until the house is sold. Andrew and Alice should write a contract similar to Michael and Helen's, showing a 50-50 ownership, and should execute a promissory note recording Andrew's loan.

PROMISSORY NOTE FOR DOWN PAYMENT MONEY

    I, Alice Adams, acknowledge receipt of a loan of $25,000 from Andrew Ames, to be used as my share of the down payment for our house located at 10 Rose Street, Oakland, California. I agree to pay this sum back, plus interest, at the rate of 10% per year, by making monthly payments of $330.38, all due in ten years.[13]

    If the loan and all interest due hasn't been repaid when the house is sold, the remaining balance owed will be paid to Andrew before Alice receives any proceeds from that sale.

Dated:_____   Signature:_____
                                            Alice Adams

Dated:_____   Signature:_____
                                            Andrew Ames

---

[13]If Alice couldn't afford the payments and Andrew was a generous sort, the note could say: "I agree to pay the entire loan and interest at 10% per year when the house is sold."

Note: A local title company can calculate for you the monthly payment necessary to pay off a loan. You need to know the original value of the loan, the interest rate and the number of payments. Alice could pay less each month, but make one large balloon payment at the end of the loan period. For example, if she paid only interest over the 10 years, her monthly payment would be $208.33 but she'd have to pay $14,646 at the end.

2. Unequal Ownership

If each person contributes the same amount for the down payment and pays equally on the mortgage and other expenses, its self-evident that each person owns 50%. It's common, however, for joint purchasers to contribute unequally. One person may have more for the down payment. The other may be able to afford larger monthly payments. Or, one person may have carpentry skills and a willingness to put in many hours renovating the house while the other sits by, beer in hand, and kibitzes.

Below we provide sample contracts for unequal ownership. Some aspects are easy to express in cash terms, while others are harder. For example, labor contributed to renovate a house can be given a cash value of an hourly wage times the number of hours worked. But how do you value someone's ability to borrow the down payment from his parents—especially in a society structured to reward the owners of capital? We're not suggesting that you arrive at a mathematically exact determination—as you'll see, we suggest rough values if that satisfies you both. But it can be reasonable to consider and value intangible factors, even though doing so is difficult and imprecise.

Let's start with Tim and Barb. Tim has more money, so he makes two-thirds of the down payment and owns two-thirds of the house. To keep things simple, Tim also agrees to pay two-thirds of the mortgage, taxes and insurance. Here's their contract:

2/3 - 1/3 OWNERSHIP AGREEMENT

We, Tim Foote and Barb Bibbige agree as follows:

1. *Property:* We'll purchase the house at 451 Morton Street, in Upper Montclair, New Jersey.

2. *Contributions:* We'll contribute the following money to the down payment:

Tim $40,000

Barb $20,000

3. *Ownership:* We'll own the property as tenants in common with the following shares:

Tim   2/3

Barb   1/3

4. *Expenses and Mortgage:* All expenses, including mortgage, taxes, insurance and repairs on the house, will be paid as follows:

Tim   2/3

Barb   1/3

5. In the event the house is sold, the initial contributions ($40,000 to Tim and $20,000 to Barb) will be paid back first; the remainder of the proceeds will be divided two-thirds to Tim and one-third to Barb.

6. *Contingencies:*

a. We agree to own the house for three years unless we agree otherwise. After three years, either person may request the house be sold. The person who doesn't want to sell has the right of first refusal; that is, he or she may purchase the house at the agreed-upon price, and must state in writing that he or she will exercise this right within two weeks of the setting of the price. He or she has 60 days to complete the purchase, or the right lapses.

b. If one owner moves out of the house before it's sold, he or she will remain responsible for his or her share of the mortgage, taxes, insurance and repairs. He or she is entitled to the fair rental value of his or her portion of the house, however, assuming it is rented. The person who stays has the first right to rent the quarters or assume the cost if he or she chooses not to seek a tenant. If the person who remains wishes to neither find a tenant nor pay the fair rental value, the person leaving shall have the right to rent his or her share, with the tenant to be approved by the person remaining (approval will not be unreasonably withheld).

c. If Tim and Barb decide to separate and both want to keep the house, they'll try to reach a mutually satisfactory agreement for one to buy the other out. If by the end of two weeks they can't, they'll ask a friend to flip a coin. The winner has the right to purchase the loser's share provided the winner pays the loser the fair market value within 90 days of the toss.

The fair market value will be determined by an appraisal conducted as follows: Tim and Barb will designate in writing one appraiser to do the job. If either party doesn't agree with the result, he or she may hire a second appraiser. If the the parties still cannot agree on a fair price, the two appraisers will be asked to jointly choose a third appraiser. The fair market value will be the average of the three appraisals. The fees of the three appraisers will be divided equally between Tim and Barb.

    d. If either Tim or Barb dies, the other, if he or she hasn't been left the deceased person's share, has the right to purchase that share from the deceased's estate or heirs in equal monthly installments over five years, at 10% interest. The value of the deceased person's share will be determined as set out in Clause 6c above.

    7. *Binding:* This agreement is binding on us and our heirs, executors, administrators, successors and assigns.

    8. *Dispute Resolution:* [Insert mediation/arbitration clause from Chapter 5, Section L.]

Signed in:_____, _____
               (City)   (State)

Dated:_____   Signature:_____
                                     Tim Foote

Dated:_____   Signature:_____
                                     Barb Bibbige

(Notarize and Record)

Substitute Clause 6

The requirement not to sell the house for three years, even if the couple separates, makes sense if you want to be pretty sure of a profit on re-sale. Jointly owning a house after separation can be complicated, however. For a simpler agreement substitute a provision that the house be sold at any time the couple breaks up, or that the person with the larger share has the first right to buy the other out.

3. Agreements For One to Buy and the Other to Fix it Up

It's common for one person to contribute a greater portion, or even all, of the down payment, while the other contributes labor and/or materials to fix the place up. Many contracts reflecting this are possible. We have a strong bias for the simple, but if your special circumstances require something more complicated, have a lawyer with lots of experience in real estate review it.

Bob and Evie are purchasing a graceful but dilapidated Victorian. Evie has the cash for the down payment and Bob the expertise and time to fix it up. They each can afford half the monthly expenses. They want to own the place equally but need guidance on how to do it. Evie will contribute $35,000 to the down payment and closing costs; thus, Bob should eventually contribute $35,000 worth of materials and labor (at $15 an hour) to fix it up and become an equal owner.

EQUAL OWNERSHIP WHERE ONE PERSON
CONTRIBUTES CASH AND THE OTHER CASH AND LABOR

We, Bob and Evie, agree as follows:

1. We'll purchase the house at 225 Peaches Street, Atlanta, Georgia for $200,000 and will own the house equally as tenants in common.

2. Evie will contribute $35,000 to be used for the down payment and closing costs.

3. Bob will contribute $20,000 for materials and 1,000 hours of labor (valued at $15 per hour) over 24 months, for a total contribution of $35,000, toward fixing up the house. If Bob doesn't fulfill this obligation within two years, or should we separate before the end of two years, at the time of separation Bob owes Evie the difference between what he contributed and $35,000.

4. All monthly expenses will be shared equally.

5. If either of us does not pay our share of the mortgage, taxes or insurance in a timely manner, the other person may make the payment, and that payment will be treated as a loan to be paid back as soon as possible, but not later than six months, plus interest at the rate of 10% per annum.

6. Either of us can terminate this agreement at any time. If this occurs, and we both want to remain in the house and can afford to buy the other out in 90 days, a third person

will flip a coin to see who keeps the house. If only one of
us wants the house, she or he'll pay the other his or her
share within 90 days. If the person who wants the house
can't pay the other within 90 days, we'll sell the house and
divide the proceeds equally, unless Bob owes Evie money
under Clause 3, in which case Evie shall recover that amount
before the proceeds are divided.

7. If we cannot agree on the fair market value of the
house, the value will be determined by an appraisal
conducted as follows: we will designate in writing one
appraiser to do the job. If either of us doesn't agree with
the result, he or she may hire a second appraiser. If we
still cannot agree on a fair price, the two appraisers will
be asked to jointly choose a third appraiser. The fair
market value will be the average of the three appraisals.
The fees of the three appraisers will be divided equally
between us.

8. This contract may be amended in writing at any time by
unanimous consent.

9. [Insert mediation/arbitration clause from Chapter 5,
Section L.]

Dated: _____   Signature: _____
                                          Evie Valery

Dated: _____   Signature: _____
                                          Bob Rosenthal

(Notarize and record)

It's easiest to establish ownership interests based on contributions made (or promised) at the time a contact is drafted. It's possible, however, to provide for ownership shares that will fluctuate over time. Doing this is considerably more complicated. If Bob and Evie want to provide that their ownership shares can vary, with Evie owning the place to start and Bob's share growing as he contributes labor and materials, they'd provide that each person's share equals his or her contributions of cash and labor. They'd need to modify Clause 1 to say:

"1. We'll purchase the house at 225 Peaches Street, Atlanta, Georgia for $200,000 and will own the house as tenants in common. Each person's ownership share will be determined by placing his or her total contribution of money and labor (valued at $15 per hour) over the total contributed by both and creating a fraction."

Bob and Evie would have to keep track of all contributions. The best way to do this is to add a clause to the contract stating: "All contributions by either of us will be entered on Attachment 1, Capital Contributions" on or about the first of each month."

**ATTACHMENT 1
19__ CAPITAL CONTRIBUTIONS**

			Contributed by:	
Nature of Contribution	Date	Value	Evie	Bob
Cash	1/29	35,000	35,000	
Paint, Roof Supplies	3/10	4,000		4,000
Wood	3/12	3,500		3,500
Floor Supplies	3/12	3,500		3,500
Labor	3/13-6/15	6,000		6,000
Cash-Hot Tub	7/20	1,000	500	500
Totals		53,000	35,500	17,500

We know couples who have taken a different tack. Rosemary and Ed, for example, wanted a very detailed contract, believing that for them, it would be fairer than a rough, general division. Rosemary is a carpenter by trade, and she and Ed agreed that her carpentry work should be valued at a higher hourly rate than the ordinary labor of either. Their contract is a bit worky, but in fairness, we've seen agreements like this work very well in several instances.

UNEQUAL OWNERS WHERE ONE PERSON CONTRIBUTES CASH AND BOTH CONTRIBUTE LABOR

Ed and Rosemary agree that:

1. They will buy the house at 15 Snake Hill Road, Cold Springs Harbor, N.Y. The initial investment (down payment and closing costs) of $44,987.07, will be contributed by Ed. Title will be recorded as Rosemary Avila and Edward O'Brien as tenants in common.

2. They will each pay one-half of the monthly mortgage, tax and homeowner's insurance payments, and will each be responsible for one-half of any costs necessary for maintenance and repairs.

3. They will contribute labor and materials to improve the house. Rosemary's labor—doing carpentry—will be valued at $16 per hour and both Ed and Rosemary's labor making

other house repairs will be valued at $9 per hour; these rates may be raised in the future if both agree. Materials will be purchased as needed and as affordable by both Ed and Rosemary and valued at their cost.

4. They will keep a ledger marked "Exhibit I - 15 Snake Hill Road Home Owner's Record." This ledger is considered a part of this contract. They will record the following information in the Home Owner's Record:

a) The $44,987.07 initial contribution made to purchase the house by Ed.

b) Monthly payments by Ed and Rosemary for the mortgage, property taxes and homeowner's insurance.

c) Rosemary's labor as a carpenter on home improvements valued as stated in clause 3.

d) Their labor on non-carpentry home improvements valued as stated in clause 3.

e) All money paid by either or both for supplies and materials necessary for home improvements.

f) Any other money spent by either to improve the home as long as the expenditure has been approved in advance by the other.

5. Their ownership shares of the house are determined as follows:

a) The dollar value of all contributions made by either will be separately totaled, using the figures set out in Exhibit I - 15 Snake Hill Road Home Owner's Record.

b) Rosemary and Ed may add interest to their investment totals at 10% per year simple interest. Interest will be calculated twice a year (January 1 and July 1), with the interest being added to each person's total investment as of that date.

c) Total equity in the house will be computed according to the following three steps:

Step 1: We will subtract all mortgages and encumbrances outstanding from the fair market value as of the date of the computation. If we can't agree on the fair market value, the value will be determined by an appraisal. The appraisal will be conducted as follows: We will designate in writing one appraiser to do the job. If either of us doesn't agree with the result, he or she may hire a second appraiser. If we still cannot agree on a fair price, the two appraisers will be asked to jointly choose a third appraiser. The fair market value will be the average of the three appraisals. The fees of the three appraisers will be divided equally between us.

Step 2: We will create a fraction. The numerator will be the larger share (as computed in Clauses 5a and 5b above) and the denominator will be the total amount of both people's shares. This fraction represents the total contribution in the house of the person with the larger share. The person with the smaller share will compute her share by either subtracting the larger share from the number "1," or by forming a fraction using the steps outlined above.

Step 3: The fraction of the house owned by each will be applied to the equity interest arrived at in Step 1.

6. If either of us does not pay his or her share of the mortgage, taxes or insurance in a timely manner, the other may make the payment, and that payment will be treated as a loan to be paid back as soon as possible, but not later than six months, plus interest at the rate of 10% per annum.

7. Either Rosemary or Ed can terminate this agreement at any time. If this occurs, and both want to remain in the house and can afford to buy the other out in 90 days, a third person will flip a coin to see who keeps the house. If only one person wants the house, she or he'll pay the other his or her share within 90 days. If the person who wants to keep the house can't pay the other within 90 days, we'll sell the house and divided the proceeds according to the shares established under Paragraph 5(c).

8. [Insert mediation/arbitration clause from Chapter 5, Section L.]

Dated: _____   Signature: _____
                                        Edward O'Brien

Dated: _____   Signature: _____
                                        Rosemary Avila

(Notarize and record)

4. Agreement for One Person to Move Into a House Owned by the Other

We're often asked how to deal with the thicket of legal, practical, and emotional problems that pop up when one person moves into another's house. Some of even the most relaxed people have problems when one invades another's turf. Let's look at a typical situation.

Our friend Alan called to say that he's just moved in to his lover Alison's house. Alison has asked Alan to share equally the monthly house payments, real property taxes, fire insurance, etc. Alan's agrees, but only if he somehow gets to own part of the house.

Alison's house is worth about $150,000; her mortgage is $100,000 and her equity $50,000. Alison agrees that if Alan makes one-half of the payments, he should get some interest in the house, but she raises a good point. Because she already has a big investment in the house, Alan can't hope to get much of a share by paying one-half of the monthly payments. So how can they have Alan get an ownership interest in the house fairly? This was getting hard to work out over the phone, so we invited Alan and Alison over for some tea and a discussion of possible solutions. Here are several:

- The simplest would be for Alan to forget buying a share of the house and simply pay Alison rent. This should, in all fairness, be considerably less than the one-half of the mortgage, tax and insurance costs because Alison is buying the house and Alan isn't. If they adopt this approach, they should check the rents being paid by people in comparable houses in the neighborhood to reach a fair amount.

- Another simple solution would be for Alan to pay Alison one-half of her net equity in the house in exchange for her deeding the house to both of them either as "joint tenants" or "tenants in common." That is, Alan would pay Alison $25,000. If they followed this approach, they'd want to make a contract to cover issues such as who keeps the house if they break up (see Section E1 above). But before we got too far, Alan stood up and turned his pockets inside out. He had $85 and a Swiss army knife with a broken can opener. Even in these days of easy credit, this wasn't going to do.

- Another approach would be for Alison to deed one-half of the house to Alan in exchange for a promisx Alison, however, wasn't quite ready to give up half ownership in her house in exchange for Alan's promise to pay.

- Our final suggestion was less simple. Alan and Alison could agree that Alan pays one-half (or any portion) of the monthly expenses in exchange for a percentage of the equity in the house equal to the proportion his payments are of the total amount of money invested in the house by both. After we all talked for a while, Alan and Alison worked out a variation on this so that Alan felt like more than a boarder, without paying one-half now.

Note: It's wise to check any agreement of this type with a knowledgeable lawyer and accountant. The cost for the few hours of time involved is likely to be well worth it.

---

a. The Person Moving in Gradually Becomes an Equal Co-Owner

An agreement to become an equal co-owner over time might look like this:

57 PRIMROSE PATH CONTRACT

Alan Martineau and Alison Salinger agree as follows:

1. That Alison owns the house at 57 Primrose Path, Omaha, Nebraska, subject to a mortgage with the Prairie National Bank in the amount of $100,000;

2. That Alan and Alison agree that the house has a fair market value of $150,000 as of the date this contact is signed and that Alison's equity interest is $50,000;

3. That beginning with the date this contract is signed, Alan shall pay all monthly expenses for property taxes, homeowners insurance, mortgage payments and necessary repairs and shall continue to do so until his total payments equal $125,000, or until the parties separate;

4. That Alan's share of the total net equity of the house shall be figured at the rate of one-fourth of one percent for every month that he pays all of the expenses as set out in paragraph 3. For example, if Alan pays all the expenses for two years, his interest in the house equity shall be 6%;

5. That Alison shall deed the house to "Alison Salinger and Alan Martineau as Tenants in Common" and record the deed and this contract;

6. That Should Alan and Alison separate prior to the time that Alan contributes $125,000, Alison shall have first right to remain in the house and Alan shall leave within 30 days of the decision to separate;

7. That once Alan contributes $125,000, the house shall be owned equally by Alan and Alison, all expenses for taxes, mortgage insurance and repairs shall be shared equally, and Alan shall have an equal right to stay if separation occurs. If they cannot agree amicably as to who will stay after they become equal co-owners, they will have a friend flip a coin, with the winner getting to purchase the share of the other and remain in the house;

8. That if separation occurs, the person leaving shall be entitled to receive his or her share as provided in this contract within 90 days of moving out. If Alan is an equal owner and they dispute the value of the property, it shall be determined as follows: Alan and Alison will designate in writing one appraiser to do the job. If either party doesn't agree with the result, he or she may hire a second

appraiser. If they still cannot agree on a fair price, the two appraisers will be asked to jointly choose a third appraiser. The fair market value will be the average of the three appraisals. The fees of the three appraisers will be divided equally between Alan and Alison;

9. That if the person who has the first right to stay can't pay off the other within 90 days, the other person shall have the right to buy out the first within an additional 30 days. If neither person is willing or able to buy out the other, the house shall be sold and the proceeds divided under the terms of this agreement;

10. [Insert mediation/arbitration clause from Chapter 5, Section L.]

11. That this agreement can be amended, but only in writing, and must be signed by both Alison and Alan;

12. That Alison and Alan agree that if a court finds any portion of this contract illegal or otherwise unenforceable, that the remainder of the contract is still in full force and effect.

_____   _____
Date   Alison Salinger

_____   _____
Date   Alan Martineau

(Notarize and record)

You may wonder why Alan and Alison decided that Alan should pay $125,000 for a one-half interest in the house and that he should get credit for one-fourth of one percent of the equity for every month that he paid all of the expenses. We didn't know for sure, and so we asked them. Here's Alison's reply:

"We were interested in our own version of fairness—not statistical accuracy—even if that were possible. We figured that, as I already had $50,000 in the house and that the house was likely to go up in value, it'd be fair to require Alan to contribute more, as his payments would be made gradually and, of course, a portion

would go to pay interest, not principal. Also, I wanted to give up my full-time job and have more time for painting miniatures, so I was anxious to have Alan pay all the expenses—taxes, repairs, insurance, as well as mortgage payments.

"$125,000 was an amount we could both live with. We gave Alan credit for all of his expenses—not just his mortgage payments, because we felt that this worked out fairly for us. To arrive at one-fourth of one percent per month (or 3% per year), we did some peasant arithmetic and concluded that it would take Alan about 16 years to contribute his $125,000 and become a one-half owner. If you divide 50% by sixteen, you come out to about 3% ownership per year or one-fourth of one percent per month. I'm aware that Alan is getting a very good deal, but so am I. I don't have to worry about any house expenses for sixteen years."

b. The Person Moving In Becomes An Immediate Equal Co-Owner

Another way to handle the problem would be for the person who owned the house to sell the person moving in one-half of the house at present fair market value, and take a second mortgage to secure the payment. The note would be paid in full if the house were be sold or refinanced. This method would be very generous to the person moving in because he would become a half owner with no money down. Fred and Faye take this approach. Their agreement looks like this:

---

10 BRIAR CLIFF DRIVE CONTRACT

We, Faye Firth and Fred Fox agree as follows:

1. Faye now owns the house at 10 Briar Cliff Drive, Oswego, Minnesota.

2. The present value of the home is agreed to be $150,000; Faye's mortgage is $100,000 and her equity $50,000.

3. Faye hereby sells one-half of the home to Fred for $25,000, retaining a one-half interest in the house.

4. The $25,000 will be paid to Faye by Fred in 48 equal monthly installments with interest of 9% per year. (Obviously, you can include any payment schedule you desire.) Payment of this obligation shall be secured by a second mortgage, which will be recorded on the public record.

5. All future costs of maintaining the property, including first mortgage payments (principal and interest), taxes, insurance, utilities and necessary repairs will be divided evenly.

6. If the property is sold before Fred's promissory note has been paid in full, Faye will be entitled to the entire balance of the note. The remaining profit (or loss) will then be divided evenly between Fred and Faye.

7. Until Fred pays the entire $25,000 plus interest, Faye shall have the first right to stay in the house if they separate. If separation occurs after the $25,000 is paid,

they shall have an equal right to stay in the house. If both want to stay a friend will be asked to flip a coin within 30 days of the decision to separate, with the winner getting to buy out the loser's share for its fair market value.

8. If Fred and Faye cannot agree on the fair market value of the house, the value will be determined by an appraisal conducted as follows: Fred and Faye will designate in writing one appraiser to do the job. If either person doesn't agree with the result, he or she may hire a second appraiser. If they still cannot agree, the two appraisers will be asked to choose a third appraiser. The value will be the average of the three appraisals. The fees of the three appraisers will be divided equally between Fred and Faye.

9. If either Fred or Faye dies, the survivor, if he or she hasn't been left the deceased person's share, has the right to purchase that share from the inheritor by paying its fair market value (to be arrived at under the terms of Paragraph 8) to the inheritors within 200 days of the date of death. [Consider modifying this clause to allow more time to pay.]

10. If one person is either unable or unwilling to make his or her share of the mortgage, tax or insurance payments in a timely manner, the other may make those payments. The extra payments will be treated as a personal loan to be paid back by the person on whose behalf they are made within six months, including 10% interest per annum (or the highest interest rate permitted under the state law, whichever is lower).

11. [Insert mediation/arbitration clause from Chapter 5, Section L.]

12. This agreement can be amended, but only in writing, and must be signed by both of us.

13. We agree that if the court finds any portion of this contract illegal or otherwise unenforceable, that the remainder of the contract is still in full force and effect.

_____	_____
Date	Faye Firth
_____	_____
Date	Fred Fox

(Notarize and record)

Tax Note: Keep in mind tax consequences when selling a share of a home. If you receive no money from the sale in a particular year, there is no taxable gain, or income, from the sale. If you do receive money from the sale, you have to determine what percent is a return on your initial capital (not taxed) and what percent is interest and profit (which is taxed). If the house has gone up in value substantially, selling a share will increase the seller's income and therefore tax liability. Spend an hour with a tax accountant, unless you are thoroughly familiar with all tax implications.

Financing Note: If you sell a share of a house already subject to a mortgage, you may need lender approval under the terms of the "due on sale" clause. The lender may not approve, for a variety of reasons, especially if your current mortgage interest rate is below the current market rate. Then, you may need to pay off the existing mortgage and refinance.

Chapter

Eight

Starting a Family

ONE EVENING, YOU dream about little feet scampering about your house. After satisfying yourself that it's not a dog, cat or hamster that you're hankering for, you and your mate decide that, even though you aren't interested in getting married, you'd like to have a child. While there are no insurmountable legal problems in having a child without being married, there are a few things you'll want to think about.[1]

A. Having a Child (or Having an Abortion)

A FATHER RECENTLY came to us and asked if he had to support his child in the following situation. He and his mate moved in together and decided not to have children. Two years later they separated. A day or two before they parted, the woman (by her own admission) ceased using her diaphragm without telling the man, in an attempt to get pregnant. She succeeded, although she didn't know she was pregnant until six weeks later.

Yes, the father has to support the child.

Courts don't care why people have children. Whether you decide to have children after signing a contract, checking the location of the planets or just letting it happen is legally irrelevant. If a child arrives, both parents have a duty to support. It makes no difference whatsoever whether or not the parents are married. But is this fair to the man

in the above situation? Perhaps not, but this book is about the law, not about fairness.

What about having an abortion? That's simple —a pregnant woman can get an abortion without the consent of the father, whether or not she's married. According to the United States Supreme Court case *Roe v. Wade,* 410 U.S. 133 (1973), an adult woman's decision to have an abortion can be regulated by the state only in the following manner:

1. Prior to the end of the first trimester (three months), the state may not interfere with or regulate a physician's decision, reached in consultation with the patient (the pregnant woman), that the pregnancy should be terminated.

2. From the end of the first trimester (three months) until the fetus becomes viable (can live outside the mother), the state may regulate abortions only to the extent that the regulation relates to preserving and protecting the health of the mother.

3. After the fetus becomes viable, the state may prohibit abortion altogether, except where it's necessary to preserve the life or health of the mother.

4. The state may declare abortions performed by anyone other than a licensed physician to be illegal.

This trimester analysis was criticized, but not overruled, in *Webster v. Reproductive Health Services,* 109 S.Ct. 3040 (1989), where the Supreme Court upheld a Missouri law stating that life begins at conception, prohibiting public employees from performing, assisting or counseling a woman to get an abortion and prohibiting abortions from being performed in public facilities. The court also upheld a requirement that doctors perform a viability test on any fetus at least 20 weeks old; if the fetus is viable, no abortion can be performed. Future limitations may come from the Supreme Court this year or next.

---

[1]We are talking about *having* a child, not adopting. The problems unmarried people face in adopting can be insurmountable. If you want to adopt, you may want to get married first. Although some states allow single parent adoptions, if the single person lives with someone or if an unmarried couple wants to adopt, approval is less likely. You might be able to adopt from a foreign country, especially a poor country with many orphans. One way to adopt is if one of you has a child that the other wants to adopt. Although you're probably better off marrying and requesting a stepparent adoption, it's possible to adopt this way, especially if you've cared for the child a long time and the child's other parent is either absent or not against the adoption. For more information, see a lawyer who specializes in adoption.

Practically speaking, if you're a woman, and you suspect you're pregnant and want an abortion, contact a physician as early as possible for verification and compare prices before selecting the physician or clinic to perform the abortion. If you're a man, there's legally nothing you can do to influence a woman's decision to have or not have a baby.

What about the "Right To Life" groups' fight for a constitutional amendment banning abortion? We're against it. While abortion makes us as queasy as the next person, we believe that a woman must have the legal freedom to choose. We've seen too many sixteen-year-olds, pregnant and miserable, for whom motherhood would be a disaster, to think otherwise. Banning abortions will simply drive tens of thousands of women out of hospitals and back to side-alley butchers. Of course, no woman should be coerced through the welfare or prison system, or any other way, to have an abortion, but at the same time, no one should have a child to salve someone else's conscience.

What about the rights of the father—isn't it unfair to leave all the decision-making to the mother? If she has the child, he must support it, but if she wants an abortion, he can say nothing. Yes, it's unfair, but no law that protects the interests of the father, as well as that of the mother and child, has been proposed. But law aside, we offer our advice: for both parents' to be responsible and care for and support their children, both must have a say in deciding when, and when not, to have children.

B. Naming the Baby

IN THE GREAT MAJORITY of states, you may give your child any name you like. This includes first, middle and last names. You don't have to give the baby the last name of either parent—Mary Jones and Jack Smith can name their child

Ephraim Moonbeam if it pleases them. A few states require a married woman's child to bear the husband's surname—but these laws are few, and being challenged. [2]

In most states, the normal procedure for naming a baby is simple. A representative of the local health department or similar agency asks the new mother the child's name and some questions about her health and the father's occupation. The mother doesn't have to name the child or identify the father at this time, though she may be pressured to do so. The information she gives is typed on a form that she signs. The state then issues a birth certificate, which usually doesn't reveal whether or not the parents are married.

If the baby wasn't born in a medical facility, the mother and/or person officiating must notify the health officials of the birth. There's no requirement that the baby be named at this time, though it's common to do.

---

[2]South Carolina law (§ 20-1-70) requires that if a child's unmarried parents marry after the birth, the child must take the father's surname.

If, in either case, the mother withheld the baby's name or father's identity (and thus the birth certificate is incomplete) and later wants it updated, she should call the state agency which furnishes birth certificates (such as the Department of Vital Statistics), to fill out a form to amend the birth certificate.[3]

⚠️ **Caution:** Do not list a person as the father if that person is not, in fact, the father. Many women are tempted to do this, especially if they no longer see the natural father and are involved with someone who they'd prefer to have raise the child. Be realistic—your current relationship may not last forever, and complicated questions of paternity and support can grow from the seemingly simple act of listing the wrong person as the father of a child. Once a person is listed, it's very difficult, sometimes impossible, to de-list him.

Similarly, been named father on a birth certificate isn't proof to a court that you're the father. If a paternity or support action is filed against you, you can contest paternity. Advances in blood chemistry research make it possible to determine paternity with better than 98% accuracy, and to disprove it with 100% accuracy.

C. Naming the Father: Paternity

PATERNITY SIMPLY MEANS "the state of being a father." For reasons discussed below, when an unmarried couple has a child, it's essential that the father sign a paper stating that he's the father

as soon as possible after the baby is born.[4] This protects the mother, the baby and especially the father. Paternity mix-ups are complicated, humiliating and expensive, and the law in the legitimacy-illegitimacy-paternity area is so confused, it's hard to know what a father's rights are unless he signs a paternity statement.

Don't let your excitement over the baby cause you to forget to fill out the statement. You can prepare it yourself quite easily. We include two samples below and tear-outs in the Appendix. The second is to be signed by both parents. It's here because in a surprising number of cases, the mother, after the father signs the first type of statement, tries to frustrate his custody and visitation rights by denying that he was, in fact, the father.

---

[3]For information on naming a baby, changing names or amending a birth certificate in California, see *How To Change Your Name* (California ed.) by Loeb & Brown, Nolo Press.

---

[4]If he waits and signs it later, he's normally okay if no dispute over custody or adoption arises. If he waits until a dispute develops, however, and then tries to legitimate his child, most courts will say it's too late unless he's had an ongoing relationship with the child. [See *Quilloin v. Walcott*, 434 U.S. 246 (1978) and *Lebr v. Robertson*, 463 U.S. 248 (1983) where the Supreme Court denied the right to block an adoption to fathers who had no real relationship with their children nor tried to legitimate the children until the adoption proceedings began.] And in some states, only a father who has established paternity must be notified of adoption proceedings. These laws effectively limit the rights of an unmarried father; if he's not notified and doesn't appear in court, he can't make his feelings known.

SAMPLE 1—ACKNOWLEDGEMENT OF PATERNITY

Lazarus Sandling hereby acknowledges that he is the natural father of Clementine Conlon Sandling, born January 1, 1990, to Rebecca Conlon in New York, New York.[5]

Lazarus Sandling further states that he has welcomed Clementine Conlon Sandling into his home and that it is his intention and belief that he has taken all steps necessary to fully legitimate Clementine Conlon Sandling for all purposes, including the right to inherit from, and through, him at the time of his death.

Lazarus Sandling further expressly acknowledges his duty to properly raise and adequately support Clementine Conlon Sandling.

_____
Date

_____
Lazarus Sandling

(Notarize)

SAMPLE 2—ACKNOWLEDGEMENT OF PARENTHOOD

Lazarus Sandling and Rebecca Conlon hereby acknowledge that they are the natural parents of Clementine Conlon Sandling, born January 1, 1990, in New York, New York.

Lazarus Sandling and Rebecca Conlon further state that they have welcomed Clementine Conlon Sandling into their home and that it's their intention and belief that Clementine is fully legitimated for all purposes, including the right to inherit from and through Lazarus Sandling.[6]

---

[5]As noted above, Clementine need not have Lazarus' last name to be legitimate. As a practical matter, however, our society's tradition is that a child be given its father's last name, and it may be easier in the long run if Clementine has Lazarus' last name, or a hyphenated version of Lazarus and Rebecca's names.

[6]A child of unmarried parents can always inherit from its mother, but in the past, there were problems in inheriting from a father in some states. See Section K below.

Lazarus Sandling and Rebecca Conlon further expressly acknowledge their legal responsibility to properly raise and adequately support Clementine Conlon Sandling.

_____   _____
Date   Rebecca Conlon

_____   _____
Date   Lazarus Sandling

(Notarize)

No matter which statement you complete, prepare it in triplicate and have your signature notarized. Notarization isn't required, but it's an excellent idea. In the event the father dies, the mother will have to present the statement to various agencies. Notarization proves that the signature wasn't forged after the father's death. The mother and father should each keep a copy and the third copy should be kept safe for the child. Some states have set up procedures to file paternity statements with the Bureau of Vital Statistics. If your state has, file yours.

D. Legitimacy

MOST STATES AND the federal government have moved away from the concepts of "legitimacy" and "illegitimacy." And about time too—there's something weird about a society that has a higher value for children whose parents happened to get married before doing what comes naturally. Many states have adopted the Uniform Parentage Act which says that "the parent and child relationship extends equally to every child and to every parent, regardless of the marital status of the parents."

The Uniform Parentage Act

The Uniform Parentage Act has been adopted in Alabama, California, Colorado, Delaware, Hawaii, Illinois, Kansas, Minnesota, Missouri, Montana, Nevada, New Jersey, North Dakota, Ohio, Rhode Island, Washington and Wyoming.

Even in states where legitimacy and illegitimacy make little difference, it's legally important to know who a child's parents are. In inheritance, child support, custody, adoption and many other areas of the law, the rights and duties of parents are clearly marked out. If a father doesn't voluntarily sign a paternity statement, the state will try to establish that he's the father in other ways.[7]

In the states that have adopted the Uniform Parentage Act, a man is presumed to be the father if:

Circumstance 1: He's married to the mother at the time the child is born, or was married to her within 300 days of the birth of the child. This means that, if the man dies or the couple divorces while the mother is pregnant, he's still presumed to be the father.

Circumstance 2: He and the mother, before the birth of the child, attempted to get married

---

[7] *Trimble v. Gordon,* 430 U.S. 762 (1977) held that states may set up different standards of proof necessary to establish paternity, but can't be completely arbitrary. To find your state law, check your state code (see Chapter 12). Look in the index under "Children," subheading "Legitimate."

(obtained a license and had a ceremony) but the marriage wasn't valid because one person was still married to someone else, the clergyperson could not perform a marriage or a similar reason.

and

The child was born during the attempted marriage or within 300 days after its termination, be it by court order, death or simple separation.

Circumstance 3: After the child's birth, he and the mother have married (or gone through a ceremony in apparent compliance with law) although the marriage could later be annulled for some reason.

and

a. He has acknowledged paternity in writing (by, for example, signing a paternity statement);

b. With his consent, he's named the father on the child's birth certificate; or

c. He pays child support under a written, voluntary promise or he has been ordered to pay support by a court.

Circumstance 4: While the child is still a minor, he receives the child into his home and openly holds out the child as his natural child.

You'll notice that these rules deal with presumptions. Legally, a presumption means that certain facts are presumed to produce a certain legal conclusion unless rebutted by strong evidence.[8] In circumstance 4, if a man takes a child into his home and says he's the father—even though he never married the mother, he's presumed to be the father. This doesn't mean that he is—he or the mother might prove that though he received a child into his home and told everyone that he was the father, he wasn't. This can lead to a court fight over blood tests and the like.

---

[8]Some states have laws conclusively presuming (they can't be rebutted) that a child born to a married couple living together at the time of conception is the husband's. These laws are under attack because of the extreme accuracy paternity blood testing.

Unfortunately, 32 states haven't adopted the Uniform Parentage Act, and many still use the terms legitimate and illegitimate. In a long line of court decisions, however, beginning with *Levy v. Louisiana,* 391 U.S. 68 (1968), the U.S. Supreme Court has struck down most state laws giving legitimate children more legal rights than illegitimate children. A few cases have gone the other way though. In *Mills v. Habluetzel,* 456 U.S. 91 (1982), for example, the court said it was constitutional to give legitimate children more time to sue for support than illegitimate children, as long as illegitimate children have an opportunity to sue.

In most states that still label children, it's possible to change the label from illegitimate to legitimate by:

• The parents marrying each other.

• The father signing a paternity statement—that is, acknowledging that the child is his in writing.

• The father welcoming the child into his home and/or holding himself out as the father.

• The parents going to court and having a judge rule that the man is the father. This can usually be done by joint petition—the parents going to court together in a non-adversary proceeding.

Children born during a marriage that is later annulled remain legitimate. And remember, a child's legitimacy is relevant only in relation to the child with the father, his family and his benefactors. The mother's relationship with her child isn't changed by the child's status.

Hint: Re-read this section and the previous one—you're likely to conclude that signing a paternity statement is the best (and maybe only) way to be sure that your child is legitimate. By signing, you needn't worry about the other legal technicalities.

E. Separating

MOST PARENTS PLAN to stay together at least until their children are grown. But the glue that held families together in former generations seems to have lost some of its stick. Whether married or living together, many parents separate and raise their children while living apart. Doing this in a constructive, humane way is a great challenge. It requires both parents to let their egos take a back seat to the best interests of their child.

Because unmarried couples don't get divorces, there's no automatic occasion to involve judges and lawyers in the child-raising responsibilities. Unmarried couples can make their own support, custody and visitation arrangements. We believe that, if possible, it's best that they do so.

Below are three sample written agreements. They're all quite different, ranging from joint support and joint custody, to dad supports and mom raises the kids. If none fits your situation exactly, use the clauses that do fit and add some others.

Remember that circumstances change; thus, approach your agreement with a spirit of flexibility and openness. Also, no custody, support or visitation agreement—even one ordered by a judge—is ever permanently binding. A fair amount of support today may not be enough tomorrow. Custody with one parent may work brilliantly for a year and then sour. Your agreement must be a living document, not a museum piece frozen under glass. It should be a statement of needs and expectations that lays a solid foundation for the changes and additions that will surely come.

Note: We assume that you've both signed a statement acknowledging parenthood, or at least the father has signed one. If you haven't, return to Section C. It's essential to everyone's interests (most especially the father's) that a paternity statement be signed.

SAMPLE 1—SEPARATION AGREEMENT

Rebecca Conlon and Lazarus Sandling, having decided to no longer live together, make the following agreement for the purpose of raising their child Clementine in a spirit of compromise and cooperation. Rebecca and Lazarus agree to be guided by the best interests of Clementine and that:

1. Custody of Clementine shall be joint. This means that all major decisions regarding visitation by the non-custodial parent, Clementine's physical location and Clementine's health, education and the like, shall be made jointly. For the first year of this agreement, Lazarus shall care for Clementine on weekday days, and Rebecca on weekday nights and weekends.

2. At the time this agreement is made, Lazarus' income as a night disc jockey and Rebecca's income as a day horse jockey are approximately equal and neither shall pay the

other child support. Lazarus shall cover Clementine's health and dental insurance through his job, and Rebecca shall contribute an equal amount ($100 per month) for clothes. Each person shall pay routine costs for food and shelter while Clementine is in his or her custody.

3. If in the future, either Lazarus or Rebecca's income increases to more than 20% over the other's, the person with the higher income shall bear a larger share of the child support with the exact amount to be worked out at that time, based on the income of both parents and Clementine's needs.

4. Both Lazarus and Rebecca will make an effort to remain in the area of Philadelphia, PA, where they presently live, at least until Clementine is in junior high school.

5. If Lazarus and Rebecca disagree as to visitation, custody support or any other problem concerning Clementine, they shall undergo a joint program of counseling to attempt to resolve their differences. Clementine shall be involved in this process to the maximum amount consistent with her age at the time.

6. Insert mediation/arbitration clause from Chapter 5, Section L]

_____   _____
Date   Rebecca Conlon

_____   _____
Date   Lazarus Sandling

(Notarize)

If communication between Lazarus and Rebecca completely breaks down and one of them filed a formal custody action in court, this agreement would probably be given serious consideration by the judge. But because the judge has the legal right to make support and custody orders that are in the "best interests of the child," the agreement would not be binding.

SAMPLE 2—SEPARATION AGREEMENT

Sam Matlock and Chris Woodling make this agreement because they have decided to stop living together, but wish to provide for the upbringing and support of their children, Natasha and Jason. Sam and Chris agree as follows:

1. That until Jason and Natasha are both in school, Chris shall have primary responsibility for child care during the week and Sam shall pay child support in the amount of $500 per month per child.

2. That Jason and Natasha shall spend most weekends and at least one month during the summer with Sam; Sam shall be available for babysitting at least two weekday nights.

3. That all major decisions regarding Jason and Natasha's physical location, support, visitation, education and the like shall be made jointly by Sam and Chris; Jason and Natasha shall be involved in the decision-making to an extent consistent with their ages at the time.

4. That when both Natasha and Jason are in school, Chris intends to return to her career as a fashion designer at least part-time and Sam intends to return to school to finish his Ph.D. Sam and Chris contemplate that during this period, Chris will earn enough to support the children and Sam will take on a larger share of the child care duties.

5. Both Sam and Chris are determined to conduct their affairs without recourse to lawyers and courts. If communication becomes difficult, they promise to participate in a program of joint counseling. If any issue becomes impossible to compromise, they will submit the dispute to binding arbitration.

6. Insert mediation/arbitration clause from Chapter 5, Section L]

_____   _____

Date   Sam Matlock

_____   _____

Date   Chris Woodling

(Notarize)

SAMPLE 3—SEPARATION AGREEMENT

Joseph Brenner and Josephine Clark agree to live separately from this time on, and wish to assure that their children, Nancy Benner born June 1, 1985, and David Clark, born May 20, 1989, have a secure financial future and receive the support that they'll need to lead a safe and happy life. Thus, Joseph and Josephine as follows:

1. Josephine shall have custody of Nancy and David reserving to Joseph liberal rights of visitation, including two months during the summer, school holidays and generally whatever time the children wish to see him.

2. For two years beginning September 1, 19__, Joseph shall pay to Josephine the sum of $1,200 per month for child support for Nancy and David. This amount is set deliberately high to allow Josephine to continue her part-time job.

3. Starting September 1, 19__, Josephine shall attempt to find employment four days per week.

4. Beginning September 1, 19__, or whenever Josephine finds a four-day-a-week job, whichever occurs later, Joseph shall pay to Josephine the sum of $1,000 per month for child support of the two minor children. This support shall continue at the rate of $500 per child per month (with yearly adjustments for inflation in September at the rate tied to the Consumer Price Index) until each child reaches the age of majority, marries or is otherwise emancipated.

5. All payments are due on the first day of each month.

6. The provisions of this agreement may be incorporated into a court order in a lawsuit brought by either party. If a lawsuit is brought, this agreement shall be presented to the judge.

7. This agreement may be modified only by written agreement of both parties or by court order.

8. Insert mediation/arbitration clause from Chapter 5, Section L]

_____   _____
Date   Joseph Brenner

_____   _____
Date   Josephine Clark

(Notarize)

Form Preparation Note: Whichever form you prepare, make two copies. Notarization isn't required, but it's a good idea. Each person should keep one copy. It's possible to have the agreement be made part of a court order, but you'll probably need an attorney to do this. If you expect possible problems with payment, you'll want to make this into a court order. Otherwise, it's probably unnecessary and perhaps even counter-productive to involve courts and lawyers.

F. Custody

IF YOU BREAK UP, you both have an equal right to custody of your child as long as the child has been legitimated. If the father refused to sign a paternity statement or otherwise legitimate the child, however, he's out of luck. A series of court decisions, the logic of which we can't explain, have set up a double standard: A father must support his children, whether legitimate or not, but has an equal right to custody if he's legitimated them. We must again emphasize the obvious—if you're dad, sign a paternity statement as soon after birth as possible. If you wait until a dispute develops, it may be too late. Of course, sign one when the dispute arises anyway—even a late legitimation is better than none for a father.

Uniform Putative and Unknown Father's Act

As of January 1990, this Act has not been adopted by any state. Over the next few years, however, it is likely that it will be introduced in many state legislatures and passed in a number.

What does it mean that both parents have equal rights to custody of a legitimate child? Neither parent has the right to deprive the other of having, or visiting with, the child unless, or until, a judge makes a different order. And if a court does give one parent custody, if an illness or similar event prevents that parent from providing for the child, the other parent is next in line to exercise custody rights.

Example 1: *Rebecca and Lazarus break-up, and Rebecca takes physical custody of Clementine. A year later Rebecca dies. Lazarus, who signed a paternity statement legitimating Clementine, has the right to custody, and any other person seeking custody would have to present evidence to a court showing Lazarus' inability to care for Clementine.*

Example 2: *Instead of dying, Rebecca marries and her husband wants to adopt Clementine. As long Lazarus has legitimated the child, she cannot be adopted by Rebecca's new husband, or any other person, without Lazarus' consent, unless he had abandoned her (failed to support and contact her for a certain length of time).[9] Even then, the adopting parent would have to prove abandonment to the court.*

---

[9]In most states it's at least two years, though some have shortened it to one. If you have no money and can't support your child, you can't be viewed as abandoning the child as long as you visit regularly.

Although the father of a child that has not been legitimated has the legal right to custody,[10] he faces an uphill battle. He will be notified and given the right to be heard, and may even win custody. But—and this is important—most courts won't view his petition seriously and award him custody. In our view, this double standard is inconsistent with both common sense and the U.S. Constitution. Let's hope the Supreme Court will eventually agree.

G. Visitation

AN UNMARRIED PARENT of a legitimate child has the same legal right to visitation that a married parent has (see Chapter 9, *You and Your Prior Family*, Section C). This means that the parent who doesn't have custody may visit with the child at reasonable times. You are entitled to arrange visitation voluntarily, like custody, but if you can't, a judge will arrange it for you. A father who hasn't legitimated the child will probably be allowed (by a court) to visit, if he's has had previous contact with the child.

If a non-custodial parent disappears, failing to contact or provide support for his or her children, custodial parents who've established new families fear the non-custodial parent's return as a ghost from the past. If the non-custodial parent requests visitation, the judge will probably be suspicious of the new-found desire to visit after years of neglect. If that parent is willing to provide support and demonstrates a genuine desire to establish a relationship with the children, however, the judge

will probably allow some visitation. Most judges believe it's in a child's best interest to have a relationship with both parents, even if they're less than perfect.

H. Adoptions

THE LEGITIMATE CHILD of an unmarried couple cannot be adopted without both parent's consent, unless one parent has abandoned the child. A father who signs a paternity statement, provides support (if he can) and maintains a relationship with his child is not in danger of the child being adopted by someone else.[11] Unmarried mothers without custody needn't sign a paternity statement, but must pay support if they can and visit. In addition, if a child is a new born, and the father has had no opportunity to support—or abandon—the child, some states allow him to prevent the adoption and obtain custody.[12]

A stepparent adoption is one where one parent marries someone other than the other parent, and the new spouse wants to adopt the child. These adoptions are approved pretty readily because the child is already in the home and will stay there even if the adoption is denied. A local social service agency will conduct a home study—visiting the home and interviewing

---

[10]In *Stanley v. Illinois*, 405 U.S. 645 (1972) the U.S. Supreme Court said "the state cannot . . . presume that unmarried fathers . . . are unsuitable and neglectful parents. The denial to unwed fathers of a hearing of fitness accorded to all other parents whose custody of their children is challenged by the state constitutes a denial of equal protection of the laws." In a similar case, the Court ruled that an unwed father (closely involved with his child) has the right to veto an adoption if the mother has that right. *Caban v. Mohammed*, 441 U.S. 380 (1979).

[11]In Georgia, this is called an "opportunity interest;" if an unwed father acts on his opportunity to establish paternity, provide support and maintain contact with his child, he'll enjoy the legal rights of any father. [*In re Baby Girl Eason*, 358 S.E.2d 459 (1987).] See also, *Lehr v. Robertson*, 463 U.S. 248 (1982) where the Supreme Court allowed an adoption without an unwed father's consent because he hadn't participated in his child's life. The court said that if an unmarried father "accepts some . . . responsibility for the child's future, he may enjoy the blessings of the parent-child relationship. . . . If he fails to do so, the federal constitution will not automatically compel a state to listen to his opinion of where the child's best interests lay."

[12]These states include Colorado, Connecticut, Illinois, Indiana, Maine, Massachusetts, Michigan, Minnesota, Nebraska, Nevada, New Mexico, New York, North Carolina, Oregon, South Dakota, Utah, Vermont and West Virginia.

custodial parent, the adopting parent and the child.

If the non-custodial parent is the mother, the agency will also have to obtain her consent or recommend that her parental rights be terminated. If the non-custodial parent is the father, the agency will determine whether he has abandoned the child or whether his consent is needed.

Here are a few scenarios:

Example 1: *Linda and Frank aren't married. Linda is pregnant with his baby, but Frank takes off before the baby is born. He doesn't send support or contact Linda or the baby (Mollie) for three years. Linda's life deteriorates and she calls an adoption agency to place Mollie for adoption. Linda must consent, but the agency need not get Frank's. It will likely, however, make a minimal effort to notify him. If he opposes the adoption, he must be given a hearing, but his opposition won't be counted for much.*

Example 2: *This time Linda keeps Mollie and later marries Herman. Herman wants to adopt her. Linda's consent is necessary, but Frank's isn't. The agency will probably make some effort to notify Frank, and he'll get a hearing if he opposes the adoption, but his abandonment will probably prevent him from successfully opposing it.*

Example 3: *This time Linda and Frank live together for several years after Mollie is born. When they split up, Linda keeps the child. Frank holds Mollie out to the world as his, visits her and pays support to Linda. He never signs a paternity statement, however. Whether Herman can adopt Mollie without Frank's consent depends on state law. If the state has adopted the Uniform Parentage Act (Section D above), Frank's*

consent is necessary as he has legitimated Mollie by welcoming her into his home and acknowledging that he's the father. Other states, however, require a paternity statement.

Example 4: *Same as 3, except when Mollie is born, Frank signs a paternity statement. Every state will require Frank's consent before allowing Herman to adopt Mollie.*

Example 5: *This time, before Linda and Frank split up, Frank signs a paternity statement, but never contacts Mollie again. If he refuses to consent to Herman adopting her or can't be found, a court will decide whether he's forfeited his parental rights by abandoning Mollie. All effort will be made to notify him of the hearing.*

Example 6: *This time, Frank keeps Mollie after they split up. Frank marries and his wife wants to adopt. Linda must consent to the adoption. If she refuses, there must be a hearing to terminate her parental rights, and she must be given a chance to oppose. If she hadn't supported or contacted Mollie for a long time, it's likely her rights will be ended.*

Note: Most states provide that parental rights can be terminated and a child "freed for adoption" for reasons other than abandonment, such as imprisonment for a felony, mental retardation or unfitness. We don't deal with these situations because contested adoption actions aren't common in these areas.

I. Support for a Child of Unmarried Parents

AS WE'VE NOTED above, a father has a duty to support his child even if the child is illegitimate and he has no right to custody.[13] (Both parents have a legal duty to support their children.) If you can arrange support to your mutual satisfaction, a court will have no reason to get involved. In Chapter 9, *You and Your Prior Family,* Section D, we discuss support in detail.

The parent with custody (usually the mother) or someone acting on the child's behalf (such as the welfare department) can sue the other parent (commonly the father) to obtain a court order setting the amount of child support the non-custodial parent must pay. If he doesn't pay, the District Attorney can prosecute him, which, if he is able to support but simply refuses, can land him in jail. County jails are full of fathers who don't take their support obligation seriously.

If the child is adopted, both parents' parental rights are terminated and their duty to support the child ends. If the child is adopted by a stepparent, the non-custodial parent no longer must support the child.

J. Public and Private Benefits for a Child of Unmarried Parents

A CHILD CAN BECOME entitled to many benefits, such as Social Security, union benefits and private insurance benefits, if his parent becomes disabled or dies. Until recently, these benefits derived through the father were often unavailable to ille-gitimate children. For example, Social Security regulations used to grant more benefits to the legitimate child of a deceased, retired or disabled father than to an illegitimate child.

In *Jimenez v. Weinberger,* 417 U.S. 628 (1974), however, the U.S. Supreme Court ruled that treating the children differently was unconstitutional. Similar discriminatory government programs have likewise been held unconstitutional and now it makes no difference whether a child is legitimate or illegitimate for purposes of receiving Social Security and similar government benefits.[14]

It's nice that children are treated equal, but their father must still take steps to protect them. Sign a paternity statement. If you die, Social Security or other federal, state or private benefits may be denied, not because your child is illegitimate, but because there's no conclusive proof that you were the father.[15]

K. Inheritance Rights of a Child of Unmarried Parents

YOU CAN LEAVE your property to anyone you want to in a will, trust, joint ownership device or other estate planning device (see Chapter 11, *Death*). In short, you don't have to to legitimate a child to leave him or her property.

If an illegitimate child's parent dies without a will, however, most states diminish the child's right of inheritance—the child can fully inherit from the mother but not from the father. Even in

---

[13]Several cases have held that a state may limit the time for the mother (or local welfare agency) to bring a paternity suit to obtain child support. Two Supreme Court cases have struck down one and two-year limits, but acknowledge that a longer time period would be acceptable *Mills v. Habluetzel,* 456 U.S. 91 (1982) and *Pickett v. Brown,* 462 U.S. 1 (1983).

[14]The mother, however, may be denied survivor's benefits if the father fails to legitimate the child. *Califano v. Boles,* 443 U.S. 282 (1979).

[15]In *Morales v. Bowen,* 833 F.2d 481 (3rd Cir. 1987), a New Jersey court awarded social security benefits to a child whose father failed to acknowledge paternity only after the mother presented clear and uncontradicted evidence of his paternity. In California, however, the court awarded benefits to the child of a man who died before learning of his lover's pregnancy. *Smith v. Heckler,* 820 F.2d 1093 (9th Cir. 1987).

states that allow illegitimate children to inherit, some limit the time the child can make a claim against the father's estate. In *Trimble v. Gordon,* 430 U.S. 762 (1977), the Supreme Court made it clear that a paternity statement will normally be adequate to guarantee the inheritance rights of children born out of wedlock if there's no will.[16]

---

[16] If your state rules allow acknowledgement of paternity for purpose of inheritance in a way other than a paternity statement, that will be sufficient. In Connecticut, for example the child can inherit if there was no will if the father admitted paternity prior to his death or paternity had been determined by a court.

Chapter Nine

You and Your Prior Family

IF YOU'VE BEEN MARRIED in the past or are currently married to someone other than the person you live with, you may encounter special problems, especially if you have children or receive alimony (called maintenance or spousal support in some states), and you and your ex-spouse left each other angry and bitter.[1] Fortunately, as more people realize that lawyers are the prime beneficiaries of domestic strife and court fights normally last only as long as the money does, the willingness to compromise with ex-mates has grown. This is wise—you and your spouse got yourselves into the relationship and, in the last analysis, you're the only ones who can get yourselves out. While paranoia may be a part of separating, and ending a relationship in a loving (or at least civilized) fashion is difficult, we urge you to try, even if it's the hardest thing you'll ever do.

A. Getting a Divorce While Living With Someone Else

IN EVERY STATE, some type of "no-fault" divorce is available. "No fault" means that a judge won't listen to any testimony about who's at fault for ending the marriage. To get a no-fault divorce, the person requesting the divorce must state either that the couple no longer gets along and wants to go separate ways (the couple has irreconcilable differences or there's been an irretrievable or irremediable breakdown of the marriage) or that the couple has been living apart for a certain period of time.

"Hooray!" you're shouting. "The fact that I left my spouse and live with someone else can't be used against me at my divorce." Not necessarily. Although every state has no-fault, 33 states and

the District of Columbia kept their traditional fault-based divorces (adultery, mental cruelty and the like) as well. This means that a spouse in one of those states can request a fault divorce and show that you mistreated him or her.

The chart below lists, state-by state, the grounds for divorce. A notation in the fault category means the state still lets you claim adultery or the like. No-fault means you can claim irreconcilable differences, or irretrievable or irremediable breakdown. For separation, we include the time needed to be apart.

---

[1]If you live in California, you'll find much information on divorce, custody, visitation, adoption and support in *California Marriage and Divorce Law,* by Warner, Elias and Ihara (Nolo Press).

GROUNDS FOR DIVORCE[2]

State	Fault Grounds	No-Fault Grounds	Separation	Length of Separation
Alabama	✔	✔	✔	2 years
Alaska	✔	✔		
Arizona		✔		
Arkansas	✔		✔	3 years
California		✔		
Colorado		✔		
Connecticut[3]	✔	✔	✔	18 months
Delaware	✔	✔	✔	6 months
Florida		✔		
Georgia	✔	✔		
Hawaii		✔	✔	2 years
Idaho	✔	✔	✔	5 years
Illinois[4]	✔	✔	✔	2 years
Indiana		✔		
Iowa		✔		
Kansas	✔	✔		
Kentucky		✔		
Louisiana	✔		✔	6 months
Maine	✔	✔		
Maryland	✔		✔	1 year
Massachusetts	✔	✔		
Michigan		✔		
Minnesota		✔		
Mississippi	✔	✔		
Missouri[5]	✔	✔		
Montana		✔	✔	180 days
Nebraska		✔		
Nevada		✔	✔	1 year
New Hampshire	✔	✔		
New Jersey	✔		✔	18 months
New Mexico	✔	✔		
New York	✔		✔	1 year
North Carolina	✔		✔	1 year
North Dakota	✔	✔		
Ohio	✔		✔	1 year
Oklahoma	✔	✔		
Oregon		✔		
Pennsylvania	✔	✔	✔	3 years
Rhode Island	✔	✔	✔	3 years
South Carolina	✔		✔	1 year
South Dakota	✔	✔		
Tennessee[6]	✔	✔	✔	3 years
Texas	✔		✔	3 years
Utah	✔		✔	3 years
Vermont	✔		✔	6 months
Virginia[7]	✔		✔	1 year
Washington		✔		
West Virginia	✔	✔	✔	1 year
Wisconsin		✔	✔	1 year
Wyoming		✔		
Washington, DC	✔		✔	6 months

---

[2]This information and chart is taken from the *Family Law Dictionary*, Leonard & Elias (Nolo Press).

[3]Separation divorce must also allege incompatibility.

[4]Must allege irretrievable breakdown and separation for no-fault; if both parties consent, 2 years reduced to 6 months.

[5]If contested, plaintiff must show adultery, abandonment, incompatibility or separation.

What this means is that if your state still has fault divorce, and your spouse is angry because you've moved in with your lover, you face the possibility that your spouse may drag your living situation (adultery) into court. For practical purposes, in some states you might be awarded less than your share of the marital property. And, even if your state has done away with fault-based divorces, it might still consider it in the division of property, awarding more property to the spouse not at fault.

For example, Hawaii has eliminated traditional fault divorces—only "irreconcilable differences" may be alleged to obtain a divorce. Hawaii courts, however, can consider marital fault when dividing property. On the other hand, Alaska still allows divorces based on one spouse's fault, but that fault cannot be used to keep that spouse

---

[6]Separation divorce allowed only if there are no children.

[7]May be reduced to 6 months if there are no children.

from getting his or her share of the marital property. The below chart gives the state-by-state breakdown.

FAULT CONSIDERATIONS IN DISTRIBUTING MARITAL PROPERTY

Marital Fault Irrelevant to Property Division	Marital Fault May Reduce Share of Property
Alaska	Alabama
Arizona	Arkansas
California	Connecticut
Colorado	Florida
Delaware	Georgia
Idaho	Hawaii
Illinois	Maryland
Indiana	Michigan
Iowa	Mississippi
Kansas	Missouri
Kentucky	New Hampshire
Louisiana	North Carolina
Maine	North Dakota
Massachusetts	Rhode Island
Minnesota	Texas
Montana	Utah
Nebraska	Vermont
Nevada	Virginia
New Jersey	Wyoming
New Mexico	
New York	
Ohio	
Oklahoma	
Oregon	
Pennsylvania	
South Carolina	
South Dakota	
Tennessee	
Washington	
West Virginia	
Wisconsin	
Washington, DC	

Living with your lover may also limit or bar your right to receive alimony in some states. This is true, for example, in California and Hawaii, which have eliminated fault divorces. Alaska, however, which allows fault divorces, prohibits that fault from being considered when establishing alimony. The below chart lists those states that may restrict alimony on the grounds of the receiving spouse's fault.

FAULT MAY BAR OR LIMIT ALIMONY

Alabama	Louisiana	South Dakota
Arkansas	Maryland	Tennessee
California	Massachusetts	Texas
Connecticut	Missouri	Utah
Florida	North Carolina	Virginia
Georgia	Oklahoma	Washington, DC
Hawaii	Pennsylvania	West Virginia
Idaho	Rhode Island	Wisconsin
Illinois	South Carolina	

Fault need not make a difference to you and your spouse. Many people get civilized divorces in states where fault-based divorces are possible. They make custody, support and property decisions in a spirit of compromise, not "who hurt whom." If you and your spouse are separating amicably, you needn't worry about the effect of living with someone else. But in case memories grow short, consider writing down your understanding; we provide a sample below.

If you and your spouse aren't divorcing amicably, and you'll possibly lose property or alimony by living with your lover, don't, if possible, until your divorce is final. This is especially true if cohabitation is illegal in your state (see Chart in Chapter 2, *Sex, Living Together and the Law*).

CO-OPERATIVE SEPARATION AGREEMENT[8]

Sean and Barbara Washington agree to the following:

1. That they've decided to go their separate ways and no longer plan to live together.

2. That John Washington, age 5, and Richard Washington, age 3, will reside with Barbara Washington, and Sean will spend as much time as possible with the children.

3. That Sean will provide a reasonable amount of support to Barbara each month, taking into consideration his salary and the needs of the children. Initially this will be $400 per month per child.

4. That as neither Sean nor Barbara plan to marry again soon, it's understood and accepted that both will very likely have personal friendships that may involve sex and that either or both may decide to live with someone of the same or opposite sex.

5. That Sean and Barbara will proceed to get a divorce as amicably as possible and that neither will try to influence the court by raising the fact that the other is having a relationship, or living, with a third person.

6. [Insert mediation/arbitration clause from Chapter 5, Section L]

_____
Date

_____
Date

_____
Barbara Washington

_____
Sean Washington

---

[8]This type of agreement isn't technically enforceable in court, especially as it relates to children. As we discuss below, a court must look at all factors when considering "the best interests of the child." Still, an amicable agreement will help if one spouse suddenly drags the other's lifestyle into court. A judge might well ask, "How come you didn't object the day you signed the agreement, but now suddenly you do?"

B. Child Custody

IF YOU AND YOUR SPOUSE agree on custody, the court will normally ratify your agreement without considering the details of your life. A judge won't know if one of you is living with another person unless it's brought to his attention. If you and your spouse are battling over custody, however, the best traditional advice is to not live with a person of the opposite sex and to be very discreet in your sexual activity, at least until the court makes a decision. This advice applies to both fault and no-fault divorces, as a parent's living arrangement is always admissible in a custody dispute on the theory that a court needs as much information as possible to determine "the best interests of the child."

As you'll notice, we use the word "traditional" to describe the "no sex, no living with anyone" advice to be followed by a parent in a custody fight. This is because many states have relaxed their uptight legal attitudes toward living together. While we can't say that most judges are enthusiastic about granting custody to a parent who lives with someone, fewer judges deny custody to a parent who lives with someone else, especially when the new relationship is stable and nurturing. Therefore, the decision to live or not live with your lover while fighting over custody should be decided situation-by-situation, state-by-state.

In all states, child custody is decided according to "the best interests of the child." This means that the judge who hears the case can take into account all evidence and allegations before him and then decide who will provide the better home. Although mothers are more often granted custody, the automatic preference is gone and many men win custody of their children.

People often ask:

"If I live with a man, can my children be taken from me?"

"If my husband is an alcoholic (or a recently recovering alcoholic), will he be able to get custody of (or visitation with) the children?"

"I was once arrested for possession of marijuana; does this mean I can't get custody?"

"My income comes from Social Security disability and other public programs while my husband has a good-paying job. Does this mean he'll get custody of the kids?"

"My son is nine years old and wants to live with me; will the court let him?"

"Is it actually possible for a father to get custody of young children?"

The answer to all of those questions is "it depends." In spite of what your next-door neighbor, best friend, or brother-in-law has said, the law doesn't say that adultery, smoking pot, drinking or whatever necessarily means you can't win, or will lose, custody. In addition, one parent's greater income isn't a valid reason to give him custody.

The bottom line is that in every state and under every test, each judge determines who gets custody; she'll necessarily apply her own standards and prejudices. Some judges don't like marijuana; some don't like arrest records; some don't like political activity; some (despite the fact that it's not proper to admit it) don't like poor people; and some, in spite of prevailing attitudes, don't like unmarried persons living together, but, as we mentioned earlier, this isn't the "no-no" it used to be; in fact, here are some typical holdings:

"We've long passed the point where sexual misconduct automatically disqualifies a mother from obtaining custody of her minor children." *Greenfield v. Greenfield,* 260 N.W.2d 493 (Neb. 1977).

"The fact of the mother's adulterous relationship is of importance in a child custody case only as it may affect the best interests of the child." *Bonjour v. Bonjour,* 566 P.2d 667 (Alaska 1977).

"Without some evidence that the living arrangement is in some way detrimental to the welfare of the child, a modification of custody, based solely upon that relationship, is improper." *Dunlap v. Dunlap*, 475 N.E.2d 723 (Ind. 1985).

"Absent a showing that the children were exposed to such activity or were in any manner damaged by reason of such activity, such sexual activity does not justify a change of custody." *Kennedy v. Kennedy*, 380 N.W.2d 300 (Neb. 1986).

"Inherent in a custody award is the right of the custodian to make basic parental decisions, such as who can or cannot associate with the children." *In re Rollins*, 760 P.2d 1381 (Ore. 1988).

To research other cases in this area, your best source of information is the *Family Law Reporter*, available in many larger law libraries. (See Chapter 12, *More Legal Help.*) You may run into cases from conservative areas where cohabitation was grounds to deny custody, but they're few and getting fewer.[9]

1. Joint Custody

For many parents—those who agree on custody and those doing battle—joint custody is a possibility. In some states, courts must award joint custody, absent an unusual circumstance. We recommend joint custody if the parents communicate well and are equally dedicated to raising the kids because it balances the power between parents and gives each an equal.share. We believe that fathers are much more likely to support and maintain close relationships with their children when they're truly involved in decision-making.

Joint custody means that the parents (and hopefully the children) plan jointly for their children's future, as they did before the divorce. Actual physical custody is worked out by the parents, taking into consideration things like the parents' and childrens' schedules, the schools and the neighborhoods. Joint custody doesn't mean that the children must spend six months of each year with each parent.

A common criticism of joint custody is that because neither parent has the final say, arguments can go on forever. This point is valid, and joint custody often works best if the parents and children attend family counseling (sometimes called "divorce" or "separation" counseling) for help through the rough spots. Few marriages are saved by counseling, but many families save anguish by family counseling. A good divorce can be as precious as a good marriage.

---

[9]Many courts study the impact of cohabitation on the child and find it not harmful. Others find the opposite. See, for example, *Nix v. Nix*, 706 S.W.2d 403 (Ark. 1986), ("appellant's ongoing relationship . . . was immoral, failed to set a proper example for the children, and resulted in harm to the children"); *LaBlane v. LaBlane*, 490 So.2d 763 (Louis. 1986) and *Gray v. Gray*, 654 SW.2d 309 (Mo. 1983). These cases resulted in either a loss of custody or a prohibition against the children staying when the parent's lover was present. See also *Parrillo v. Parrillo*, 554 A.2d 1043 (R.I. 1989), *Small v. Small*, 412 So.2d 283 (Ala. 1982) and *In re Marriage of S*, 641 S.W.2d 776 (Mo. 1982).

2. Anatomy of a Contested Custody Case

Judges don't decide custody cases simply by inviting the parents to present their rival arguments. Long before the parents get to court, government agencies, such as the County Juvenile Probation Department, Social Services Department or the Department of Child Welfare, have been involved.

What normally happens is that the parents' lawyers (or the parents themselves if they're handling the case) notify the court that, as part of a divorce, there's a fight over custody. The judge assigns the case to a relevant government social worker, who makes an investigation and presents a written report and recommendation to the court. An investigation can include interviews with the parents and children, checking background information, arrest records, health records and references, and sometimes psychological testing.

Social workers have different degrees of skill and time in interviewing and assessing personalities. Some offices are so understaffed they effectively preclude in-depth investigation. Also, social workers have their own biases and their recommendations will reflect those prejudices. While most social workers are younger and more tolerant than many judges, they will probably feel compelled to mention your living situation in the report. Even if your particular social worker does not think it's important, the judge may feel differently.

Once the judge gets the report, your attorney (or you if you represent yourself) will have the opportunity to read it before you go to court and discuss it. The judge isn't compelled to follow the report, but most do. If the social worker recommends that you get custody, you've won more than half the battle. If not, you're at a serious disadvantage, but you can still proceed to the trial, and you may ask the social worker to come to court to be cross-examined about the report.

At the trial, the judge may ask your children where they want to live. Some judges ask only older children; other judges never ask any children. Most judges will pay little—if any—attention to the opinion of a child under 7, will probably respect the wishes of a teenager if the chosen parent is otherwise suitable and will possibly consider the wishes of children between 7 and 12. Judges also tend to keep brothers and sisters together, though not always.

⚠ **Caution:** During a divorce proceeding, a judge needn't award custody of the children to either the husband or the wife; she can award custody to a relative, a friend or even the local juvenile court, but must find both parents unfit before taking this drastic step. This law is noted to warn hostile parents that too much mudslinging may convince the judge that neither parent is fit.

C. Visitation of Children

IF A COURT GRANTS you (or your former spouse) custody of the children, the other parent (or you) will be given the right to visit, unless the court believes that the non-custodial parent's physical presence would be detrimental to the children.[10] If you and your ex-spouse can communicate enough to agree on a visitation schedule, the court will probably grant "reasonable visitation rights," and leave it to you to work out the details.

If, however, you and your ex-spouse cannot communicate to the degree of agreeing on when, where and how visitation will take place, the court will specifically define the visitation rights. The court might say, for example, that "Barbara Washington shall have the right to visit with the children every Saturday from 10:00 a.m. to 5:00 p.m., plus three weeks during the summer months, the weeks to be agreed upon by the parties;" or "Sean Washington shall have the right of visitation on the first weekend of every month from 6:00 p.m. on Friday to 6:00 p.m. on Sunday provided he picks the children up from and delivers them to Barbara Washington's home."

Sometimes, courts impose restrictions on visitation beyond times and places, such as requiring the non-custodial parent to tell the other of her desire to visit 24 hours in advance, prohibiting the non-custodial parent from removing the child from the county, state or, in rare cases, the child's own home, prohibiting the non-custodial parent from drinking alcohol while he's with the children, or where there's evidence of abuse, requiring another adult to be present during the visit.

In addition, a court may prohibit a parent from visiting the children in the presence of the person he lives with, or prohibit his children from spending the night if his lover is present in the house.[11] These cases are not the rule, however, and if you've been given such an order, speak to an attorney regarding your obligations, your rights and a possible appeal. It's rarely wise to violate a court order.

D. Child Support

THE FAMILY SUPPORT ACT of 1988, a federal law, requires every state to adopt a formula setting a minimum amount of child support depending on the financial resources of the parents, the needs of the children and other factors.[12] A state that did not comply by October 13, 1989 is in jeopardy of losing its federal government AFDC reimbursement.

The effect of this law is that child support—or at least a minimum amount of child support—is no longer set by the judge, as it's set by a formula. Although the law has resulted in higher child support awards than in the past, this has been offset by the decrease in litigation because there's less to fight about. Your state's formula may be available from court clerk's offices or law libraries.

If you have custody of your children and live with someone else, your ex-spouse is still required to support the children. He may be angry at your new living arrangement and tempted to get out of

---

[10]See, for example, California Civil Code § 4601, which reads: "Reasonable visitation rights shall be awarded to a parent unless it's shown that such visitation would be detrimental to the best interests of the child."

[11]For example, in *Commander v. Commander*, 493 So.2d 530 (Fla. 1986), the court held that a mother couldn't have overnight visits with her children because she and her lover slept together on the living room sofa when the children slept over, giving the children a "distorted view" of acceptable family life. And in *Lasseigne v. Lasseigne*, 434 So.2d 1240 (La. 1983), the court prohibited overnight visits when the father's lover was present, even though the couple was discreet, because such visits might undermine "the children's respect for the family institution." But in *Hackley v. Hackley*, 380 So.2d 446 (Fla. 1979), the court declared that a father's cohabitation shouldn't terminate his overnight visitation with his five-year-old child unless the living together situation had an adverse impact on the child.

[12]For information on computing child support in California, see *How to Modify and Collect Child Support in California*, Matthews, Segal & Willis (Nolo Press).

paying by quitting his job or refusing to look for work, but the court will then order him to pay on his ability, not inclination, to work.[13]

The person you live with has no obligation to support your children. The amount of child support your ex-spouse is ordered to pay shouldn't be affected by the fact that you live with someone else. If your lover provides shelter or buys food, clothing or other items for you, however, a court may rule that you have a higher amount of income available to support your children, thus resulting in a lower child support payment by the ex-spouse.

> Example—New York's Formula: *Barbara and Sean divorce and Barbara is awarded custody of the two children. Sean earns $30,000 a year and Barbara earns $10,000. Under New York's law, the incomes are combined ($40,000) and multiplied by 25% ($10,000). Sean, because he earns 3/4 of the income must pay 3/4 of the support, or $7,500 ($625 per month).*
>
> *A year later, Harold, who earns $100,000 per year, moves in with Barbara; Sean asks the court to reduce his child support obligation. The judge won't, as the amount of support is set by formula, unless Sean show's that Harold pays many of Barbara and the children's expenses, freeing up most of Barbara's income.[14]*

---

[13]Refusing to support your children when you have the ability to do so is a crime in all states. Many people don't take their obligation seriously and end up with a free education at a county school with high grey walls and bars on the windows.

[14]New York's law, like most state's, allow the judge to deviate from the formula if the amount is unjust or inappropriate, based on factors such as the financial resources of the custodial parent. If you receive child support and live with your lover (or new spouse) and don't want to lose what you receive, consider signing an agreement to keep all earnings and property separate. One California court ruled that joint income could not be considered in making a child support award when the custodial parent and new spouse had such an agreement.

If you're a non-custodial parent and live with someone—perhaps even support that person and her children—will your child support be reduced?. Because you have no legal duty to support these people, a judge won't reduce your support obligation. Your primary duty is to your own children, not your lover's. At the same time, if your living expenses are reduced because you share them with another person, a judge may deviate from the child support formula because a greater amount of your income has been freed up.

And be aware that states are buckling down in collecting child support. All states have laws to attach the wages of a parent who falls behind in child support. A wage attachment means that an amount to cover the child support is taken out of a paycheck and paid directly to the custodial parent or a government agency. Also, states, with the help of the federal government, are cooperating to collect child support from parents who move to another part of the country. In short, paying child support is not only morally good, but also it can keep you out of jail.

E. Alimony

ALIMONY (ALSO CALLED spousal support or maintenance), was necessary a generation ago when papa went to the office and mama stayed home to tend the babies and the spaghetti. Today, however, it's slowly dying. Among younger people especially, alimony is granted less frequently (or for short periods only) and isn't even requested in many cases. Any alimony that is paid terminates upon the recipient's remarriage, absent an agreement or court order to the contrary. But what happens if the recipient cohabitates, not remarries?

If your written separation agreement states that alimony will terminate upon cohabitation, a court will likely enforce it.[15] If you have no agreement, states vary. Some have laws requiring termination, regardless of whether the recipient's economic need diminished by cohabiting.[16] Others, such as New York, require that the recipient "hold herself out as the wife" of the man she lives with before alimony is terminated. Still in other states, such as California, Tennessee and Connecticut, cohabitation creates a "rebuttable presumption" that the recipient's need for support has been reduced—that is, the court will assume you need less alimony, unless you prove otherwise.

In states without these specific laws, alimony can be terminated or modified only on a showing of change of circumstance. Thus, if the recipient lives with someone who doesn't support him or otherwise alter his financial situation, then his alimony probably won't change because his economic circumstances haven't changed.

In rare cases, cohabitation may alter the payor's situation as well. A California Court recently held that a payor's whose economic circumstances changed for the better when his female friend moved in with him must pay more alimony to his ex-wife.[17]

⚠ **Warning:** If receiving alimony is important to you, don't live with someone until you thoroughly check the law in your state. Go to a public law library (in the county courthouse); find your state Code and look in the index Alimony or Spousal Support. Also, check the staple-bound pages (called pocket parts) in the

back of the book that contain recent changes. And, ask the law librarian if there are any books on domestic relations in your state, such as those published by the Continuing Education of the Bar (CEB) in California or the Practicing Law Institute (PLI) in New York. Also check the *Family Law Reporter,* which contains a digest of significant cases from all states. If you're still in doubt, check with a lawyer (see Chapter 12, *More Legal Help*).

F. Cohabitation After a Divorce

YOUR MARRIAGE IS LEGALLY FINISHED and you're settling down to a new life with your new partner. If you've no minor children and receive no alimony, you need not worry about cohabiting. If you do, however, you can't forget that your living with someone may affect you custody and visitation arrangements. These matters may be changed by the court if it finds that circumstances have changed since the making of the original order.

> Example: *When you were awarded custody of your children, you were a Sunday school teacher whose only recreation was attending afternoon piccolo concerts. Now, you and the children live with your new lover in a community for ex-alcoholic slide trombone players. If your ex asks for a change in custody, will the court grant it? That depends on what the judge thinks of your new lifestyle. You'll have less trouble if you show that the children are secure, well taken care of and doing well in school; you'll have a serious problem if it looks like you're raising the kids in an unstructured zoo.*

There's very little that you can do to keep your ex-spouse from taking you back to court. Your ex has the right to ask the court to change a

---

[15]Some courts won't enforce it if it's imposed by a judge acting on his own (see *Else v. Else,* 367 N.W.2d 701 (Neb. 1985)), but will if it's suggested and agreed to by the couple (see *Bell v. Bell,* 468 N.E.2d 859 (Mass. 1984)). Also, some states (such as Florida, New Jersey and New York) require that the cohabitating couple be economically interdependent before terminating alimony.

[16]These states include Alabama, Georgia, Illinois, Louisiana, Pennsylvania and Utah.

[17]*In re Marriage of Tapia,* 211 Cal.App.3d 628 (1989).

custody or visitation order at any time. You have the same right. As living with someone will influence some judges, but not others, your best approach, if possible, is to maintain amicable relations with your ex.

For example, if you're extremely cooperative about visitation, your ex-spouse probably won't ask the court to change custody if you begin living with someone. Likewise, if you're prompt and reasonably generous with your child support and alimony payments, your ex is much less likely to hassle you about visitation if a friend moves in. If, however, in spite of your efforts your ex is hostile to your planned cohabitation, contact a lawyer to check the legal implications of living together in your state.

Chapter

Ten

Moving On—Dividing Things

EVEN THE NICEST RELATIONSHIPS can end, usually bringing some sticky moments. This is so even if both of you try to be sensitive and caring, and even more so if one of you does not. An important loss can't help but affect you in powerful ways. It's easy to let your feelings of loss (anger, guilt, hostility, resentment) manifest themselves as bitter arguments over who'll get the coffee pot, dessert forks, children or house. If you're splitting up, think for a moment of how you'd advise your closest friends in a similar situation. Then take the advice yourself.

In years passed, many people were pressured by door-to-door salesmen into signing expensive contracts for things they didn't really want, resulting in the unlucky buyer making many months (or years) of payments. Eventually, Congress halted this practice with a law giving a person who signed a door-to-door contract a three-day "cooling-off period" to cancel the contract without reason. The idea is that folks shouldn't be stuck permanently with their own hasty actions committed in an emotion-charged atmosphere.

The same can be said about breaking off a relationship. You've been arguing, you're tired of each other and you've likely said things that hurt. Don't stomp out with your back scratcher and the check books and announce that you'll never return. Give yourself at least three days to "cool off," preferably away from where you live. If, after this time, you still want to split, and both of you can discuss matters rationally, sit down and divide. But, if one of you is still yelling or crying, wait awhile to settle financial matters. Of course, dividing property isn't important compared to what's really going on, but a year from now you'll feel better if you feel you got a fair share of your property. And neither of you will be able to complain that it wasn't a fair split or fool yourself into thinking that that was what really concerned you.

A. Dividing Property

IF YOU'VE ORDERED your economic affairs along the lines of the sample agreements in Chapter 5, *Contracts,* or Chapter 7, *Buying a House,* you're in good shape—maybe not emotionally, but at least materially. You can easily divide things according to your written agreement. If you disagree on the interpretation of a contract clause, apply your mediation/arbitration clause, or the principals of mediation and arbitration we discuss in Chapter 5. Avoid court, however—unless the property is very valuable (a home, for example) the legal fees will probably be more than the property is worth.

If you and your partner never wrote down anything, however, and after discussing property division and making every effort to divide things fairly, you can't reach an agreement, do one of the following:

1. *Forget it:* Simply stop arguing and let your friend take what he wants. We strongly advise this if the disputed items aren't valuable. Thousands of people fight bitterly over objects never worth the trouble. And a little generosity may work wonders in getting your friend to be more reasonable on other issues.

2. *Mediate:* Consult a friend, or professional mediator, to help you work out a mutually satisfactory compromise. Many cities and counties provide mediation services at low or no cost. If public mediation isn't available, private mediation certainly is. A consumer organization may be able to refer you. Failing that, mediators are listed in the Yellow Pages. But before you hire someone you don't know, check references carefully. (See Chapter 5, Section L for more on mediation.)

3. *Arbitrate:* Find a third person (or a panel of people) and empower her, in writing, to make a binding decision. Arbitration is warranted only if the disputed items are quite valuable (a house, boat, antique car) and attempts to settle matters

through mediation have failed. (Again, see Chapter 5, Section L.)

4. *Go to Court:* Engage in an all-out war, with attorneys, in court. We don't recommend this unless a lot is at stake and all other sensible efforts to resolve the dispute have failed. If you decide on court, you'll need to know your state's laws governing the property rights and obligations of unmarried couples. The principals of the *Marvin v. Marvin* case and other legal decisions may apply. So re-read Chapter 4, *Living Together Contracts and the Law,* and carefully consider whether your situation resembles any of those that would qualify for a *Marvin* (or similar case) remedy. If you feel you've a good claim, see an attorney.

As you must understand by now, the law involving the rights of unmarried couples is highly complex and changing. Most lawyers know little about it. We discuss finding one who does in Chapter 12, *More Legal Help.* But even if you find a competent lawyer, the wheels of justice in America don't spin quickly—indeed, they often barely move. Most litigants spend lots of money and time and still don't achieve a satisfactory result. So take a moment to contemplate the Gypsy curse, "May you have a lawsuit in which you know you are right."

B. If Paternity is Denied

BEFORE REACHING THE QUESTIONS of child custody and support, some mothers will have to cope with a father who refuses to acknowledge that he's the father. This can be a serious legal problem if you don't have an acknowledgment of paternity (see Chapter 8, *Starting a Family*). If you face this problem and need financial help to raise the children, see an attorney, or if you have very little money, the district attorney. Paternity actions are unpleasant, but children shouldn't suffer because of an irresponsible father. For-

tunately, blood tests can normally resolve paternity questions without the need for extended or expensive litigation.

C. Support for Children

WE HOPE THAT WHEN your child was born, you both signed a parenthood agreement, or at least the father signed an acknowledgment of paternity. If not, address this oversight—sign a statement—now. Even if your breakup is bitter, you must protect the rights of your child. Once a statement is signed, your must decide the question of child support.

Both parents are legally obligated to support their child. If you're fortunate enough to work out a satisfactory child support arrangement with your child's other parent, write it down (along with your arrangement for custody and visitation). This may be all that you'll ever need. If a problem with that agreement arises, however, it may not be enforced by a court if the court feels its not "in the best interests of the child."

If you've worked out a child support agreement but are concerned that support won't be paid voluntarily, have your agreement confirmed by a court order. If your settlement is in your child's best interest,[1] it shouldn't cost much to have a lawyer present it to a court.

---

[1]As discussed in Chapter 9, *Your and Your Prior Family,* a federal law now requires every state to adopt a formula setting a minimum amount of child support. If you bring your agreement to court, the court will make sure that your arrangement is consistent with your state's formula.

The best way to figure out child support is to follow the method used by your state. After all, it's what a court would do, and is considered in your child's best interest. Your state's formula should be available from the court clerk's offices or a law library.

Formulas usually require the parents to total their combined yearly incomes and then determine the percentages of the total each earns. If, for example, Burt earns $35.000 and Monica earns $15,000, for a yearly total of $50,000, Burt's share is 70% and Monica's is 30%.

The state then multiplies the total yearly income by the percentage it feels it costs to raise kids. In New York and other "expensive" states, the factor is about 25%; state's with lower costs of living assign lower numbers. If Burt and Monica lived in a state assuming 20%, the total annual child support would be set at $10,000 ($50,000 * 20%). Burt, who earned 70% of the total income would be responsible for $7,000 a year ($583 per month) and Monica for $3,000 ($250 a month).

If Monica had custody, she's considered meeting her support obligation by virtue of the child living with her, and Burt would be obligated to pay her (for the child) $583 a month. If Burt had custody, Monica would be obligated to pay $250. A court may alter these figures if one parent's expenses were unusually high or had another source of assets.

If you can't come to an agreement, follow our suggestion for mediation in Chapter 5, Section L.

Unfortunately, few low or middle income families can support two households on one income. If there's only one wage earner, no one will be well off. We can't say much to help except pay attention to your ex-lover's needs as well as your own, try to avoid being paranoid or vindictive, and remember that in addition to a decent place to live, good food and a feeling of being loved, a child needs a lollipop once in a while.

If you and your child's other parent are seriously disputing child support and mediation has not helped, you'll probably have to go to court to get it resolved. For married couples, it's included as part of a divorce lawsuit. For unmarried couples, child support disputes are resolved as a part of paternity actions.

D. Support for Each Another

SOME PEOPLE SEPARATE and agree that one owes the other support. This can occur if one person has paid the other's school expenses, given up a job to move a long distance to join the other or a myriad of other reasons. We discuss providing support, and written agreements to cover it in Chapter 5. Most people don't plan ahead, however, and must do the best in the here and now.

If you agree that one person will support the other for a while, sign an agreement so stating. Below are two samples. Both include language making payment contingent upon the waiver of other current legal claims. If you're tempted to cross this out, thinking that the support is a gift, not something given in exchange for giving up legal rights, be aware that a promise of a future gift can't be enforced in court, while a contract agreement where one person gives up a valuable right in exchange for another normally can be.

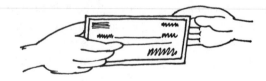

SAMPLE 1—SEPARATION AGREEMENT

Roger Bane and Mildred Perkins have decided to live separately from this time on. For the past five years, they've lived together; Mildred has provided household services for Roger and has foregone any paid employment.

Mildred and Roger hereby agree that, in exchange for Mildred waiving any and all contractual and equitable claims for property accumulated during the living together relationship against Roger, Roger shall pay to Mildred $400 a month for 12 months, for a total of $4,800. The payments shall be made on the first of every month, commencing March 1, 19__.

[Insert mediation/arbitration clause from Chapter 5, Section L.]

_____   _____
Date   Roger Bane

_____   _____
Date   Mildred Perkins

SAMPLE 2—SEPARATION AGREEMENT

Sue Jessup and Eric Smallwood agree as follows:

1. That for most of the last three years Eric has supported Sue while she got her Doctor of Divinity degree and that the amount of support provided was approximately $18,000.

2. That in exchange for Eric waiving any and all claims against Sue, Sue agrees to pay Eric $18,000.

3. That commencing July 1, 19__ Sue will pay Eric $450 per month. Payments shall be made on the first of each month and shall continue for a total of forty months.

4. [Insert mediation/arbitration clause from Chapter 5, Section L.]

_____   _____
Date   Sue Jessup

_____   _____
Date   Eric Smallwood

Like other agreements, this should be prepared and signed in duplicate. Notarization is optional unless the contract covers real property. If your ex-lover won't voluntarily sign an agreement to pay you some support and you believe you're entitled, there's the possibility of a lawsuit. You'll have to either prove an express (oral or written) agreement or rely on an equitable remedy of your not being fairly paid for your labor, or your ex unfairly profiting from something in your living together relationship. (We discuss these issues in Chapter 4, *Living Together Contracts and the Law*.)

Tax Consequences of Support Payments:

If money paid by one unmarried partner to the other at separation is the repayment of a loan, the recipient isn't taxed except on the portion for interest. If the money is for agreed-upon work performed by one person for the other, it's taxed as income. If the money, however, is given because one person needed it and the other was generous, it's considered a gift for tax purposes. The recipient has no tax liability, but the donor may owe gift taxes if the amount exceeds $10,000 per year.[2] If your payments will total more than $10,000, consider spreading them over more than one year.

E   Custody of Children

IN CHAPTERS 8, *Starting a Family*, and 9, *You and Your Prior Family*, we discuss child custody issues and include several sample agreements for people who work out an arrangement. If you can't, try to get a third party to help. A counselor or mediator with experience in family issues should be able to help you work out a fair compromise (many family courts provide this service for free). Only if all else fails, see an attorney. Representing yourself in a contested custody case is very difficult (see Chapter 12, *More Legal Help*).

F.   Conclusion

ONCE YOU'VE SETTLED the property, debts, support and custody, you've come through one of the most important and toughest periods of your life. Probably you've had to call on more maturity, patience, intelligence and plain courage than you thought you had. Congratulations.

---

[2]Under federal law, you can give away up to $10,000 per year to the same person tax free. If you go over $10,000, when you die the amount in excess is added on to your total estate's value for gift tax purposes. If that exceeds $600,000, taxes are assessed.

Chapter

Eleven

THIS IS YOUR FOURTH—and final—vocabulary lesson:

Administration (of an estate)—the distribution of the estate of a deceased person. The person who manages the distribution is an **administrator** (male) or **administratrix** (female).

Beneficiary—the person or organization who is entitled to receive benefits. Often used in trusts.

Codicil—a signed and witnessed supplement to a will containing a modification, amendment or explanation.

Community Property—property owned equally by spouses in Arizona, California, Louisiana, Idaho, Nevada, New Mexico, Texas, Washington and Wisconsin. It is property acquired by either spouse during the marriage except property inherited by, or given to, one. Unmarried couples cannot have community property.

Estate—all the property of a person who has died.

Executor—another term for administrator.

Heir—a person who inherits.

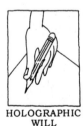

HOLOGRAPHIC
WILL

Holographic Will—a will that is completely handwritten. Such a will is valid in many states.

Inherit—to receive from someone who has died.

Issue—the children, grandchildren, direct lineals and blood descendants of a person.

PERSONAL
PROPERTY

Intestate—without a will. To die intestate means to die without having a will. **Intestate succession** is the distribution of a deceased person's property if he didn't leave a valid will or alternate estate plan.

Life Estate—the right to use property, most often real estate, during one's lifetime. This is a valuable property interest.

Living Trust—also called an "inter vivos trust;" a living trust is set up while a person is alive and remains under her control during her life—that is, she can change the beneficiary, revoke it or add to it at any time. The person who sets it up (the settlor) funds it with any money or property (the trust corpus) and appoints herself as trustee with full power to sell or transfer the trust contents. At her death, the trust assets pass directly to her beneficiary(ies) free of probate.

Personal Property—all property which isn't real property. Money, securities, autos, furniture and animals are all personal property.

Probate—a time-consuming and expensive court procedure designed to prove a will authentic and distribute the property according to the will. Many people with substantial assets plan their estate to avoid probate.

Real Property—land and those items attached to the land such as buildings.

Residue—the property which remains in the estate after all the debts are paid and gifts are made. It's usually used in a will, where the deceased had named a residuary beneficiary to inherit all property (the residue) not specifically left to a named beneficiary.

Separate Property—the property of a married couple that belongs to one spouse only, not both.

Succession—who gets what when someone dies. **The Laws of Succession** regulate who will share in the estate.

Survive—to be alive when someone dies. Some wills require that a beneficiary survive the deceased by a certain number of days (often 90) in order to inherit.

Testate—to die with a valid will.

Testator—a person leaving property by will.

Trust—a relationship where one person (the trustee) holds property for the benefit of another person (the beneficiary). A testamentary trust is commonly used when money is left to a child or as a tax saving device.

Will—a legal document in which a person states who he wants to inherit his property. Wills can also nominate guardians for a minor child (if the child's other parent isn't around), disinherit people, forgive debts and establish trusts.

A. Why Make a Will or Estate Plan

MANY OF US TURN off when the subject of death is raised, no matter what the context. We act as though, by ignoring death's inevitability, we can somehow get death to ignore our mortality. We don't plan what will happen to our property, who will care for our children, whether we'll be buried or cremated, and the like. Many people let society's laws cope with these problems.

The laws that govern what will happen to our property if we die without planning are called "intestate succession" laws. Intestate succession laws are designed to pass property to blood relatives only. If a member of an unmarried couple dies without a will or other protection for the survivor, the survivor will inherit nothing.

To insure that property is transferred, actually and legally, to your friend, you must arrange that transfer by a proper legal device, such as a will, living trust, joint tenancy designation, insurance policy or pay on death bank account. Any uncertainty regarding what property each partner owns should, of course, be resolved in advance, in a clearly-defined living together contract. (See Chapter 5, *Contracts.*)

Beyond defining who owns what, a living together contract, even one that provides that the survivor owns property covered by the contract on the other's death, is not a safe substitute for a will or living trust. The contract will very likely not cover all the couple's property, and if the deceased person makes a will leaving her share of property to someone other than her surviving partner, legal confusion (always expensive) will ensue and the will may prevail.

In addition to passing property, estate planning lets you nominate a personal guardian for your child, if you're a parent, appoint a person to supervise the distribution of your property, summarize your funeral/body disposition wishes or specify who will make the arrangements. If you don't nominate a guardian or appoint a supervisor, the court will. And if you don't plan your funeral/body disposition, your blood relatives will, and they can cut out your lover.

This chapter presents two approaches to estate planning for unmarried couples. Sections E and F discuss wills, and contain a sample you can adapt for yourself. Transferring property by a will can have drawbacks, however, principally probate—where your will is filed with a court, your assets identified, your debts paid and your property distributed to your inheritors. Probate usually involves substantial attorney's and other fees, and considerable delay. By planning ahead, you can often eliminate the need for probate, and sometimes save on taxes as well. Section G gives information to accomplish these goals. For now, it's enough to know that if your estate is "small" (roughly, under $50,000) it may not be worth the bother to do more than prepare a will.

B. If You or Your Partner Die Without a Will

IF YOU DON'T LEAVE a will or other estate planning device, intestate succession laws will pass your property to your relatives if you have any, and to the state if you don't. Most states' intestate succession laws are alike. If you want to know exactly what your's say, visit a public or law library and get a copy of your state's legal code.

1. Intestate Succession Laws

We don't include each state's intestate succession laws because of space considerations and because we believe you should complete a will or other estate planning device. The below summary is what would happen under a typical intestate succession law, assuming you die single.[1] Details vary from state to state.

- If you have children, all your property will be divided equally among them. The only exception is if you have a deceased child who left children (your grandchildren). These grandchildren will divide the deceased child's share.

- If you leave no children or grandchildren, all of your property goes to your parents equally if they're alive.

- Next in line are your brothers and sisters, who share equally unless any have died leaving children, in which case they (your nieces and nephews from your deceased sibling) share with your living siblings.

- If you leave no children, grandchildren, parents or siblings, your nephews and nieces share your estate equally unless you have grandnephews and grandnieces whose parents have died, who would receive their deceased parent's share.

- If you have none of the above relatives, your estate passes half to your paternal grandparents and half to your maternal grandparents. If they're not alive, their children (your parents' first cousins and your first cousins once removed) take equally. If any of these cousins have died, their share goes to their children.

- If you have none of these relatives, your property goes to the state.

---

[1]You're not single unless you have a final decree of divorce. If you die intestate still married to someone, she'll inherit a large part of your property.

2. Death and Living Together Contracts

Marvin and similar decisions can have a considerable effect on your property if you die without a will or other estate plan. As we discuss in Chapter 4, *Living Together Contracts and the Law,* most states enforce written living together contracts that cover property. If you have a contract stating that you're the half-owner of specific property, your partner has no power to dispose of your share. And if the contract says that you become the sole owner at the other's death, this provision should be honored unless he leaves a will to the contrary.

If you've no written contract, many states will enforce an oral or implied contract if you can prove its existence, and some courts will invoke an equitable remedy if one partner has been very unfairly treated. But to do this, the surviving partner would have to sue the heirs who inherit by intestate succession and prove the oral or implied contract existed, or that an equitable remedy should govern.

No hard and fast rules govern when the survivor might be able to prove that an oral or implied contract existed in order to get a share of the deceased's estate. Courts have made few rulings in this area. But if you're the survivor of a person who left no will (or who left a will but disposed of property you believe is yours by contract), you may have a case if any of the following situations exist:

- You worked in the home and your friend earned the money, but you agreed to share everything. In some states, you may be able to claim property under an oral contract. In some other states, your claim might be under an implied contract or other equitable remedy on the theory that you worked with the expectation of being paid, which never happened.

- You and your partner bought items jointly, and had agreed that all property belonged to both, with the survivor taking 100% if the other died. With a written agreement you'd probably have little trouble prevailing, but even with an oral agreement, you may succeed. It will depend on the attitude of the deceased's relatives entitled to inherit. If they are supportive of you, or will work out a compromise, a probate court will likely go along.

- You and your partner jointly contributed to the purchase of real property, but the property was put in only the deceased's name. In most states, it's difficult to rebut the legal presumption that the person whose name is on the deed is the legal owner, but you may be able to establish the legal grounds necessary to support an equitable remedy.

For information on proving an oral contract, implied contract or other equitable remedy reread Chapter 4.

C. Beginning an Estate Plan

WE HOPE WE'VE CONVINCED you to plan ahead for death. Before making a sensible will, living trust or other estate plan, however, you obviously need to know what property is yours. Don't laugh. If you've lived with a person for a long time, your property may be so mixed up with your friend's that you can't tell who owns what. If this is your situation, sit down and make an agreement as to who owns what.

SAMPLE PROPERTY OWNERSHIP AGREEMENT

Tomas Finnegan and Keija Adams agree as follows:

1. That they've been living together for ten years and that during that time much of their property has been mixed together so that it isn't completely clear who owns what.

2. That the purpose of this agreement is to divide all of Keija's and Tomas's real and personal property owned on January 10, 199_ into three categories as set out below.

3. That from the date of this agreement, all property listed in category 1 belongs solely and absolutely to Tomas, all property listed in category 2 belongs solely and absolutely to Keija and all property listed in Category 3 belongs to both in the shares noted.[2]

Category 1 (Tomas)

1. 1986 Ford Mustang

2. G.E. washer & dryer

3. 100 shares of stock in Melt-in-Your-Mouth Popcorn, Inc.

Category 2 (Keija)

1. 1987 Yamaha Cycle

2. BMX Stereo & related stereo equipment

3. $12,000 deposited in the Restaurant Workers Credit Union

Category 3 (Tomas and Keija)[3]

1. House at 2547 Jones Street owned in equal shares and held in joint tenancy under an agreement dated January 27, 1991.

2. Living room furniture owned 70% by Keija and 30% by Tomas.

Date _____   Keija Adams _____

Date _____   Tomas Finnegan _____

(Notarize and record)

---

[2]For real property (and personal property with title documents, such as a car), make sure that ownership indicated on the deed (or title slip) conforms with this agreement.

[3]If you already have an agreement defining ownership shares of jointly-owned property, make sure this agreement conforms to it. You can incorporate the earlier agreement into this one as Keija and Tomas have done.

D. An Introduction to Wills

MOST OF US KNOW what a will is—a document where you specify who gets your property when you die. A will is relatively easy to make and you can leave your property to anyone you wish, including the person you live with (or anyone else for that matter). It's easy to change or revoke; you're not stuck with it once you make it. And it's your own business. Discussing it with your lover is probably a good idea, but you don't have to.

As we stated earlier, however, the one drawback of a will is probate.[4] Thus, you may decide after reading Section G, to prepare a living trust or other probate avoidance document. Even if you do, though, you still need to make a will for the following reasons:

- You may have property at your death that you hadn't thought of, or don't yet own at the time of planning your estate, such as a suddenly-inherited house, a gift of an expensive stereo, lottery winnings or a personal injury lawsuit recovery. If you have a will, your residuary clause (all property not left to a specific person) will pass this property to your friend (or whomever else you name).

- To forgive debts owed to you.

- To disinherit anyone.[5]

- To nominate a personal guardian for your minor children.

- To name a custodian under the terms of the Uniform Transfers to Minors Act (if it's applicable in your state) to manage property left to your minor child.

or

- To set up a children's trust to manage property for your minor or young adult child.

- To name your executor—the person who will wind up your affairs after your death.

Once you decide what property you want to transfer by will, prepare the paperwork promptly. Postponement brings no benefit, while the risk—your property going to relatives chosen by your state legislature, not your friend—is great.

Let's consider some common questions about wills.

1. Can I Make a Legally Binding Will?

Yes. Anyone who's legally an adult[6] and "of sound mind" can make a valid will. The form in this book can be used by residents of all states except Louisiana, which has a different legal system (one derived from French law) than the rest of the country. If you live in Louisiana, you'll need to see a lawyer to prepare your will.

A person has to be pretty far gone to not be "of sound mind." If you're reading this book, you pass.

And we firmly believe that most wills can be prepared without the help and cost of a lawyer. If you have a large estate and want extensive estate planning, you'll need to see a lawyer. But if your estate is moderate-sized and you're not planning a complex distribution, you can do it yourself. A lawyer may try to scare you into buying her services by claiming that your will requires "expert, professional attention," but she'll then have her secretary prepare the same fill-in-the-blanks form she's used for a generation.

---

[4]Many states, however, provide simplified probate, or require no probate at all, for small estates, somewhere between $5,000 and $60,000. These laws are summarized in *Plan Your Estate: Wills, Probate Avoidance, Trusts and Taxes* by Clifford (Nolo Press).

[5]In some states, you cannot disinherit a spouse—a problem few of you should face. If you are not yet divorced, however, and this issue concerns you, see *Plan Your Estate: Wills, Probate Avoidance, Trusts and Taxes*, Clifford (Nolo Press).

---

[6]As defined by state law. It is 18 or older in all states, except Georgia, where you must be 19 to leave real estate in a will.

⚠️ **Caution:** If you have relatives who vehemently object to your relationship (and you own valuable property), it's possible that if you leave your property to the person you live with, those relatives will challenge your will on the ground that you were incompetent, or under "undue influence,"[7] when you made it. Although will contests are rare, they do occur. If there's any reasonable possibility a relative will challenge your will, establish that you're not under undue influence when you signed it. One way is to write your will yourself, but pay a lawyer to review it and be present at the signing. Another possibility is to have it prepared and signed in a lawyer's office, so someone can later testify that you were obviously competent. And if you're really concerned, videotape the signing and look into the camera and tell the world just how competent you are.

2. What Are the Technical Requirements in Preparing a Valid Will?

You must comply with few technical requirements to prepare a valid will. Do all of the following and your will is valid in every state except Louisiana.

- Type (or print) it.
- State that it's your will ("this is the will of (your name)" suffices).
- Sign and date it
- Declare to three witnesses,[8] when you sign it, that it's your will. (Some authorities recommend you say, "This is my will," and the witnesses answer, "He says it's his will." It sounds like Gilbert and Sullivan.) The witnesses must know that the document is a will, but aren't expected (or required) to read it.
- Have the witnesses sign and date the will after watching you sign and date it. The witnesses can't receive anything under the will. It's best to use younger witnesses who will likely outlive you and will be available to authenticate your signature, if necessary.

3. Are Handwritten Wills Legal?

In 26 states, "holographic" (handwritten) wills—ones you sign, but don't have witnessed—are valid. In the other states, they're not. Regardless of your state's rule, it's better to type your will and have it witnessed. Even states that allow holographic wills treat them suspiciously. And if they contain cross-outs, additions or machine-printed type (such as a date or heading), they may be invalidated. If you're trapped in the woods and the wolves are coming, write out a will (if you don't have a previously prepared one) and say your prayers. Otherwise, type one and have it witnessed.

---

[7]To make a will, a person must be able to exert his own free will. Undue influence is one person exerting the mental power causing the other to leave property in a way he otherwise would not have.

[8]In many states, only two witnesses are required. Using a third, however, can't hurt and means the will is valid in all states.

4. What Is a Joint Will?

A joint will is one document through which two people leave their property. After the first person dies, the joint will specifies what happens to the property of the second person when she dies. We don't recommend joint wills; the survivor, we believe, should have the freedom to dispose of her property as she wishes. If, despite our recommendation, you're thinking of using a joint will, see a lawyer.

5. What Happens If I Move to a New State After I've Made My Will?

If you use the form in this book, your will is valid in every state except Louisiana. This is true even if you move from one state to another. It's a good idea to draft a new will after a permanent move, however, especially if the executor no longer resides in your new state. To make a change, you can revoke your will and write a new one, or complete a "codicil." (We discuss both options below.)

E.   Preparing a Basic Will

THE WILL BELOW is basic and can be used by most unmarried couples with a moderate-sized estate. You can leave your property to whomever you want and nominate a guardian for your minor children. But many complexities aren't covered. For example, we include no provision for stating how to pay your death taxes.[9] Nor can you make a gift under the Uniform Transfers to Minors Act or establish a children's trust to delay the age when minor children inherit past 18. If your situation warrants a complex will, consult a lawyer or another Nolo comprehensive will-

---

[9]We discuss death taxes in Section G3.

preparation resource (see Estate Planning resources box at the end of this chapter).

After you read this chapter and form your overall estate plan, prepare a rough draft of your will, using or adapting the one we provide. Complete only the sections that pertain to you and renumber the remaining clauses. If, for example, you were never married and have no children, delete Clause II, "Prior Marriage and Children" and renumber the rest. When you're satisfied you've covered everything, type the will carefully on 8 1/2" x 11" typing paper. Gather your witnesses and date and sign the will at the end—you need not sign each page.

It's legal, though never advisable, to alter your draft prior to your and the witness' signing by crossing something out and initialing the change. Instead, retype it. Once your will is signed and witnessed, you can't legally cross out a provision or add a new one. You must formally amend it or revoke it.

What Happens If you Don't Follow Formalities?

If your will doesn't comply with technical requirements (for example, you have only one witness), the court will toss it out and your property will pass by intestate succession to your blood relatives. A will's not hard to do correctly. But check and double-check to be sure you do!

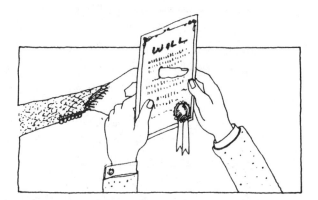

WILL OF (YOUR NAME)

I, ___[your name]___, a resident of ___[your county]___ County, ___[your state]___, declare that this is my will.

I.   REVOCATION

I revoke all wills and codicils that I have previously made.

II.   PRIOR MARRIAGES AND CHILDREN

A. I was married to ___[name of former spouse]___ and am now divorced.

B. I have ___[number]___children now living, whose names and dates of birth are:

_____   _____

Name   Date of Birth

(repeat as often as needed)

I have the following children of my deceased child _____[name]_____:

_____   _____

Name   Date of Birth

(repeat as often as needed)

The terms "my children" as used in this will shall include any other children hereafter born to or adopted by me.

C. If at my death any of my children are minors, and a guardian is needed, I recommend that _____[name]_____ be appointed guardian of the persons of my minor children, and _____[name]_____ as property guardian of my minor children.

III. GIFTS

A. I make the following gifts of money or personal property:

1. I give every child or grandchild listed in Clause II $1.00 (one dollar) in addition to any other property I may give them elsewhere in this will, or otherwise.

2. I give the sum of $_[amount]_ to _____[name]_____ if _[he/she/it]_ survives me by 60 days; if _[he/she/it]_ doesn't, this gift shall be made to _____name]_____.

(repeat as often as needed)

3. I give _____[identify item of property]_____ to _____[name]_____ if _he/she/it_ survives me by 60 days; if _he/she/it_ doesn't, the gift shall be made to _[name]_.

(repeat as often as needed)

4. I forgive and cancel the debt of $__[amount]__ owed to me by ___[name]___.

(repeat as often as needed)

B. I make the following gifts of real estate:

1. I give my real estate in _[county]_ _[state]_, commonly known as _[address and street]_, to _[name]_ if _[he/she/it]_ survives me by 60 days. If _[he/she/it]_ doesn't survive me by 60 days, that property shall be given to ___[name]___.

(repeat as often as needed)

IV. RESIDUE

I give the residue of my property subject to this will as follows:

A. To _[name]_, if _[he/she/it]_ survives me by 60 days;

B. If not, to _[name]_ if _[he/she/it]_ survives me by 60 days;

C. If neither ___[name in 1]___ nor ___[name in 2]___ survives me by 60 days, then to ___[name]___.

V. EXECUTOR

A. I nominate ___[name]___ as executor of this will, to serve without bond. If ___[name]___ shall for any reason fail to qualify or cease to act as executor, I nominate ___[name]___ to serve without bond.

B. I grant to my executor the right to place my obituary of _[her/his]_ choosing in the papers _[she/he]_ thinks appropriate.

VI. NO CONTEST

If any person or persons named to receive any of my property under my will, in any manner contests or attacks this will or any of its provisions, that person or persons shall be disinherited and shall receive none of my property, and my property shall be disposed of as if that contesting beneficiary had died before me leaving no children.

VII. FUNERAL/BURIAL ARRANGEMENTS

I have made funeral arrangements with _____[name of organization]_____. I also direct that _____ _____[specify instructions]_____ and I direct my executor to take all steps necessary to carry out my funeral/burial arrangements.

VIII. SIMULTANEOUS DEATH

If __[name of lover]__ and I should die simultaneously, or under such circumstances as to render it difficult or impossible to determine who pre-deceased the other, I shall be conclusively presumed to have survived _[name of lover]_ for purposes of this will.

I subscribe my name to this will this _[day]_ of _[month]_, _[year]_, at _[city, county]_, _[state]_.

[your full name]

IX. SIGNATURE AND WITNESSING

On this _[day]_ of _[month]_, _[year]_, _[your full name]_ declared to us, the undersigned, that this instrument was _[his/her]_ will, and requested us to act as witnesses to it. _[He/she]_ thereupon signed this will in our presence, all of us being present at the time. We now, at _[his/her]_ request, in _[his/her]_ presence, and in the presence of each other, subscribe our names as witnesses and declare we understand this to be [his/her] will, and that to the best of our knowledge the testator is competent to make a will, and under no constraint or undue influence.

Witness's Signature	Address
Witness's Signature	Address
Witness's Signature	Address

Your Name and Address

Use your full name as it appears on legal documents such as your driver's license or passport. If you use a second name, list both, separated by a.k.a. (also known as), such as, "John Q. Jones a.k.a. John Quincy Jones."

If you maintain residences in two states, each may try to impose state death taxes.[10] Listing your residence here will help minimize this, and help establish which state will probate your will. (It's probated in the county where you made your home.) If your ties to more than one state are strong, you'll need to take steps—such as registering vehicles, voting and conducting banking and other business affairs—to establish one as your residence. If you have a good-sized estate, see a lawyer to help in choosing which state.

---

[10]Many states don't impose death taxes. See Section G3.

I. Revocation

This clause covers all prior wills, including any hand written document that could possibly be construed as a will.

II. Prior Marriages and Children

If you've been married, mention the marriage and that it has ended (we're assuming it has). List all of your children, and any children of a child who has died (that is, your grandchildren of a deceased child). The box below discusses disinheriting a child. To do so, name that child and leave him or her $1.00 as in done in Clause III(A)(1).

How to Disinherit a Child

You must take affirmative steps to disinherit a child (or children of a deceased child. If you don't, state laws designed to prevent the accidental disinheritance of a child will kick in, and a child you didn't want to leave property will get some anyway. These laws are called "pretermitted heirs" statutes and provide that an unmentioned child (or child of a deceased child) receive a set percentage of your estate.

To disinherit a child, you can do one of two things. You can state the disinheritance in your will, such as, "I disinherit my son William Jones and direct that he receive nothing from my estate." Or, you can leave a child a minimal sum, such as $1.00, which shows that you didn't overlook this child, you just didn't want to give him anything of value.

Our form has you name each child (and each child of a deceased child), and leave them each $1.00, in addition to any other property you leave them. If you want to disinherit one of them, simply leave that child no property beyond the $1.00. If you want to use an express disinheritance clause, you'll find samples in *Nolo's Simple Will Book* by Denis Clifford.

In Clause II(C), you can nominate a personal guardian for your minor children and can name a property guardian to supervise any property you leave your children. We discuss these options in more detail in Section F below, "Providing for Children."

IIIA. Gifts of Money or Personal Property

Clause IIIA lets you to name beneficiaries of your money and personal property (everything but real estate). This clause is appropriate for direct, unconditional gifts to a single beneficiary, either a person or organization. If you want to leave a gift to two or more beneficiaries, see Nolo's other will resources, or a lawyer. And if you want to place conditions on a gift ("my car to Charley Parker, but only if he gives up smoking"), you'll need to see a lawyer.

If you're giving specific items of property, especially major items, describe them with sufficient detail to avoid later confusion. For example, if you leave someone a savings bond, identify the bond by number. If you have a lot of minor personal items, however, and don't want to list them all, you can give "all my furniture (or my tools or my musical instruments) to [name]."

You can also provide that if a beneficiary named to get a certain item doesn't survive you, an alternate beneficiary receive it. If you don't provide, and the beneficiary dies before you, the property becomes part of the "residue" (see Clause IV).

Many people don't want to leave something to someone who will never benefit from it, so they require the beneficiary to survive them by a specified period of time. This form specifies 60 days. You can state any reasonable period you want, such as 30 days or 100 days (two years isn't reasonable).

How to Leave All Your Property to One Person

To leave all your property to one person, or divided equally among several, make no specific gifts in Clauses IIIA and IIIB, except the $1.00 to any children, or children of deceased children. Instead, list the beneficiary or beneficiaries you want to receive your estate in Clause IV, the residuary clause. Because you're making no other gifts, your residuary beneficiary or beneficiaries get it all.

In Clause III(A)(4), you can forgive a debt owed to you. Forgiving a debt is a way to make a gift to the debtor.

IIIB. Gifts of Real Estate

First, remember that all real property you own in joint tenancy goes automatically to the surviving joint tenant or tenants; to leave it to someone else in your will, you take steps to end the joint tenancy.

As with your personal property and money, you name a beneficiary and can name an alternate beneficiary. If neither survives you, the property goes to your residuary beneficiary. We recommend including a survivorship period.

Note: When you leave real property to someone, she gets it along with the mortgages unless you otherwise provide. If you want to give real estate free of a mortgage, see one of Nolo's other estate planning resources (resource box is at the end of the chapter).

IV. Residue

The "residue" of your estate is what remains after all the gifts in Clause III have been distributed. You can select any person or organization to receive your residue—this person is called your residuary beneficiary. It's prudent to name two alternate residuary beneficiaries in the event your first choices predecease you. If you want to leave all of your property to one person simply leave it all to the residuary beneficiary.

V. Executor (Personal Representative)

Your executor is the person who will wind up your affairs when you die, and see that the desires you expressed in your will are carried out. You should name someone you trust and can rely on, and someone who will almost certainly be available and competent when you die. Also, you should name at least one successor in case your first choice dies before you, or refuses or is unable to serve. (If the will names no executor, the probate court appoints one.)

If you don't state that the executor is "to serve without bond," the probate court will probably require the executor to post a bond (a sum of money). This means either that a large amount of cash from the estate will be tied up, or that the estate must pay an insurance company a fee (usually 10% of the amount of the bond).

If you name an out-of-state executor, the court may require a bond, even if you stated "to serve without bond."

VI. No Contest

This clause is designed to discourage will contests. Children, however, are special cases and must be disinherited specifically if that's your wish.

VII. Funeral/Burial Arrangements

In most states, a will clause giving your funeral, burial or cremation wishes is given immediate effect, even if the will is otherwise invalid. For this reason, it's a good idea to insert any specific directions. For example, if you've provided a scientific or medical institution to be given your body, or parts, specify that here. Because wills aren't always located and read immediately, however, it's even more important that you leave parallel instructions in a more easily accessible place.

VIII. *Simultaneous Death*

If you die at the same time as a beneficiary (e.g., in a car crash or plane wreck) and it's impossible to know who died first, most states presume that the beneficiary died first. This way, your property passes to your alternate beneficiaries, not to the briefly surviving beneficiary and then to her beneficiaries. If you require a beneficiary to survive you by a certain number of days and name an alternate if she doesn't, you've solved the problem of "simultaneous death". Adding this general clause doesn't add extra protection.

If you own insurance, and you and the beneficiary die simultaneously, like the property in your will, the policy proceeds are distributed as if the beneficiary had died first.

If you own property in joint tenancy, however, and you and the other joint tenant died simultaneously, you're presumed to have died last. Thus your share passes through your will (in this will, through the residuary clause) and the other joint tenant's share passes in her will.

IX. *Signature and Witnessing*

Sign and date your will in front of your three adult witnesses, who you tell it's your will. Then ask them to sign the witness clause in front of each other. (See Section E2 above for more on witnesses and the signing ceremony.)

In some states, a "self-proving affidavit" can be added to a will. It does nothing to make the will more effective, but, in those states, can simplify—

or even eliminate—the witnesses' need to appear in probate court after you die. Explanations of self-proving affidavits and sample forms are included in *Nolo's Simple Will Book* and *Will-Maker*. (See Estate Planning Resources box at the end of this chapter.)

1. Storing and Copying Your Will

Store your will in a safe place, one that your executor has ready access to; normally a fireproof box or home safe is adequate. If you want to store your will in a bank safety deposit box, be sure your executor knows where it is and has access to the box after your death. Your bank should help you with this. Also, make sure that no state laws require safety deposit boxes to be sealed for an extended time after the death of an owner.

You can make copies of your will for any person you want to have one. Mark them clearly "COPY." Never sign a copy. (A photocopy of your original with your signature is okay.) You want to avoid signing a copy of your will to prevent any possibility of its being considered a duplicate original. Duplicate originals can cause trouble if you add a codicil (see below) or write a new will.

2. Making Changes After Your Will Is Signed

Suppose you want to make a minor change in your will. For example, your friend Cliff died, and you want to leave your library of fiction to Nina instead. Do you have to redo your entire will? Or what if you want to make a major change (you and your friend just split up)? Anyone who drafts a will should know how to change it.

To do so, you must follow will-making rules—you cannot just ink out a provision. You must use a codicil, which lets you make additions, amendments or alterations after a will has been drafted, signed and witnessed. It's a sort of legal "P.S." It should be typed on the last page of the will itself or on an additional page or pages. It must be dated and signed by you and three witnesses.[11]

Codicils should be used for small changes only. For major revisions, it's best to draft a new will from scratch. A will that has been substantially rewritten by a codicil is awkward to read, and there is a risk that it will contain material conflicting with the original will.

A codicil should be titled. You can use or adapt the following sample to make a codicil:

FIRST CODICIL TO THE WILL OF <u>(YOUR NAME), DATED <u>(DATE OF YOUR WILL)</u>

    I, <u>[your name]</u>, a resident of <u>[name of county]</u> County, <u>[name of state]</u>, declare this to be the first codicil to my will dated <u>[date of your will]</u>.

    FIRST: I revoke Section <u>[letter or letter and number]</u> of Clause <u>[roman numeral]</u>, and substitute the following: (Add whatever new provision is desired.)

    SECOND: I add the following new Section <u>[letter or letter and number]</u> to Clause <u>[roman numeral]</u>: (Add whatever is desired.)

    THIRD: In all other respects I confirm and republish my will dated <u>[date of your will]</u>, this <u>[day]</u> day of <u>[month]</u>, <u>[year]</u>, at <u>[county]</u>, <u>[state]</u>.

    <u>   [your full name]   </u>

    On the date written below, [your full name] declared to us, the undersigned, that this instrument, consisting of [number] pages, including this page signed by us as witnesses, was the first codicil to [his/her] will and requested us to act as witnesses to it. [He/she] thereupon signed this codicil in our presence, all of us being present at the same time. We now, at [his/her] request, in [his/her] presence, and in the presence of each other, subscribe our

---

[11]They don't have to be the ones who witnessed the will, but try to use them if possible. Witnesses may have to be located after your death; the fewer there are, the better.

names as witnesses, and declare we understand this to be
[his/her] will, and that to the best of our knowledge the
testator is competent to make a will, and under no
constraint or undue influence.

    Executed on [date], at [county], [state].

    We declare under penalty of perjury that the foregoing is
true and correct.

_____   _____
Witness's Signature   Address

_____   _____
Witness's Signature   Address

_____   _____
Witness's Signature   Address

3. Revoking Your Will

Wills can be revoked easily. All you need to do is:

    1. Write a new will, expressly stating that you're revoking all previous wills, or

    2. destroy the old will.

    As a practical matter, it's best to do both. Also, if you handed out copies of your will, tell the recipients that you've revoked it.

F. Providing For Children

LEAVING PROPERTY TO adult children raises no special problems. Simply name your children in your will and leave them whatever you want. Providing for minor children, however, raises concerns. If you die before they're grown, who will care for them and how will they be supported? Let's look at each of these concerns separately.

1. Custody

If two biological or adoptive parents[12] are willing and able to care for their child, and one dies, the other normally assumes custody. This is true if the parents are married, divorced or had never married, as long as both are around. But what if both die? Or what if one abandoned the child at birth, but the other dies?

    If no competent and willing parent is available, another adult must take care of the child, unless he's legally emancipated.[13] This adult is called the child's personal guardian. In your will, you should nominate the person you want to serve as personal guardian for your minor children. You can also nominate an alternate, in case the first choice can't serve.

---

[12]By adoptive, we mean people who have legally adopted a child, not people functioning informally as stepparents.

[13]An emancipated minor is one who has achieved legal adult status. Emancipation usually comes at marriage, military service, or by living independently with a court order of emancipation. Emancipation is rare. You cannot emancipate your child in your will. If you fail to name a guardian for your minor child, a judge will choose one for you.

You must use a will to do this. You cannot use other estate planning devices, such as a living trust.

Most parents probably know who they want to name as their child's personal guardian. But remember the obvious: You can't draft someone to parent your kids. Be sure any person you name is willing and able to do the job. If both parents are alive, they should agree on who to nominate. It's best not to name a couple as personal guardians, even if they will function that way. It raises potential problems, especially if the couple splits up.

If you die, the person you nominated as personal guardian doesn't become guardian until formally appointed by a court. The judge has the authority to name someone other than your choice if the judge is convinced it's in the child's best interests. Children aren't property; nominating a personal guardian doesn't have the same automatically-binding effect as a provision giving a lamp to your uncle. In practice, however, guardianship nominations are rarely contested, and a court will almost certainly confirm the person you nominate.

For some parents, naming a personal guardian is, unfortunately, not cut-and-dry. If the parents are separated or divorced, one parent may not want the other to have custody, believing that someone else would be a better parent. Before you do this, however, understand that if the other parent disputes your choice in court, he or she will almost certainly prevail unless he or she has:

a. abandoned the child,[14] or

b. is unfit as a parent.

It's usually difficult to prove unfitness, absent serious problems such as drug abuse or mental illness. The fact that you don't like or respect the other parent is never enough, by itself, to deny custody. If you honestly believe the other parent is incapable of properly caring for your child, or simply won't assume the responsibility, state your reasons in writing. We show you how to do this in *Nolo's Simple Will Book* by Denis Clifford (Nolo Press).

2. Support

Before you can worry about leaving money or property to minor children, you must have something to leave. If you have little beyond a big mortgage and car payments, consider buying a moderate amount of term life insurance to cover your children until they're on their own. Because term life insurance pays benefits only if you die during the covered period (often five or ten years), it's far cheaper than other types of life insurance. Remember, too, that the dependent children of a wage earner who dies can receive Social Security survivor's benefits.

Assuming you have property to leave to your children, your first concern is who will manage it if you die before your children are mature enough to have it. Most states prohibit minors from having more than $5,000 in their own names. More than that and an adult must manage it for them. If you don't designate a manager in your estate plan, a court will appoint one for you. These procedures are time-consuming, costly and may produce a result you wouldn't approve of. Here's how to do it yourself:

- *Leave property directly to your children's other parent.* This is an excellent approach if you've a close knit family and the other parent is a competent financial manager. Especially if moderate amounts are involved, it often doesn't make sense to create a more elaborate plan. You can use the will in this book to do this.

---

[14]Abandonment must be declared in a court proceeding, where a judge finds that a parent has substantially failed to contact or support a child for an extended period of time, usually (depending on state law) a year or two. Abandonment can be declared in a guardianship hearing if, after your death, the other parent contests the choice in your will.

- *Use the provisions of the Uniform Transfers to Minors Act (UTMA).* In many states, you can use the UTMA to name a custodian to manage property you leave to your minor children until the children are either 18 or 21 (up to 25 in California). The UTMA works particularly well for leaving $50,000 or less. You use the UTMA with this book—or you can use one of Nolo's specialized estate planning or will-drafting products (see Estate Planning Resources box at the end of this chapter).

- *Create a children's trust.* For large estates, $50,000 or more, consider establishing a simple children's trust, in either your will or living trust. In using a children's trust, the trustee manages the money for your children and doles it out for education, health and other needs under the terms of the trust. The trust ends, and any remaining money is turned over to your child outright, at whatever age you designate. Again, see the Estate Planning Resources box for Nolo products that will allow you to do this.

Note on custody and support: It's wise to name the same person as custodian of your children's money and other property (in your will, under the UTMA or in a living trust) as you named personal guardian, unless that person doesn't have good financial sense. Then, name one person as personal guardian and another financial custodian.

---

3. Example Estate Plans to Provide For Children

The information in this chapter may be overwhelming at first. Here are two examples to help you plan for your children.

Example 1: *John and Liz have two children, Tommy and William. Also, Paul, John's son from an earlier relationship, lives with them. Paul's mother hasn't been heard from in many years. John's will names Liz personal guardian for all three children; Liz's will names John for Tommy and William. In the event they die simultaneously, they name John's brother Peter as alternate personal guardian, after getting his ok.*

John and Liz have some savings and equity in their jointly-owned house, but neither amounts to much. Thus, they buy a 10-year term life insurance policy to pay $100,000 if either dies and $200,000 if they both do. Each names the other as primary beneficiary and name the children alternate beneficiaries.[15] In their wills, they leave all their property to each other, with the children as alternate beneficiaries under the UTMA and Peter custodian.

Example 2: *Now assume John and Liz have a large estate. They forego the term life insurance because the children will inherit plenty without it. They use a living trust, not a will, to transfer their property to each other (or the children if they die simultaneously). In naming the children as alternate beneficiaries, they establish three separate children's trusts. They name Peter as trustee of each, with the power to manage and dole out the money until each son*

---

[15] While this approach is sensible, it raises the remote possibility that if John and Liz die simultaneously while at least one child is still a minor, a court will have to appoint a guardian to manage the money. This is time-consuming and can cost more than the money managed totals. To avoid this, they can establish a revocable living trust (see Section G2 below) and have it continue after their death as a children's trust. They would name the trust as the alternate beneficiary of the insurance policy. If there isn't enough other property to set up a children's trust, however, it's probably not worth doing it solely to protect against simultaneous death.

is in his mid-20s, at which time he'd get what is left in his trust.

G. Introduction to More Extensive Estate Planning

IF YOU HAVE SUBSTANTIAL amounts of property, you can take steps so that your surviving beneficiaries avoid probate and pay less federal estate taxes. If your property is of modest value, however, this kind of planning (it involves more than writing a will) probably won't result in enough savings to be worth the trouble. Even if you own considerable property, if you both are reasonably young and in good health, you can postpone estate planning beyond a will until you're older or seriously ill. It results in no savings until your death and, if done too soon, must be repeatedly and boringly redone.

People plan their estates to avoid probate because probate fees are a lot. On a $200,000 estate, for example, they can be $12,000 or more, depending on your state and the lawyer's billing rate. These fees are taken out of the deceased's property and obviously reduce the amount received by the beneficiaries. If property is transferred by a device that avoids probate, you can eliminate the fees. And avoiding probate normally means that inheritors get their property sooner than through probate.

Estate planning to reduce federal estate taxes is normally not necessary for estates under $600,000. Below that, there's no estate tax unless more than $10,000 was given away to any one person in one year.

1. Estimate the Value of Your Property

Your first step in estate planning is to estimate your net worth. Making a written list of your assets and debts can help you do this. Here's an example:

NET ESTATE OF KEIJA ADAMS

PERSONAL PROPERTY	VALUE	LOCATION OR DESCRIPTION
Cash	$ 500	Safe Deposit Box
Savings accounts	2,500	Tyson Bank
Checking accounts	1,500	Tyson Bank
Government bonds	0	
Listed (private corporation) stocks and bonds	5,000 2,000	Matco Corporation Break-Monopoly Company
Unlisted stocks and bonds	0	
Money owed you including promissory notes and accounts receivable (including mortgages owed you, leases, etc.)	5,000	Jason Michaels (sold him my car)
Vested interest in profit-sharing plan, pension rights, stock options, etc.	7,000	Death benefit from Invento Corporation Pension
Automobile and other vehicles (include boats and recreation vehicles; deduct any amounts owed)	3,000 7,000	Honda Motorcycle Toyota
Household goods, net total	10,000	In my house
Art works and jewelry	1,000	3 lithographs in my bedroom
Miscellaneous	3,000	Silver set

REAL ESTATE
(list each piece owned
separately)

Current market value	175,000	1807 Saturn Drive, Newkirk, Delaware
Mortgages and other liens that you owe on the property	<u>85,000</u>	

Equity (current
market value less
money owed)   90,000

Your share of that equity   45,000
if you have less than sole
ownership

BUSINESS/PROPERTY INTERESTS
(including patents & copyrights)

Name and type of business   Invento Corporation;
                                         patentor of telephone
                                         related inventions

Percentage you own   33%

When acquired   1980

Estimated present (market)   250,000
value of your interest

LIFE INSURANCE
(list each policy separately)

Company and type (or number)   AETCO
of policy

Name of insured   Keija Adams

Owner of policy   Keija Adams

Beneficiary of policy   Tomas Finnegan

Amount Collectible   50,000

Cash surrender value, $1,000
if any

TOTAL VALUE OF ASSETS $392,500

Debts (not already
calculated; i.e.,
excluding mortgage
on real estate)   3,000

Taxes (excluding
estate taxes)   12,000

Total (other) liabilities   15,000

TOTAL NET WORTH $377,500

2. Avoiding Probate

Probate is a court proceeding where your will[16] is filed, assets gathered, debts and taxes paid and remaining property distributed to your beneficiaries. Today, it's normally as unnecessary as it is time-consuming and expensive.[17]

There are several well-established methods of transferring property to avoid probate. These include:

a. revocable living (inter vivos) trusts

b. pay on death (informal bank) account trusts

c. joint tenancy

d. life insurance

e. gifts

Each method has advantages and drawbacks, which we briefly discuss below.

a. Revocable Living Trusts

A revocable living or "inter vivos" (Latin for "among the living") trust is usually the best way for members of an unmarried couple to avoid probate. The trust is created in a trust document and given a name (e.g., "The R.P. Payne Trust"). In the trust document, you name yourself as both settlor (the person setting up the trust) and initial trustee (the person who manages the trust property). You also name a beneficiary or beneficiaries —the people who receive the trust property after you die. And you name a successor trustee to transfer the trust property to your beneficiaries after you die. The successor trustee, who can be a beneficiary, can also be empowered to manage the trust if you become incapacitated.

[16] Or your property transferred under "intestate" succession, if you wrote no will or other valid transfer device.

[17] Although computation methods vary, fees are usually based on the size of the estate. Rest assured that they are generous, no matter how calculated. For example, the fees for the attorney and executor in California on a $200,000 estate are about $10,300; court fees and appraisals will raise the total. If $100,000 is passed outside of probate, the attorney and executor fees are reduced to $6,300, for a savings of $4,000.

You must sign the trust document and have it notarized. It doesn't have to be witnessed or recorded. You must also transfer all documents included in the trust to the trust entity. For example, if you place your house or car in the trust, you must execute the deed or registration necessary to transfer the item to the trust.

While you're alive, the trust is essentially a paper transaction with no real world effects. You maintain full control over the property in the trust (you can spend, sell or give it away) and can end the trust whenever you want. Trust transactions are reported as part of your regular income tax return and require no extra tax forms. When you die, the successor trustee transfers the trust property to your beneficiaries without any court proceedings.

If this sounds simple, that's because it is. The only downside to using a living trust is that it takes a certain level of time and trouble to create and maintain one.

Example: Robert creates a living trust, with his friend Kate as successor trustee. In the trust, Robert leaves several small items to friends, and names Kate as the beneficiary of his principle assets, a house and an apartment building. Robert executes and records deeds transferring title to those buildings into the name of the trust. When Robert dies, Kate, as successor trustee, distributes the small gifts to Robert's friends and executes deeds transferring the house and apartment building to herself.

Will Note: As we discuss in Section D, "Introduction to Wills," if you establish a living trust, you should also have a will to deal with property not covered by the trust and to name a personal guardian for any minor children.

b. *Pay on Death Account Trusts*

A pay on death bank account, also called an "informal trust" or "Totten trust," is a bank account that avoids probate. You manage the account as you would any other account and name whomever you want to receive the money when you die, as beneficiary of the account. During your life, you retain full and exclusive control over the account—you can remove any funds in the account for any reason, make deposits or close the account. At your death, the account passes to the beneficiary without probate.

There are no drawbacks to a pay on death bank account trust. Most banks have standard forms allowing you to create one either by opening a new account or transferring an existing account. And bank account trust fees are normally no higher than the fees for other types of bank accounts.

Government Securities Note: A pay on death designation can also be used for most types of United States government securities.

---

c. *Joint Tenancy*

We discuss joint tenancy in Chapter 7, *Buying a House.* Joint tenancy is a form of shared property ownership that can be used for both real and personal property. What sets joint tenancy apart from other forms of joint ownership is its "right of survivorship" feature—when one joint tenant dies, her share automatically passes to the surviving joint tenant.[18] Indeed, it's not possible to leave a share of joint tenancy property to someone other than the other joint tenant. Any attempt to do so in a will will be ignored.

Joint tenancy is an excellent probate avoidance device for property you and your friend acquire together, 50-50, assuming, you each want your share to pass to the other at your death. Because joint tenants must own equal shares, it won't work if one person owns a larger share than the other.

Joint tenancy ownership can be created in property solely owned by one person by the owner transferring title to herself and her friend "as joint tenants with right of survivorship." For living together couples, establishing a joint tenancy simply to avoid probate is usually a poor idea:

- Unlike placing property in a revocable living trust, placing property in joint tenancy constitutes an outright transfer. Any joint tenant can sell his or her interest in the joint tenancy at any time.

- If the property transferred into joint tenancy has appreciated in value since it was purchased, or is likely to appreciate in the future, there are unfavorable tax consequences.

Negative Tax Consequences of Transferring Appreciated Property into Joint Tenancy

Property that goes up in value shortly before death will not qualify for a stepped-up tax basis[19] if it's transferred by joint tenancy; it will if it's transferred by will or living trust. In joint tenancy, however, half of the property retains the tax basis of the original joint tenant. When the property is sold after being transferred to the surviving joint tenant, he must pay a capital gains tax on the difference between sales price and the tax basis of the original joint tenant.

---

[18]If there's more than one survivor, each acquires an equal share of the deceased's original interest.

[19]Stepped-up tax basis is the value of property necessary to determine taxable profit on a sale. Usually the tax basis of real estate is its purchase price plus the cost of capital improvements.

Example: *John buys property for $50,000 —his tax basis. Twenty years later, he transfers the property into joint tenancy with Evie, whose tax basis on her half is $25,000 (half of John's basis). John dies and Evie becomes the sole owner. She sells it for $500,000 and her taxable gain is $225,000. The tax basis on John's half is stepped up to $250,000 (half the market value at sale). But Evie's tax basis remains at $25,000—the $225,000 gain is $250,000 (the value of her half) less her $25,000 tax basis. Had the property been transferred at John's death by will or living trust, the tax basis of the entire property would have been stepped up to $500,000, and no tax would have been due.*

d. Life Insurance

Life insurance proceeds are paid to the policy's beneficiary directly, without going through probate. The only exception is if the proceeds are payable to the deceased's estate, as opposed to a specific beneficiary, in which case they are subject to probate, and included in the value of the probate estate. The only reason to name the estate as beneficiary is to pay the debts, taxes and probate costs of a large estate with no other liquid assets. See Section 3c below for information on how giving life insurance away while you're alive can save on death taxes.

e. Gifts

Obviously, any property given away prior to death, even immediately before, isn't in your estate when you die, and doesn't have to be probated. See Section 3c below for a discussion of how gifts can be used to reduce estate taxes.

3. Death Taxes

All property owned when you die is theoretically subject to federal estate (death) taxes, although in practice, many exemptions result in some estates paying no estate tax. Also, many states impose death (inheritance) taxes.

Both types of death taxes are imposed whether the property is transferred by will (through probate) or another device (outside of probate). Death taxes are harder to reduce or avoid than are probate fees, but there are some ways to achieve savings.

a. Federal Estate Taxes

Federal estate taxes are assessed against the net worth of the estate (called the "taxable estate") of a person who died. There's an exemption for moderate estate—property with a net worth of up to $600,000 can be transferred free of federal estate taxes, assuming the deceased hasn't made any large gifts during life (see section 4 below). This means many people don't have to worry about federal taxes being paid from their estate.

Other items exempt from federal estate taxes include:

- The expenses of your last illness, burial costs and probate fees and expenses.
- Certain debts, such as any state death taxes.
- All bequests made to tax-exempt charities.
- All property left to a surviving spouse.

The Marital Deduction

It may pay to get married after all. All property left to a surviving spouse is tax exempt. This can be a powerful reason for people living together with individual or combined estates over $600,000, planning to leave their property to each other, to consider marriage.

If you're an older couple with a large estate (married or not), however, you should consider leaving property to each other in a life estate trust. The survivor receives trust income for life, but the principal goes to another named beneficiary. As is more thoroughly discussed in *Plan Your Estate: Wills, Probate Avoidance, Trusts and Taxes,* by Denis Clifford (Nolo Press), this allows each person to take advantage of the $600,000 exemption. By contrast, if large amounts are left to the survivor, all of the property over $600,000 will be taxed when that person subsequently dies.

In valuing your estate, keep in mind these rules:

- All valuable property you legally own will be included in your federal taxable estate.

- For tax purposes, your net worth is what you own, less what you owe.

- Only the value of your share of jointly-owned property (including community property) is included in your estate (but see Joint Tenancy box).

Estate Tax Valuation of Joint Tenancy Property

The *total* value of property held in joint tenancy is included in your taxable estate, less the portion the surviving joint tenant can prove she contributed. The government presumes that the deceased contributed 100% of any joint tenancy property, and the survivor contributed nothing. If the survivor can prove otherwise, the taxable portion will be reduced accordingly.

Example: *Eighteen years ago, Joe and Eva bought a lemon-yellow Jaguar XKE together, and have preserved it in mint condition. It's always been owned in joint tenancy, but the records proving each person's one-half contribution to the purchase price have long since been lost. Joe dies. The government will include the current market value of the entire car in Joe's taxable estate unless Evie can somehow prove that she contributed half the cost.*

Estimating your likely federal estate tax liability takes a few steps. You first determine the net worth of your estate, as discussed above. Then, you add in any gift of more than $10,000 you've made in any one year to any one individual or non-tax exempt organization. If the total is under $600,000, you owe no taxes.[20] If the total exceeds $600,000, you'll be taxed according to the table below. Let's look at several examples:

Example 1: *Ben's net estate amounts to $520,000. This is below $600,000, so no federal tax is assessed.*

Example 2: *Eva's net estate is $700,000, $100,000 above the exempt $600,000 amount. Eva needs to look at the following table to figure out the tax:*

---

[20]If you added back any gifts in excess of $10,000, your estate will be assessed a tax—and then given an exemption—which means the net tax will be $0.

UNIFIED FEDERAL ESTATE AND GIFT TAX RATE SCHEDULE

Column A total net taxable excess estate over	Column B but not over	Column C tax on amount in Column A	Column D rate of tax on over amount in Column A
$ 0	$ 10,000	$ 0	18%
10,000	10,000	1,800	20
20,000	40,000	3,800	22
40,000	60,000	8,200	24
60,000	80,000	13,000	26
80,000	100,000	18,200	28
100,000	150,000	23,800	30
150,000	250,000	38,800	32
250,000	500,000	70,800	34
500,000	750,000	155,800	37
750,000	1,000,000	248,300	39
1,000,000	1,250,000	345,800	41
1,250,000	1,500,000	448,300	43
1,500,000	2,000,000	555,800	45
2,000,000	2,500,000	780,800	49
2,500,000	infinity	1,025,800	50

How to Read the Chart

1. Locate the numbers in Column A and Column B between which the anticipated value of your estate falls.

Estate	=	$700,000
Column A	=	500,000
Column B	=	750,000

2. Subtract the number in Column A from value of your estate

$700,000
- 500,000
$200,000

3. Multiply the difference by the percentage in Column D.

$200,000
x   .37
$ 74,000

4. Add the product of Step 3 to the tax in Column C.

$ 74,000
+ 155,800
$229,800

5. Subtract the federal estate tax credit ($192,800) from the total in Step 4. The difference is your federal estate tax liability. (Again, the federal estate tax credit is the tax on $600,000, which, as we've discussed, isn't taxed.)

	$229,800
Eva's Estate	- 192,800
Tax Liability =	$ 37,000

b. State Death Taxes

The states listed below impose no death taxes. If you live in one of these states, you don't need to worry about state death taxes:

STATES WITHOUT DEATH TAXES

Alabama	Georgia	Texas
Alaska	Hawaii	Utah
Arizona	Illinois	Vermont
Arkansas	Maine	Virginia
California	Missouri	Washington
Colorado	New Mexico	Wyoming
Florida	North Dakota	

If you live in any other state, your estate will be subject to state death taxes. Worse, many state death tax rules discriminate against beneficiaries not legal family. The amount of death taxes (or an exemption from death taxes) is based on the legal relationship of the deceased to the beneficiary. Usually, the largest exemption is for property left to a spouse, the next largest for property left to minor children, then for property given to other blood relatives and finally for property left to "strangers" (this includes the person you live with).

A few states, North Carolina, for one, provide no exemption for property left to "strangers." And some states vary the tax rate, not just the exemption, depending on who gets the property. Generally, the lowest rate is for property left to a spouse, the highest for property left to "strangers." You can get a copy of your state rules from your state tax office.

State tax rates are substantially less than the federal rate. Unfortunately, however, because "strangers" are taxed the most, the taxes will be much higher on property you leave your friend than they'd be if you were married—one more inequity resulting from the law's insistence that love and marriage be synonymous.

The state of your residence (generally, where your address is) when you die is the state that imposes death taxes. If you own real property (land, real estate) in another state, however, that state will impose its death taxes on the property in that state.

A Word Of Advice: As noted in the discussion on wills, figuring out your residence isn't always simple. If your voting records, driver's license and other permission slips say the same, you'll have no problems. If you divide your time between more than one state, however, you risk having your estate subjected to more than one state death tax. Pick a place (presumably, the state with lower inheritance taxes) and declare that your legal home. If you're very wealthy, get some legal advice on this point.

---

c. Avoiding or Reducing Death Taxes

Estate tax planning is often thought to be a form of lawyer's magic, or chicanery, to escape death taxes. Certainly there's some gimmickry in many schemes the rich use to escape or reduce death taxes, although tax law changes have reduced this considerably from former years. The sad truth, however, is that for most folks with estates somewhat over the $600,000 tax threshold, but not truly large, death taxes aren't easy to escape. But there are a few legal ways to reduce death taxes, such as:

1. *Making gifts:* Federal estate and gift taxes are unified, so, with a few exceptions, the tax is the same whether you give property away during life or at death. Taxes are unified so that a rich person cannot give away all his property tax-free just before death. The rule, stated simply, is that *gifts of up to $10,000 per person per year are tax-*

free. Everything else is subject to tax if the gift-giver's estate is large enough.

Example: *If Max gives $13,000 to Gabrielle, gift taxes are assessed on $3,000; if Max gives $10,000 to Gabrielle and $10,000 to Megan, no gift taxes are assessed. If Max gives $10,000 a year to Gabrielle for three years, no gift taxes are assessed.*

Let us repeat that the tax rates and dollar exemptions for gift and estate taxes are the same—the $600,000 federal exemption can be used for gift taxes as well as estate taxes. If Keija gives Tomas $60,000 in one year, $50,000 is subject to a gift tax and $10,000 is exempt. But Keija doesn't herself pay the tax; she applies the $50,000 toward her Gift/Estate tax credit of $600,000 and her heirs at her death avoid paying the tax. If Keija makes no other taxable gifts, $550,000 of her estate would pass tax free.

The $10,000 annual assessed gift tax exemption can be used to lower the eventual value of one's estate.

Example: *Joe and Ruth, both in their sixties, want their daughter Angie to have their summer house after they both die. The house is worth $200,000. They transfer title to Angie in exchange for a "loan" of $100,000 each, at 10% interest, and payments are set at $10,000 a year. Angie signs promissory notes, but each year Joe and Ruth each make a "gift" of $10,000 to Angie by forgiving the payment due. They do this until the property is fully owned by Angie with no tax liability.[21]*

---

[21]Obviously, this takes a lot of trust. Also, if either Joe or Ruth died, the estate might insist that the remaining payments be paid back—although the debt could be forgiven in a will.

Note—charge interest or be taxed: If you make an interest-free loan of $50,000 to a friend, you've also made a gift of the interest you didn't charge. A Supreme Court case said if you don't charge reasonable interest, you'll be taxed for what you should have charged.

If you're truly wealthy, other gift options—including "pooled income" funds, transfers to charitable pools and charitable remainder annuity trusts—are available. These devices don't work for people with average incomes or estates, so we don't cover them. But if your estate is over $1,000,000, consult an experienced tax attorney or tax accountant.

Gifts of Life Insurance

Making a gift of a life insurance policy you own on your life while you're alive may save your beneficiaries federal estate taxes. If you own a policy on your life, proceeds paid to your beneficiaries at your death are included in your taxable estate. But if someone else owns the policy, the proceeds can't be taxed when you die. To take advantage of this, you must transfer ownership of the policy more than three years before your death.

Example: *Norm's total estate, including life insurance policies that will pay $450,000 at his death, amounts to $1,000,000. His plan is to leave all his property to his lover Trudy. If he keeps ownership of his life insurance policy, $400,000 of his estate will be subject to estate taxes of $150,000. But if Norm gives ownership of the policy to Trudy, Norm's taxable estate will be reduced to below the $600,000 level.*

The main risk in transferring ownership of a life insurance policy is obvious—once the policy is given, it's gone. You have no rights over the policy; you can't get it back, or cancel it or change the beneficiary. The new owner has total power over the policy. In the above example, Norm can't make Trudy keep up the policy or prevent her from cashing it in. In short, make a gift of a life insurance policy only to someone you fully trust.

Making a gift of a life insurance policy requires a little paperwork. Simply naming a beneficiary doesn't transfer ownership. You must sign a document, available from the insurance company (called a "Notice of Assignment") transferring complete ownership to the new owner.

2. *Establishing trusts:* Because of the complex nature of trusts, a serious discussion is beyond the scope of this book. But if you have a substantial estate, you may save considerable death taxes by using trusts, particularly if:

- the bulk of your estate will be left to a person who's old or ill and likely to die soon. When you die, the estate is taxed; when the old or ill person dies, the property you left is taxed again. To avoid this second tax, you can establish a trust in your will leaving the old or ill person only the income from the trust, with the principal eventually going to someone else; or

- you leave all your property to your children. It'll be taxed when you die and then when they die. For years, one death tax dodge of the very rich was to leave their wealth in trust for their grandchildren, escaping taxation on the children. Tax law changes curtailed this by introducing a "generation-skipping transfer tax." You can now leave only $1,000,000 in a trust for your grandchildren to escape taxes on the middle generation. Any amount over this $1,000,000 is subject to federal estate taxes in each generation. If you have children, grandchildren and a truly huge hunk of money, consider establishing a generation-skipping trust. To do, you'll need to see a lawyer.

H. What About My Body?

MANY PEOPLE MAKE burial or cremation plans informally, trusting their loved ones to take care of the details after death. This works fine if you're confident your plans will be carried out. Often, however, families ignore wishes after death and substitute their own, especially if they dislike the person you live with.

If you're concerned about funeral, burial or cremation arrangements, you can do the following:

- Make the practical arrangements yourself. Get a burial plot or arrange for cremation, and plan your ceremony.

- Leave instructions in your will, for example:

    "Upon my death I wish to be buried in the Green Meadow Cemetery in Lancastershire, Massachusetts in plot number _____ which is reserved and paid for [or which will be paid for by my burial insurance through Carpenters Union 18]. I wish no elaborate ceremony and wish my remains to be prepared for burial by the Fraternal Brothers Burial Society under the contract that I have signed with them. Any decisions not already made, or necessitated by circumstances that I cannot now foresee, I entrust to my friend of many years, Lucinda Whitehorse."

- Leave a letter of instruction in a place where it will be available immediately at your death. It should contain the same information that is in your will. If your will is in a safe deposit box at your death, it may take several days to get it and a letter of instructions will be a great aid to family and friends.

⚠️ **Warning:** Don't leave a signed copy of your will in an accessible place. A signed copy accidentally destroyed is revoked in some states. Your instruction letter should contain only burial instructions and instructions as to where your actual will is located.

Nolo's Estate Planning Resources

Nolo publishes the following estate planning guides:

- *Nolo's Simple Will Book,* by Denis Clifford gives all the instructions necessary for drafting and updating a will.

- *Plan Your Estate: Wills, Probate Avoidance, Trusts and Taxes,* by Denis Clifford covers every significant aspect of estate planning and gives all instructions needed for preparing a living trust.

- *The Power of Attorney Book,* by Denis Clifford, shows you how to legally authorize a friend or family member to make financial or health care decisions on your behalf.

- *WillMaker* (with Legisoft) is software for the Apple II, Macintosh and IBM (and compatibles) computers to create, in a step-by-step, question and answer format, your own legally valid will.

All of Nolo's estate planning resources are good in every state but Louisiana.

More Legal Help

CONGRATULATIONS! BY GETTING THIS book and reading this far, you've made a personal declaration of independence. You could have purchased this information at $125 to $250 an hour from a lawyer; instead, you've committed the time and effort to inform yourself.

Although we've explained, in some detail, the law as it relates to unmarried couples living together, we haven't come close to covering everything. To even make a start would require a legal encyclopedia, much of which would be irrelevant for most readers. That said, here are some suggestions for those of you who wish to expand on what you learned here or get additional help from an expert.

The major types of follow-up are:

- **Legal Research:** When you want more information on an issue raised in this or another self-help book, and want to find the information yourself.

- **Self-Help Law Resources:** When you're ready to begin a routine legal proceeding such as an uncontested divorce or child support modification, and want to use a self-help book.

- **Typing Services (Independent Paralegals):** When you're ready to initiate a legal proceeding and want to do it yourself, but want some help in filling out the forms.

- **Legal Advice:** When you want specific information from a lawyer or want a form such as a living together contract or will reviewed.

- **Mediation:** When you and your friend (former friend) are disputing who owns what, how to divide jointly-owned property or another issue, and you want help in attempting to work out a consensual solution.

- **Legal Representation:** When you want to explore the possibility of initiating a lawsuit, and want a lawyer to handle it for you. For example, if you claim you and the person you

lived with had an oral contract to share property, but that person denies it, formal legal help may be necessary.

A. Legal Research

IF THIS BOOK leaves you with some questions unanswered, you may be able to find the answers by visiting a local law library.

In many states, county law libraries, commonly located in larger courthouses, are open to the public. Also, most state-supported law schools (and some private ones) let the public use their libraries. Finally, large public libraries (main branches) often maintain a modest collection of legal materials.

Although some law libraries have more books than others, most will contain your state's statutes, written court opinions and some expert commentary. You can find and read any statute or case we've referred to at the law library by looking it up. But to do this, you'll need some guidance in understanding the legal hieroglyphics (called "citations") used to identify cases and statutes.

Understanding Case Citations

A case citation is the way to locate a particular court case. It normally has five elements:

1. The case name.

2. The series or book set where the case is located.

3. The specific volume of the set.

4. The page number.

5. The year the case was decided.

The California case that established the right of unmarried couples to contract is cited as:

Marvin v. Marvin, 557 P.2d 106 (1976).

"Official" sets of cases are published by each state, for appellate and Supreme Court cases. Each has its own form of citation. For example, in California, the *Official Reports of the California Supreme Court* is abbreviated as Cal. or Cal.2d or Cal.3d, representing the first, second and third series in the volume.

Cases are also published "unofficially" by private publishing companies, principally, West Publishing Company.[1] For the California Supreme Court, this is the *California Reporter* (Cal. Rptr.) and *Pacific Reporter* (P. or P.2d). Thus, a complete cite for *Marvin v. Marvin* would be 18 Cal.3d 660, 557 P.2d 106, 134 Cal. Rptr. 815 (1976). The *Marvin* decision is the same, word for word, in all three reports.

Locating Your State's Laws

The laws (called statutes) of your state are published in a collected form, called code books. Some states group all their laws in one lengthy code book, with each law numbered sequentially. Others divide their laws into manageable sub-groups, such as corporations code, vehicle code, civil code and so on. In either case, if you have the citation of a statute, it will be easy to locate. If you must start from scratch, consult the subject matter index.

---

[1] A few states have stopped publishing their "official" reports and have let West and other publishers take it over.

Codes are normally published in hardbound books in two forms—an annotated and unannotated version. Annotated means that after each statute is set out, excerpts from relevant judicial cases and cross-references to related laws and explanatory materials, such as law reviews and other articles, are included.

The hardbound books are updated and republished every ten years or so. In the interim, law changes and new laws are collected in paperback supplements called pocket parts. These slip inside of the back cover of each code book. Thus, in 1991, if you look up a statute in a hardback book published in 1990, check the same statute number in the pocket part to be sure the law hasn't been changed. You should also check an updated master index to see if new laws have been passed in the area of your concern.

If you want to find the answer to a legal question you have, rather than simply look up a specific statute or case to which you already have the citation, you'll need some guidance in basic legal research techniques. Good resources that may be available in your law library are:

- *How to Find and Understand the Law,* 2nd ed., by Steve Elias (Nolo Press, 1986).

- *How to Prepare a Legal Citation,* by Elaine Maier (Barron's, 1986).

- *The Legal Research Manual: A Game Plan for Legal Research and Analysis,* 2nd ed., by Christopher and Jill Wren (A-R Editions, Madison, WI, 1986).

- *Introduction to Legal Research: A Layperson's Guide to Finding the Law,* by Al Coco (Want Publishing Co., 1985).

- *How to Find the Law,* 9th ed., by Morris Cohen and Robert Berring (West Publishing Co., 1989).

To find specific answers to questions involving family law, find a good background resource. Here are several:

- *The Family Law Reporter*—a newsletter, published by the Bureau of National Affairs, containing the text and synopses of important cases as they're decided. Older copies are bound together in volumes, with a subject index at the back to help you find what you need.

- *The Family Law Series*—a set of books, published by Shepard's Company, which provides detailed analyses of selected topics, including summaries of relevant cases. The volume entitled *Marriage & Family Law Agreements* contains much information about living together contracts. The books are updated annually, with a pocket part tucked inside the back cover.

- *Family Law Quarterly*—a journal published by the American Bar Association. Every year, in the winter issue, the journal summarizes family law in an article "Family Law in the 50 States—An Overview," which lays out trends and new developments and contains much material on cohabitation.

- *American Law Reports*—a series of articles, published in five sets. Each article is about a particular point of law, and attempts to survey the field and gather all relevant cases on the topic. If you check the index under "cohabitation," you'll find many articles. These volumes contain pocket parts, to add new cases to the articles are they're decided.

B. Self-Help Law Resources

GETTING INFORMATION ABOUT domestic relations law is one thing; acting on it is another. If you need a divorce, adoption, guardianship or any other court proceeding, you'll need guidance to get the job done correctly, no matter how simple the procedure. Fortunately, in some states, self-help law books can help people do many uncontested legal tasks.

1. Finding a Book

Here is a brief overview of how to locate and use self-help law books. Because most legal areas vary by state-to-state, publishers of self-help material tend to be small and local. Thus, we can't include a comprehensive list of all self-help law resources. Finding materials of interest in your area will involve some detective work. Check with several large local book stores. Any self-help law books specific to your state should be in the law section. What they don't carry they may know of. Reference librarians at local law libraries and public libraries usually have a pretty good idea of what's available.

2. Evaluating a Book

Many excellent self-help law books are published. Unfortunately, many inadequate one are also published. Here are some thoughts on separating the good from the bad:

- Many self-help law books provide basic overviews of legal topics, but don't give practical advice on how to carry out a particular procedure. When selecting a self-help law book for guidance through a task, make sure detailed step-by-step instructions are included.

- No matter how routine your situation appears at first, it's always possible that complications will arise. A good book will scrupulously alert you to circumstances not covered, and point out when additional help or research is required.

- If the instructions don't seem adequate to solve your problem, supplement it by locating a law book written for attorneys. These are in law libraries; many can easily be used by non-lawyers.

- As a general rule, you'll need more than a self-help book if you're in a dispute and the other side hires a lawyer. With very few exceptions, involving an attorney makes a case unpredictable, and self-help law books require predictability to be most effective.

3. Other Nolo Publications on Family Matters

Nolo Press publishes over sixty self-help law books. Many are specific to California, but we also have a number of books and software packages applicable nationally. For more information, see the advertisements at the back of this book.

C. Legal Typing Services (Independent Paralegals)

UNTIL RECENTLY, PEOPLE who didn't want to hire a lawyer to help with a legal problem had two choices: handle the problem themselves or not handle it at all. Now, especially in Western states, businesses known as "typing services" or "independent paralegals" have emerged to assist people in filling out the forms necessary to complete their own legal work. Typing services can help in routine family law matters such as uncontested divorces, guardianships, stepparent adoptions, name changes, paternity declarations, child and spousal support modifications and temporary restraining orders for domestic violence.

Typing services are very different from lawyers. They cannot give legal advice or represent you in court—by law, only lawyers can do those things. When you consult a typing service, it will still be up to you to decide what steps to take in your case, and to gather the information needed to complete forms. Typing services can, however:

- Provide the written instructions and legal information needed to handle your own case;

- Provide the appropriate court forms; and

- Type your papers so they'll be accepted by a court.

As an added bonus, typing services charge much less—usually 60% to 80% less—than attorneys charge.

Generally, the longer a typing service has been in business, the better. People at a typing service should be up-front about not being attorneys and not providing legal advice. The following statement, posted in Divorce Centers of California, a prominent typing service near San Francisco, summarizes its services well:

> **WE ARE NOT ATTORNEYS:**
>
> *We are pro per assistants. Attorneys represent people. We assist people to represent themselves. If you want someone to represent you, you will need to hire an attorney. If you want to "do it yourself," we can help. We believe that representing yourself is the only way to gain, and keep, control over your own life and your own legal problems. You don't need legal training to use the courts or manage your own legal affairs. You have a constitutional right to represent yourself without an attorney. Let us assist you!*

A recommendation from someone who has used a typing service is the best way to find a reputable one in your area. Barring that, services often advertise in classified sections of newspapers under Referral Services, usually immediately following attorneys. Also check the Yellow Pages under "divorce assistance" or "legal help." A local legal aid office may provide a reference, as will the occasional court clerk. Also, many offices advertise in local throwaway papers. Finally, a list of reputable typing services is maintained by the National Association For Independent Paralegals (NAIP).[2]

---

[2]NAIP is a national association of state independent paralegal groups that conducts paralegal training and compiles information about typing services. Write to NAIP at 585 Fifth Street West, Suite 111, Sonoma, CA 95476, or call (800) 542-0034.

D. Lawyers

LAWYERS ARE EXPERTS at recycling information and charging plenty for this often limited service. There's no guarantee that the attorney's advice will be correct or wise. Still, at times you may need the help of a lawyer. Here are some suggestions as to how to go about it.

1. Hiring a Lawyer as a Consultant

If you've put some time and work into preparing a legal document or planning a course of action, you may want a lawyer to check your work or conclusions. A lawyer should listen to you describe your situation, examine your documents, educate you about your rights and possible alternatives and, if necessary, help you decide on a plan of future action. This is a basic consultation; it should involve an office call or two and a little additional time to review documents. The fee should be modest.

We outline finding a lawyer in Section 3 below. Keep in mind these two additional important points:

- Lawyers sometimes try to sell you services you don't need. Carefully evaluate any suggestion

that you need additional expensive legal services. At the very least, get a second opinion.

- A lawyer best suited to give you practical or legal advice may not be the best to represent you if you need to go to court. Because advice by itself doesn't require a longer-term working relationship, your most important goal in seeking advice is to find someone with experience with your type of legal problem. The fact that a lawyer doesn't litigate or charges top dollar, shouldn't disqualify her as a consultant if you can get a lot of valuable information in a short time.

2. Hiring a Lawyer To Handle Your Case

In certain situations you should see an attorney. The main ones are:

- You're involved in a contested court case and the other side hires a lawyer. But even in this situation, try and get the other party to mediate, not litigate (see Chapter 5, Section L).

- You believe your rights are being seriously violated and there's a lot of money at stake. For example, if you and your living together partner have only an oral contract to share all property, and he dies with no will or other estate plan, you'll likely need a lawyer to help you assert your claim that a portion of the property in his name actually belongs.

- You have a legal problem and you don't want to do the work. This can make good sense if you inform yourself of the issues involved and can afford $125-$250 per hour.

3. Finding a Lawyer

No matter what you need a lawyer for, realize that only a few lawyers know enough about living together issues to be worthy of serious consideration. Unfortunately, lawyers who don't know much about the law in this area (or who are even hostile to the idea of living together) can't always be trusted to decline this type of work. It's up to you to be sure any lawyer you consult has the skills you need.

There are several ways to find a good lawyer:

- **Personal Referrals:** This is your best approach. If you know someone who was pleased with the lawyer hired for a family law matter, call that lawyer first. If that lawyer can't take on your case, or doesn't have the experience necessary, he or she will likely be willing to recommend someone else who is experienced, competent and available.

- **Pre-Paid Legal Insurance:** If you're a member of, or join, a pre-paid "legal insurance"[3] plan which offers a certain amount of free advice for a yearly fee, your initial membership fee may be worth the consultation you receive, even if you use it only once. This is especially true if you only need a document reviewed, or want advice on a fairly routine issue.

The plans are sold by large companies such as Bank of America, Montgomery Ward and Amway, and often offered to credit card holders, or sold door to door. There's no guarantee that the lawyers available through these plans are of the best caliber; sometimes they aren't. Whenever you avail yourself of any service offered by these prepaid insurance plans, be forewarned: The lawyer is probably getting only $2 or $3 per month from the plan for dealing with you and may have agreed to this minimal amount in the hope of selling customers other legal services not covered by the monthly premium. If the lawyer recom-

---

[3]It's a misnomer to refer to these programs as legal insurance. The programs provide an initial level of service for a low fee and then charge specific fees for additional or different work. Thus, most pre-paid plans are more a marketing device for the participating lawyers than they are an insurance plan.

mends an expensive legal procedure, get a second opinion.

- **Group Legal Practice:** Some unions, employers and consumer action organizations offer group legal plans to their members or employees. The idea behind these plans is to allow members to obtain comprehensive legal assistance free or at low rates. If you're a member of such a plan, and the service you need is covered for free, start there. But many of these plans offer only a few free services, with the rest covered at a supposedly reduced rate. This is often a poor deal. You may be referred to a lawyer not an expert in family law, but who has agreed to handle a high volume of cases on the cheap.

- **Legal Clinics:** Law clinics such as Hyatt Legal Services and Jacoby and Meyers loudly advertise their low initial consultation fees. This generally means that a basic consultation is cheap (often about $20); anything beyond that isn't. In addition, many group plans hire inexperienced lawyers, pay poorly and load them down with too much work. If you consult a law clinic, the trick (for you) often is to extract the information you need at a reasonable price and to closely scrutinize any attempt to convince you that you need further services. Again, if you are told an expensive procedure is necessary, get a second opinion.

- **Lawyer Referral Panels:** Most county bar associations will give names of some attorneys who practice in the area. You can usually get a referral to an attorney who claims to specialize in family law, and an initial consultation for a low fee. A problem is that the referrals usually provide minimal screening for the attorneys listed, so those who participate may not be the most experienced or competent. Indeed, many lawyers well regarded in their community don't list with these services, as they have more than enough business. You may find a skilled attorney willing to work for a reasonable fee following this approach, but check out the credentials and experience of the person to whom you're referred.

- **Self-Help Clinics.** Many county bar associations and some law schools set up do-it-yourself clinics at little or no cost. These clinics often provide an overview of the procedure involved, assistance in completing forms, and preparation for appearing in court, in areas such as obtaining temporary restraining orders, uncontested divorces, and guardianships. Many of these clinics are open only to low-income people and most are limited to serving residents of a particular geographical area.

- **Yellow Pages:** The Yellow Pages have extensive names of lawyers listed under Attorneys by both specialty and alphabetical order. Many of the ads quote initial consultation rates. If all else fails, let your fingers do the walking. But before you get extensively involved with a lawyer you don't know, ask for and check his or her references.

4. What To Look For in a Lawyer

No matter what approach you take to finding a lawyer, here are some suggestions on how to make sure you have the best possible working relationship:

- **Determine the type of lawyer you need:** Some lawyers specialize in one type of law, such as bankruptcy, some are good negotiators, and a few pride themselves on being fang dog litigators. There's no such thing as a lawyer for all occasions. To avoid the serious initial mistake by hiring the wrong type of lawyer, ask yourself if you want a document reviewed, help in meditating a dispute, or someone to represent you in court? In making this choice, consider that most court actions are extremely expensive and rarely warranted (no matter who is right or wrong) unless large amounts of money are at stake.

- **It's your call:** Don't be intimidated or overly impressed by the first lawyer you meet. Your legal situation affects your life, and you're in the best position to decide what you feel comfortable doing about it. You're the one who is hiring the lawyer to perform a service for you. Shop around until you feel truly satisfied.

- **Do some personality testing:** You must be comfortable with any lawyer you hire. When making an appointment, ask to talk directly to the lawyer. If you can't, this may be a hint as to how accessible he is. When you talk to or meet with him, ask specific questions. Do you get clear, concise answers? If he says little except to suggest that he handle the problem (with a substantial fee, of course), watch out. You're talking with someone who doesn't know the answer and won't admit it (common), or someone who pulls rank (even more common). Don't be a passive client or deal with a lawyer who wants you to be one.

  Pay particular attention to how the lawyer responds to your already having considerable information. You've read this book, so you're already better informed about the law than most clients. Many lawyers are threatened when the client knows too much (in some cases, anything), while others are pleased to deal with an informed person. Find out which type you're dealing with at the outset.

- **Look for a family law specialist:** Keep in mind that lawyers learn mostly from experience and special training, not from law school, which rarely imparts any practical information. Ask any lawyer you're considering hiring what percentage of the practice is in family law and how experienced he is in dealing with the problems of unmarried couples.

- **Money matters:** Fees—how much you'll pay for legal services—are one of the biggest bones of contention and biggest areas of misunderstanding between a lawyer and client. Don't be afraid to bring up the subject. In many states (and good practice everywhere), whenever you'll likely have to pay a lawyer a substantial fee, the lawyer must give you a written contract. That contract must explain the fees and charges, define the services to be provided and describe the lawyer's, and your, responsibilities.

  If you're in doubt, ask some straight questions about what the quoted fee covers. Lawyers will charge you for the costs of filing and serving legal documents and often for other things, like copying charges. Get estimates on both the legal fees and incidental costs of your case. You should be able to find an attorney willing to represent you for either a flat rate or an hourly rate of $100 to $200, depending on where the lawyer's office is (city lawyers tend to be pricier) and how complex your case is (extensive court time will cost). Contingency fee cases, where the lawyer takes money only if your case is won, are generally prohibited in family law cases.

- **Think it over:** Once you find a lawyer you like, make an one or two hour appointment to fully discuss your situation. Be ready to pay on the spot and then go home and think about what the lawyer recommends and how much it will cost. If the lawyer's advice doesn't make complete sense, or you have other reservations, call someone else.

5. Firing a Lawyer

One major problem people often have when dealing with lawyers is knowing when and how to fire them. Basically, you have the right to fire a lawyer at any time, although you're obligated to pay for any services you've authorized which have been performed.

Sometimes when a lawyer is fired, it's because a client believes she has received incompetent or unethical service, or has been overcharged. If this is your case, immediately call your state bar association and ask for information on how to file a formal complaint against a lawyer. Pending their looking into the matter, it's usually best not to pay for services you haven't received.

E. Alternatives To Court: Mediation and Arbitration

WE DISCUSS THIS important topic in Chapter 5, Section L.

Appendix

Below is a list of the tear-out documents contained in this appendix, in the order set out. The pages are not numbered (and some documents are not specifically identified) so you can tear them out and use them without retyping. Before doing this, however, make sure the document fully meets your needs. If you want to customize an agreement to fit your specific situation, carefully re-read the pertinent sections of the book and Chapter 5, Section A on making additions and deletions.

⚠ **Caution:** If you've any doubt as to the legal or practical consequences of any changes you want to make to any of these agreements, check them with an expert (see Chapter 12, *More Legal Help*).

Table of Contents

LIVING TOGETHER CONTRACT
(KEEPING EVERYTHING SEPARATE)

_____ and

_____ agree as follows:

1. That we have been living together and plan to do so indefinitely.

2. That all property, whether real or personal, owned by either of us as of the date of this agreement, shall remain the separate property of its owner [an itemization of valuable items is included].

3. That we will share our love and good energy, but we agree that the income of each, and any accumulations of property traceable to that income, belong absolutely to the person who earns the money. Any joint purchases shall be made only under the terms of paragraph 7 below.

4. That in the event of separation, neither of us has a claim upon the other for any money or property, for any reason, unless there is a subsequent written agreement to the contrary under paragraph 7.

5. That we shall each use our own name and will maintain our own bank accounts, credit accounts, etc.

6. That the monthly expenses for rent, food, household utilities and upkeep and joint recreation shall be shared equally.

7. That if, in the future, we decide to purchase any item jointly (such as a house or car), joint ownership of the item will be reflected on the title slip to the item, or by use of a separate written agreement which shall be dated and signed by both of us. Any joint agreement to purchase or own property shall only cover the property specifically set out in the agreement and shall in no way create an implication that other property is jointly owned.

8. That property owned now, or acquired in the future, as the separate property of either of us, can only become the separate property of the other, or our joint property, under the terms of a written agreement signed by the person whose property is to be re-classified.

9. That this agreement replaces any and all prior agreements, whether written or oral, and can only be added to or changed by a subsequent written agreement.

10. If a court finds any portion of this contract to be illegal or otherwise unenforceable, the remainder of the contract is still in full force.

11. That any dispute arising out of this agreement shall be mediated by a third person mutually acceptable to both of us. The mediator's role shall be to help us arrive at a solution, not to impose one on us. If good faith efforts to arrive at our own solution with the help of a mediator prove to be fruitless, either may make a written request to the other that the dispute be arbitrated.

Our dispute will be submitted to arbitration under the rules of the American Arbitration Association. One arbitrator will hear our dispute. The decision of the arbitrator shall be binding on us and shall be enforceable in any court which has jurisdiction over the controversy.

_____   _____
Date   Signature

_____   _____
Date   Signature

LIVING TOGETHER CONTRACT
(SHARING INCOME AND PROPERTY)

_____ and

_____ agree as follows:

1. That we plan to live together beginning _____ and to continue to live together indefinitely.

2. That while we are living together, all income earned by either of us, and all property accumulated with the earnings of either person, whether real or personal, belong in equal shares to both and that, should we separate, all accumulated property shall be divided equally.

3. That all real and personal property earned or accumulated by either of us prior to our getting together, and any income produced by this property, belongs absolutely to the person earning or accumulating it [an itemization is included].

4. Should either of us inherit or be given property, it belongs absolutely to the person receiving the inheritance or gift.

5. That the separate property of either one of us covered in paragraphs 3 and 4 of this agreement can become the separate property of the other, or the joint property of both, only under the terms of a written agreement.

6. That should we separate, neither has any claim for money or property except as set out in paragraph 2.

7. That this agreement represents our complete understanding regarding our living together and replaces any prior agreements, written or oral. It can be amended, but only in writing, and must be signed by both of us.

8. That if the court finds any portion of this contract to be illegal or otherwise unenforceable, that the remainder of the contract is still in full force and effect.

9. That any dispute arising out of this agreement shall be mediated by a third person mutually acceptable to both of us. The mediator's role shall be to help us arrive at a solution, not to impose one on us. If good faith efforts to arrive at our own solution with the help of a mediator prove to be fruitless, either may make a written request to the other that the dispute be arbitrated.

Our dispute will be submitted to arbitration under the rules of the American Arbitration Association. One arbitrator will hear our dispute. The decision of the arbitrator shall be binding on us and shall be enforceable in any court which has jurisdiction over the controversy.

_____   _____
Date   Signature

_____   _____
Date   Signature

LIVING TOGETHER CONTRACT
(KEEPING EVERYTHING SEPARATE)

BETWEEN _____

AND _____

We make this agreement to set out the rights and obligations of our joint living arrangement. It is our intention to follow this agreement in a spirit of good faith and cooperation.

Article I

We choose to live together outside the formal state regulations governing marriage and divorce. This is our free choice and desire and we specifically state that we do not intend our relationship to be interpreted as a common law marriage. We further state that we each make this agreement in consideration of the agreement of the other, and that the provision of sexual services by either of us is not the basis of this contract. We further state that this agreement will remain in full force and effect until such time as we separate, or replace or amend it with a subsequent written agreement signed by both of us.

Article II

We are each equal and independent people, willing and able to support ourselves. We will share our love and good energy, but we reject the idea that one of us should be dependent upon the other for support.

Article III

We agree that all income, however derived, and any accumulations of property traceable to that income, belong absolutely to the person who earns or otherwise acquires the income. At the time of signing this contract, we have each prepared a list of major items of property that each of us owns. This list is marked as Exhibit 1 and is attached to this contract and by this reference made a part of this contract. We shall update this list as it becomes necessary. Any and all joint purchases shall be made under the terms of Article VII below.

Article IV

We agree that any gifts or inheritances that either of us receives shall be the separate property of that person. Should a gift or inheritance be made to us jointly, we shall consider that we own it in equal shares unless otherwise specified by the donor.

Article V

We agree that the separate property of either of us can become the separate property of the other, or the joint property of both of us, only under the terms of a written agreement signed by the person whose separate property is to be reclassified.

Article VI

We agree that each of us will keep our own money in our own separate bank accounts and that we shall not open joint bank or credit accounts. We each further agree to return any credit cards that are issued to both of us, and, in addition, not to make any purchases using the credit or credit cards of the other.

Article VII

As set forth in Article III above, we will separately own all property purchased with the money we separately earn or otherwise accumulate. From time to time, however, we may need or want to pool our money to buy a particular item. If so, we will make a separate written agreement to cover each particular item of property that we acquire jointly. These agreements shall be marked Exhibit 2 and shall be attached to and incorporated in this agreement. As part of each joint agreement, we shall include a clause providing for what happens to the property if we separate. If for some reason we fail to provide for the contingency of our separation, we agree to divide all jointly-owned property equally. If we can't agree as to an equal division, we shall sell the jointly-owned property and equally divide the proceeds.

Article VIII

We agree to share equally all monthly household expenses. This includes food, incidental supplies necessary to home maintenance, rent and utilities, not including long distance phone charges which shall be paid by the person making the call.

Article IX

We each agree to own, insure and pay for the maintenance of our own motor vehicles. If at any time we wish to share ownership of a motor vehicle, we shall make a separate written agreement as to ownership under the terms of Article VII and shall have the fact of joint ownership recorded on the motor vehicle title slip.

Article X

We do not at present jointly own any real property. Should we jointly buy a house, land in the country, investment property or any other real property, we agree that a copy of a deed to the property and any and all supplementary contracts or agreements covering the property shall be marked as Exhibit 3 and attached to this contract and that when this is done they shall be incorporated into this contract. We further agree that neither of us shall have any rights to, or financial interest in, any separate real property of the other, whether acquired before or after the signing of this contract, unless such interest is set forth in a written agreement signed by both of us.

Article XI

We realize that our power to contract as far as children are concerned is limited by state law. With this knowledge, and in a spirit of cooperation and mutual respect, we wish to state the following as our agreement should we have children:

1. The father shall sign a written statement acknowledging that he is the father within ten days after birth.

2. Our child(ren) shall be given the following last name: _____.

3. We reject the idea that one of us should do most of the child care tasks while the other provides the income. We will do our best to jointly share the responsibilities of feeding, clothing, loving and disciplining our child(ren).

4. Because of the possible trauma our separation might cause our child(ren), we shall each make a good faith effort to participate in a jointly-agreed upon program of counseling before we separate.

5. If we separate, we shall do our best to see that our child(ren) has (have) a good and healthful environment in which to grow up. Specifically, we agree to:

a. Do our best to see that our child(ren) maintain a close and loving relationship with each of us;

b. Share in the upbringing of our child(ren) and, on the basis of our respective abilities to pay, support them;

c. Make a good faith effort to make all major decisions affecting the health and welfare of our child(ren) jointly;

d. Should circumstances dictate that our child(ren) spend a greater portion of the year living with one of us than the other, the person with physical custody shall be sensitive to the needs of the other to have generous rights of visitation and shall cooperate in all practical steps necessary to make visitation as easy as possible;

e. If after separation we have problems communicating as to the best interests of our child(ren), we shall seek help in the form of a jointly-agreed upon program of counseling to try and work out our differences without having to take our problems to court;

f. At the death of either of us, our child(ren) shall be cared for and raised by the other whether or not we are living together at the time of the death.

Article XII

We agree that either of us can end our agreement to live together at any time by simply ceasing to live with the other. If this is done, neither of us shall have any claim upon the other for money or support, except as provided for by the terms of this agreement pertaining to the division of jointly-owned property (Article VII).

Article XIII

We agree that from time to time this contract may be amended. All amendments shall be in writing and shall be signed by both of us.

Article XIV

We agree that if any court finds any portion of this contract illegal or otherwise unenforceable, that the rest of the contract is still valid and in full force.

Article XV

We agree that any dispute arising out of this agreement shall be mediated by a third person mutually acceptable to both of us. The mediator's role shall be to help us arrive at a solution, not to impose one on us. If good faith efforts to arrive at our own solution with the help of a mediator prove to be fruitless, either may make a written request to the other that the dispute be arbitrated.

Our dispute will be submitted to arbitration under the rules of the American Arbitration Association. One arbitrator will hear our dispute. The decision of the arbitrator shall be binding on us and shall be enforceable in any court which has jurisdiction over the controversy.

Signed at _____

_____
Date   Signature

_____
Date   Signature

EXHIBIT 1

The following is the separate personal property of _____:

The following is the separate personal property of _____:

EXHIBIT 2

The following property is jointly-owned by both of us under the terms and in the proportions set forth:

LIVING TOGETHER CONTRACT
(SHARING INCOME AND PROPERTY)

BETWEEN _____

AND _____

We make this agreement to set out the rights and obligations of our joint living arrangement. It is our intention to follow this agreement in a spirit of good faith and cooperation.

Article I

We choose to live together outside the formal state regulations governing marriage and divorce. This is our free choice and desire and we specifically state that we do not intend our relationship to be interpreted as a common law marriage. We further state that we each make this agreement in consideration of the agreement of the other, and that the provision of sexual services by either of us is not the basis of this contract. We further state that this agreement will remain in full force and effect until such time as we separate, or replace or amend it with a subsequent written agreement signed by both of us.

Article II

From the date this contract is signed, we will share all of our income and property accumulated with that income without regard to which of us earns or otherwise receives it. This does not include inheritances or gifts made to one of us. These shall remain the separate property of the person receiving the gift or inheritance under the terms of Article IV.

Article III

At the time of signing of this contract, we have each prepared a list of major items of property that each of us already owns as separate property. This list is marked as Exhibit 1 and is attached to this contract and by this reference made a part of this contract. We shall update this list as it becomes necessary. All separate property of each of us, and any income earned by this property or proceeds received from its sale shall remain the separate property of its owner unless it is transferred to the other person, or to joint ownership under the terms of a written document.

Article IV

We agree that any gifts or inheritances that either of us receives shall be the separate property of that person. Should a gift or inheritance be made to us jointly, we shall consider that we own it in equal shares unless otherwise specified by the donor.

Article V

We agree to maintain such joint and separate bank accounts and joint and separate credit accounts as appear to be reasonable from time to time. We agree to consult one another on all purchases whether for cash or credit which exceed $500 and to make a good faith effort to live within our joint incomes.

Article VI

At present each of us owns a motor vehicle. Under the terms of Article III above, each of us owns our own vehicle as separate property. If in the future either or both of us purchases another vehicle, this vehicle or vehicles shall be jointly owned, except to the extent that money from the sale of an existing separate property vehicle or other separate property is used to pay for the new vehicle(s). If separate property is used to pay for all or part of the new vehicle, it shall belong to the person providing these funds.

Article VII

We do not at present jointly own any real property. Should we jointly buy a house, land in the country, investment property or any other real property, we agree that a copy of a deed to the property and any and all supplementary contracts or agreements covering the property shall be marked as Exhibit 2 and attached to this contract and that when this is done they shall be incorporated into this contract. We further agree that neither of us shall have any rights to, or financial interest in, any separate real property of the other, whether acquired before or after the signing of this contract, unless such interest is set forth in a written agreement signed by both of us.

Article VIII

We realize that our power to contract as far as children are concerned is limited by state law. With this knowledge, and in a spirit of cooperation and mutual respect, we wish to state the following as our agreement should we have children:

1. The father shall sign a written statement acknowledging that he is the father within ten days after birth,

2. Our child(ren) shall be given the following last name: _____,

3. We reject the idea that one of us should do most of the child care tasks while the other provides the income. We will do our best to jointly share the responsibilities of feeding, clothing, loving and disciplining our child(ren).

4. Because of the possible trauma our separation might cause our child(ren), we shall each make a good faith effort to participate in a jointly-agreed upon program of counseling before separation.

5. If we separate, we shall do our best to see that our child(ren) has (have) a good and healthful environment in which to grow up. Specifically, we agree to:

a. Do our best to see that our child(ren) maintain a close and loving relationship with each of us;

b. Share in the upbringing of our child(ren) and, on the basis of our respective abilities to pay, support them;

c. Make a good faith effort to make all major decisions affecting the health and welfare of our child(ren) jointly;

d. Should circumstances dictate that our child(ren) spend a greater portion of the year living with one of us than the other, the person with physical custody shall be sensitive to the needs of the other to have generous rights of visitation and shall cooperate in all practical steps necessary to make visitation as easy as possible;

e. If after separation we have problems communicating as to the best interests of our child(ren), we shall seek out help in the form of a jointly-agreed upon program of counseling to try and work out our differences without having to take our problems to court;

f. At the death of either of us, our child(ren) shall be cared for and raised by the other whether or not we are living together at the time of the death.

Article IX

We agree that either of us can terminate this agreement by simply choosing not to live with the other. Should this be done, all jointly-owned property shall be equally divided at the time of the separation. Neither of us will have any obligation to support the other after separation.

Article X

We agree that from time to time this contract may be amended. All amendments shall be in writing and shall be signed by both of us.

Article XI

We agree that if any court finds any portion of this contract illegal or otherwise unenforceable, that the rest of the contract is still valid and in full force.

Article XII

We agree that any dispute arising out of this agreement shall be mediated by a third person mutually acceptable to both of us. The mediator's role shall be to help us arrive at a solution, not to impose one on us. If good faith efforts to arrive at our own solution with the help of a mediator prove to be fruitless, either may make a written request to the other that the dispute be arbitrated.

Our dispute will be submitted to arbitration under the rules of the American Arbitration Association. One arbitrator will hear our dispute. The decision of the arbitrator shall be binding on us and shall be enforceable in any court which has jurisdiction over the controversy.

Signed at _____

_____   _____
Date   Signature

_____   _____
Date   Signature

EXHIBIT 1

The following is the separate personal property of _____:

The following is the separate personal property of _____:

EXHIBIT 2

The following property is jointly-owned by both of us under the terms and in the proportions set forth:

ACKNOWLEDGEMENT OF PATERNITY

_____ hereby acknowledges that he is the natural

father of _____ born

_____, 19___ to_____ in

_____.

_____ further states that he has welcomed

_____ into his home and that it is his intention to take,

and he believes that he has taken, all steps necessary to fully legitimate _____

_____ for all purposes, including the right to inherit from,

and through, him at the time of his death.

_____ further expressly acknowledges his duty to

properly raise and adequately support _____.

_____   _____
Date   Signature

NOTARIZATION

State of _____

County of _____

On this ___ day of _____, in the year 19___, before me a Notary Public, State of

_____, duly commissioned and sworn, personally appeared

_____, personally known to me (or proved to me

on the basis of satisfactory evidence) to be the person whose name is subscribed to in

the within instrument, and acknowledged to me that _____ executed the same.

   IN WITNESS WHEREOF, I have hereunto set my hand and affixed my official seal in the

_____ County of _____ on the date set forth above.

                              _____
                              Notary Public

                              State of _____

                              My commission expires _____

ACKNOWLEDGEMENT OF PARENTHOOD

_____ and
_____ hereby acknowledge that they are the
natural parents of _____ , born _____ , 19___
in _____ .

_____ and
_____ further state that they have welcomed
_____ into their home and that it is their
intention and belief that _____ is fully legitimated for all
purposes, including the right to inherit from and through _____ .

_____ and
_____ further expressly acknowledge their
legal responsibility to properly raise and adequately support _____ .
_____ .

_____   _____
Date   Signature

_____   _____
Date   Signature

NOTARIZATION

State of _____

County of _____

On this ___ day of _____, in the year 19___, before me a Notary Public, State of _____, duly commissioned and sworn, personally appeared _____, personally known to me (or proved to me on the basis of satisfactory evidence) to be the person whose name is subscribed to in the within instrument, and acknowledged to me that _____ executed the same.

IN WITNESS WHEREOF, I have hereunto set my hand and affixed my official seal in the _____ County of _____ on the date set forth above.

_____
Notary Public

State of _____

My commission expires _____

LANDLORD-TENANT CHECKLIST

The following summarizes the conditions of the premises at _____
_____, on the dates indicated below.

	Condition on Arrival	Condition on Departure
Living Room		
Floors & Floor Covering		
Drapes		
Walls & Ceilings		
Furniture (if any)		
Light Fixtures		
Windows, Screens & Doors		
Other		
Kitchen		
Floor Covering		
Stove & Refrigerator		
Windows, Screens & Doors		
Light Fixtures		
Sink & Plumbing		
Cupboards		
Other		
Dining Room		
Floor & Floor Covering		
Drapes		
Walls & Ceilings		
Furniture (if any)		
Light Fixtures		
Windows, Screens & Doors		
Other		

Bathroom(s)		
Toilet(s)		
Sink(s)		
Shower(s)		
Floor, Walls & Ceiling		
Light Fixtures		
Windows. Screens & Doors		
Other		
Bedrooms		
Floor & Floor Covering		
Walls & Ceilings		
Furniture (if any)		
Light Fixtures		
Windows, Screens & Doors		
Other		
Other Areas		
Floors & Floor Covering		
Windows, Screens & Doors		
Walls & Ceilings		
Furnace		
Air Conditioning (if any)		
Lawn, Ground Covering		
Patio, Terrace or Deck		
Other		

Checklist filled out on moving in on _____, 19_____, and approved by _____, LANDLORD, and _____ _____, TENANT.

Checklist filled out on moving out on _____, 19_____, and approved by _____, LANDLORD, and _____ _____, TENANT.

LIVING TOGETHER CERTIFICATE

and _____

commit themselves to one another as lovers, friends and housemates with
the promise that kindness, good will and a sense of humor shall guide them
through both the rainbows and rainstorms in the days ahead.

AT _____

SIGNATURE _____

DATE _____

SIGNATURE _____

DATE _____

ABOUT RALPH

Ralph is the leader of the "do your own law" movement on the West Coast. As a co-founder of Nolo Press and the author of numerous books and articles aimed at giving the non-lawyer so-called "legal information" to deal with their own life decisions, he has constantly tried to expand the areas in which people can help themselves. He is currently working on his 11th Nolo book, *How to Buy a House in California: Strategies for Beating the Affordability Gap*, and along with Toni, he is the author of *29 Reasons Not to Go to Law School*. Ralph lives in Berkeley with Toni, their daughter Miya, and Annie, a neurotic but sweet orange cat.

ABOUT TONI

Toni is an anthropologist turned lawyer turned graphic artist. She is also the co-author of *California Marriage and Divorce Law*. Toni is an original member of the Nolo Press family and has been involved in the people's law movement since its inception. Her articles have appeared in *New West, Ms.* and *Harper's Bazaar*.

SOFTWARE

willmaker

Nolo Press/Legisoft

Recent statistics say chances are better than 2 to 1 that you haven't written a will, even though you know you should. WillMaker makes the job easy, leading you step by step in a fill-in-the-blank format. Once you've gone through the program, you print out the will and sign it in front of witnesses. Because writing a will is only one step in the estate planning process, WillMaker comes with a 200-page manual providing an overview of probate avoidance and tax planning techniques. National 3rd Ed.

Apple, IBM PC 5 1/4 & 3 1/2, Macintosh $59.95

california incorporator

Attorney Mancuso and Legisoft, Inc.

About half of the small California corporations formed today are done without the services of a lawyer. This easy-to-use software program lets you do the paperwork with minimum effort. Just answer the questions on the screen, and California Incorporator will print out the 35-40 pages of documents you need to make your California corporation legal.

California 1st Ed. (IBM PC 5 1/4 & 3 1/2) $129.00

the california nonprofit corporation handbook— computer edition with disk

Attorney Anthony Mancuso

This is the standard work on how to form a nonprofit corporation in California. Included on the disk are the forms for the Articles, Bylaws and Minutes you will need, as well as regular and special director and member minute forms. Also included are line-by-line instructions explaining how to apply for and obtain federal tax exempt status—this critical step applies to incorporating in all 50 states.

California 1st Ed.

Macintosh, IBM PC 5 1/4 & 3 1/2 $69.00

how to form your own texas corporation— computer edition with disk

Attorney Anthony Mancuso

how to form your own new york corporation— computer edition with disk

Attorney Anthony Mancuso

More and more business people are incorporating to qualify for tax benefits, limited liability status, the benefit of employee status and financial flexibility. These software packages contain all the instructions, tax information and forms you need to incorporate a small business. All organizational forms are on disk.

1st Edition

Macintosh, IBM PC 5 1/4 & 3 1/2 $69.00

for the record

Attorney Warner & Pladsen

A book/software package that helps to keep track of personal and financial records; create documents to give to family members in case of emergency; leave an accurate record for heirs, and allows easy access to all important records with the ability to print out any section.

National 1st Ed.

Macintosh, IBM PC 5 1/4 & 3 1/2 $49.95

ESTATE PLANNING & PROBATE

nolo's simple will book

Attorney Denis Clifford

We feel it's important to remind people that if they don't make arrangements before they die, the state will give their property to certain close family members. If you want a particular person to receive a particular object, you need a will.It's easy to write a legally valid will using this book.

National 2nd Ed. $17.95

plan your estate: wills, probate avoidance, trusts & taxes

Attorney Denis Clifford

A will is only one part of an estate plan. The first concern is avoiding probate so that your heirs won't receive a greatly diminished inheritance years later. This book shows you how to create a "living trust" and gives you the information you need to make sure whatever you have saved goes to your heirs, not to lawyers and the government.

National 1st Ed. $17.95

the power of attorney book

Attorney Denis Clifford

The Power of Attorney Book concerns something you've heard about but probably would rather ignore: Who will take care of your affairs, make your financial and medical decisions, if you can't? With this book you can appoint someone you trust to carry out your wishes.

National 3rd Ed. $19.95

how to probate an estate

Julia Nissley

When a close relative dies, amidst the grieving there are financial and legal details to be dealt with. The natural response is to rely on an attorney, but that response can be costly. With How to Probate an Estate, you can have the satisfaction of doing the work yourself and saving those fees.

California 4th Ed. $24.95

the california nonprofit corporation handbook

Attorney Anthony Mancuso

Used by arts groups, educators, social service agencies, medical programs, environmentalists and many others, this book explains all the legal formalities involved in forming and operating a nonprofit corporation. Included are all the forms for the Articles, Bylaws and Minutes you will need. Also included are complete instructions for obtaining federal 501(c)(3) exemptions and benefits. The tax information in this section applies wherever your corporation is formed.

California 5th Ed. $29.95

how to form your own corporation

Attorney Anthony Mancuso

More and more business people are incorporating to qualify for tax benefits, limited liability status, the benefit of employee status and the financial flexibility. These books contain the forms, instructions and tax information you need to incorporate a small business.

California 7th Ed.	$29.95
Texas 4th Ed.	$24.95
New York 2nd. Ed.	$24.95
Florida 2nd Ed.	$24.95

california professional corporation handbook

Attorney Anthony Mancuso

Health care professionals, marriage, family and child counsellors, lawyers, accountants and members of certain other professions must fulfill special requirements when forming a corporation in California. This edition contains up-to-date tax information plus all the forms and instructions necessary to form a California professional corporation. An appendix explains the special rules that apply to each profession.

California 4th Ed. $34.95

marketing without advertising

Michael Phillips & Salli Rasberry

Every small business person knows that the best marketing plan encourages customer loyalty and personal recommendation. Phillips and Rasberry outline practical steps for building and expanding a small business without spending a lot of money.

National 1st Ed. $14.00

the partnership book

Attorneys Clifford & Warner

Lots of people dream of going into business with a friend. The best way to keep that dream from turning into a nightmare is to have a solid partnership agreement. This book shows how to write an agreement that covers evaluation of partner assets, disputes, buy-outs and the death of a partner.

National 3rd Ed. $18.95

nolo's small business start-up

Mike McKeever

Should you start a business? Should you raise money to expand your already running business? If the answers are yes, this book will show you how to write an effective business plan and loan package.

National 3rd Ed. $17.95

the independent paralegal's handbook: how to provide legal services without going to jail

Attorney Ralph Warner

A large percentage of routine legal work in this country is performed by typists, secretaries, researchers and various other law office helpers generally labeled paralegals. For those who would like to take these services out of the law office and offer them at a reasonable fee in an independent business, attorney Ralph Warner provides both legal and business guidelines.

National 1st Ed. $12.95

getting started as an independent paralegal (two audio tapes)

Attorney Ralph Warner

This set of tapes is a carefully edited version of Nolo Press founder Ralph Warner's Saturday Morning Law School class. It is designed for people who wish to go into business helping consumers prepare their own paperwork in uncontested actions such as bankruptcy, divorce, small business incorporations, landlord-tenant actions, probate, etc. Also covered are how to set up, run, and market your business, as well as a detailed discussion of Unauthorized Practice of Law.

National 1st Ed. $24.95

JUST FOR FUN

devil's advocates:
the unnatural history of lawyers

Jonathan & Andrew Roth

This book is a painless and hilarious education on the legal profession from its rude beginning through its ruder history to its rudest present. Laugh or weep as you learn the historical underpinnings of how and why lawyers have solidly become their own worst enemies.

1st Ed. $12.95

29 reasons not to go to law school

Ralph Warner & Toni Ihara

Lawyers, law students, their spouses and consorts will love this little book with its zingy comments and Thurberesque cartoons, humorously zapping the life of the law.—Peninsula Times Tribune Filled with humor and piercing observations, this book can save you three years, $70,000 and your sanity.

3rd Ed. $9.95

poetic justice

Ed. by Jonathan & Andrew Roth

A unique compilation of humorous quotes about lawyers and the legal system, from Socrates to Woody Allen. $8.95

how to file for bankruptcy

Attorneys Stephen Elias, Robin Leonard & Albin Renauer
Here we show you how to decide whether or not filing for
bankruptcy makes sense and if it does, we give you step-by-step
instructions as to how to do it. *How To File For Bankruptcy*
covers the procedure for completing a Chapter 7 and includes a
discussion of Chapter 13 to help you decide which process is
appropriate for you.
National 1st Ed. $24.95

collect your court judgment

Scott, Elias & Goldoftas
After you win a judgment in small claims, municipal or superior
court, you still have to collect your money. Here are step-by-step
instructions on how to collect your judgment from the debtor's
bank accounts, wages, business receipts, real estate or other assets.
California 1st Ed. $24.95

simple contracts for everyday use

Attorney Stephen Elias
Here are clearly written legal form contracts to: buy and sell
property, borrow and lend money, store and lend personal property, make deposits on goods for later purchase, release others
from personal liability, or pay a contractor to do home repairs.
National 1st Ed. $12.95

social security, medicare & pensions: a sourcebook for older americans

Attorney Joseph L. Matthews & Dorothy Matthews Berman
Social security, medicare and medicaid programs follow a host
of complicated rules. Those over 55, or those caring for someone over 55, will find this comprehensive guidebook invaluable
for understanding and utilizing their rightful benefits. A special
chapter deals with age discrimination in employment and what
to do about it.
National 4th Ed. $15.95

everybody's guide to small claims court

Attorney Ralph Warner
So, the dry cleaner ruined your good flannel suit. Your roof
leaks every time it rains, and the contractor who supposedly
fixed it won't call you back. The bicycle shop hasn't paid for the
tire pumps you sold it six months ago. This book will help you
decide if you have a case, show you how to file and serve papers,
tell you what to bring to court, and how to collect a judgment.
California 8th Ed. $14.95
National 4th Ed. $14.95

for sale by owner

George Devine
In 1986 about 600,000 homes were sold in California at a
median price of $130,000. Most sellers worked with a broker
and paid the 6% commission. For the median home that meant
$7,800. Obviously, that's money that could be saved if you sell
your own house. This book provides the background information and legal technicalities you will need to do the job yourself
and with confidence.
California 1st Ed. $24.95

homestead your house

Attorneys Warner, Sherman & Ihara
Under California homestead laws, up to $60,000 of the equity
in your home may be safe from creditors. But to get the maximum legal protection you should file a Declaration of Homestead before a judgment lien is recorded against you. This book
includes complete instructions and tear-out forms.
California 7th Ed. $9.95

the landlord's law book: vol. 1, rights & responsibilities

Attorneys Brown & Warner
Every landlord should know the basics of landlord-tenant law.
In short, the era when a landlord could substitute common
sense for a detailed knowledge of the law is gone forever. This
volume covers: deposits, leases and rental agreements, inspections (tenants' privacy rights), habitability (rent withholding),
ending a tenancy, liability, and rent control.
California 2nd Ed. $24.95

the landlord's law book: vol. 2, evictions

Attorney David Brown
Even the most scrupulous landlord may sometimes need to evict
a tenant. In the past it has been necessary to hire a lawyer and
pay a high fee. Using this book you can handle most evictions
yourself safely and economically.
California 2nd Ed. $24.95

tenants' rights

Attorneys Moskowitz & Warner
Your "security building" doesn't have a working lock on the
front door. Is your landlord liable? How can you get him to fix
it? Under what circumstances can you withhold rent? When is
an apartment not "habitable?" This book explains the best way
to handle your relationship with your landlord and your legal
rights when you find yourself in disagreement.
California 10th Ed. $15.95

the deeds book: how to transfer title to california real estate

Attorney Mary Randolph
If you own real estate, you'll almost surely need to sign a new
deed at one time or another. *The Deeds Book* shows you how to
choose the right kind of deed, how to complete the tear-out
forms, and how to record them in the county recorder's public
records.
California 1st Ed. $15.95

dog law

Attorney Mary Randolph

There are 50 million dogs in the United States—and, it seems, at least that many rules and regulations for their owners to abide by. *Dog Law* covers topics that everyone who owns a dog, or lives near one, needs to know about disputes, injury or nuisance.

National 1st Ed. $12.95

the criminal records book

Attorney Warren Siegel

We've all done something illegal. If you were one of those who got caught, your juvenile or criminal court record can complicate your life years later. The good news is that in many cases your record can either be completely expunged or lessened in severity. *The Criminal Records Book* takes you step by step through the procedures to: seal criminal records, dismiss convictions, destroy marijuana records, reduce felony convictions.

California 2nd Ed. $14.95

draft, registration and the law

Attorney R. Charles Johnson

This clearly written guidebook explains the present draft law and how registration (required of all male citizens within thirty days of their eighteenth birthday) works. Every available option is presented along with a description of how a draft would work if there were a call tomorrow.

National 2nd Ed. $9.95

fight your ticket

Attorney David Brown

At a trade show in San Francisco recently, a traffic court judge (who must remain nameless) told our associate publisher that he keeps this book by his bench for easy reference.
If you think that ticket was unfair, here's the book showing you what to do to fight it.

California 3rd Ed. $16.95

how to become a united states citizen

Sally Abel Schreuder

This bilingual (English/Spanish) book presents the forms, applications and instructions for naturalization. This step-by-step guide will provide information and answers for legally admitted aliens who wish to become citizens.

National 3rd Ed. $12.95

how to change your name

Attorneys Loeb & Brown

Wish that you had gone back to your maiden name after the divorce? Tired of spelling over the phone V-e-n-k-a-t-a-r-a-m-a-n S-u-b-r-a-m-a-n-i-a-m?
This book explains how to change your name legally and provides all the necessary court forms with detailed instructions on how to fill them out.

California 5th Ed. $19.95

legal research: how to find and understand the law

Attorney Stephen Elias

Legal Research could also be called Volume-Two-for-all-Nolo-Press-Self-Help-Law-Books. A valuable tool for paralegals, law students and legal secretaries, this book provides access to legal information—the legal self-helper can find and research a case, read statutes, and make Freedom of Information Act requests.

National 2nd Ed. $14.95

family law dictionary

Attorneys Leonard and Elias

Written in plain English (as opposed to legalese), the Family Law Dictionary has been compiled to help the lay person doing research in the area of family law (i.e., marriage, divorce, adoption, etc.). Using cross referencs and examples as well as definitions, this book is unique as a reference tool.

National 1st Edition $13.95

patent, copyright & trademark: intellectual property law dictionary

Attorney Stephen Elias

This book uses simple language free of legal jargon to define and explain the intricacies of items associated with trade secrets, copyrights, trademarks and unfair competition, patents and patent procedures, and contracts and warranties.—IEEE Spectrum
If you're dealing with any multi-media product, a new business product or trade secret, you need this book.

National 1st Ed. $17.95

the living together kit
Attorneys Ihara & Warner
Few unmarried couples understand the laws that may affect them. Here are useful tips on living together agreements, paternity agreements, estate planning, and buying real estate.
National 6th Ed. $17.95

how to do your own divorce
Attorney Charles E. Sherman
This is the book that launched Nolo Press and advanced the self-help law movement. During the past 17 years, over 400,000 copies have been sold, saving consumers at least $50 million in legal fees (assuming 100,000 have each saved $500—certainly a conservative estimate).
California 15th Ed. $14.95
Texas 2nd Ed. (Sherman & Simons) $12.95

california marriage & divorce law
Attorneys Warner, Ihara & Elias
For a generation, this practical handbook has been the best resource for the Californian who wants to understand marriage and divorce laws. Even if you hire a lawyer to help you with a divorce, it's essential that you learn your basic legal rights and responsibilities.
California 10th Ed. $15.95

practical divorce solutions
Attorney Charles Ed Sherman
Written by the author of *How to Do Your Own Divorce* (with over 500,000 copies in print), this book provides a valuable guide both to the emotional process involved in divorce as well as the legal and financial decisions that have to be made.
California 1st Ed. $12.95

how to modify and collect child support in california
Attorneys Matthews, Siegel & Willis
California has established landmark new standards in setting and collecting child support. Payments must now be based on both objective need standards and the parents' combined income. Using this book, custodial parents can determine if they are entitled to higher child support payments and can implement the procedures to obtain that support.
California 2nd Ed. $17.95

the guardianship book
Lisa Goldoftas & Attorney David Brown
Thousands of children in California are left without a guardian because their parents have died, abandoned them or are unable to care for them. *The Guardianship Book* provides step-by-step instructions and the forms needed to obtain a legal guardianship without a lawyer.
California 1st Ed. $19.95

a legal guide for lesbian and gay couples
Attorneys Curry & Clifford
A Legal Guide contains crucial information on the special problems facing lesbians and gay men with children, civil rights legislation, and medical/legal issues.
National 5th Ed. $17.95

how to adopt your stepchild in california
Frank Zagone & Attorney Mary Randolph
For many families that include stepchildren, adoption is a satisfying way to guarantee the family a solid legal footing. This book provides sample forms and complete step-by-step instructions for completing a simple uncontested adoption by a stepparent.
California 3rd Ed. $19.95

how to copyright software
Attorney M.J. Salone
Copyrighting is the best protection for any software. This book explains how to get a copyright and what a copyright can protect.
National 3rd Ed. $34.95

the inventor's notebook
Fred Grissom & Attorney David Pressman
The best protection for your patent is adequate records. The Inventor's Notebook provides forms, instructions, references to relevant areas of patent law, a bibliography of legal and non-legal aids, and more. It helps you document the activities that are normally part of successful independent inventing.
National 1st Ed. $19.95

legal care for your software
Attorneys Daniel Remer & Stephen Elias
If you write programs you intend to sell, or work for a software house that pays you for programming, you should buy this book. If you are a freelance programmer doing software development, you should buy this book.—Interface
This step-by-step guide for computer software writers covers copyright laws, trade secret protection, contracts, license agreements, trademarks, patents and more.
National 3rd Ed. $29.95

patent it yourself
Attorney David Pressman
You've invented something, or you're working on it, or you're planning to start...Patent It Yourself offers help in evaluating patentability, marketability and the protective documentation you should have. If you file your own patent application using this book, you can save from $1500 to $3500.
National 2nd Ed. $29.95

nolo

ORDER FORM

Quantity	Title	Unit Price	Total

Sales Tax (CA residents only):

7 1/4%   Alameda, Contra Costa, San Diego, San Mateo & Santa Clara counties

6 3/4%   Fresno, Inyo, LA, Sacramento, San Benito, San Francisco & Santa Cruz counties

6 1/4%   All others

Subtotal _____

Sales Tax _____

TOTAL _____

Method of Payment:

☐ Check enclosed

☐ VISA   ☐ Mastercard

Acct # _____ Exp._____

Signature _____

Phone (   )_____

Ship to:

Name _____

Address _____

_____

Mail to:

NOLO PRESS
950 Parker Street
Berkeley CA 94710

For faster service, use your credit card and our toll-free numbers:

Monday-Friday 9-5 Pacific Time

US		1-800-992-6656
CA	(outside 415 area)	1-800-445-6656
	(inside 415 area)	1-415-549-1976
General Information		**1-415-549-1976**

Prices subject to change

Please allow 1-2 weeks for delivery

Delivery is by UPS; no P.O. boxes, please

ORDER DIRECT AND WE PAY POSTAGE & HANDLING!

One Year Free!

Nolo Press wants you to have top quality and up-to-date legal information. The **Nolo News**, our "Access to Law" quarterly newspaper, contains an update section which will keep you abreast of any changes in the law relevant to **The Living Together Kit**. You'll find interesting articles on a number of legal topics, book reviews and our ever-popular lawyer joke column.

Send in the registration card below and receive FREE a one-year subscription to the **Nolo News** (normally $9.00).

Your subscription will begin with the first quarterly issue published after we receive your card.

NOLO PRESS
The Living Together Kit Registration Card

We would like to hear from you. Please let us know if the book met your needs. Fill out and return this card for a FREE one-year subscription to the *Nolo News*. In addition, we'll notify you when we publish a new edition of **The Living Together Kit.** (This offer is good in the U.S.only)

Name _____

Address _____

City _____ State _____ Zip _____

Your occupation_____

Briefly, for what purpose did you use this book?

_____

_____

_____

Did you find the information in the book helpful?

(extremely helpful) 1   2   3   4   5   (not at all)

Where did you hear about the book?

Have you used other Nolo books?____Yes, ____No

Where did you buy the book? _____

Suggestions for improvement:_____

_____

_____

_____

_____

_____

_____

_____

_____

_____

_____

_____

_____

▲

[Nolo books are]..."written in plain language, free of legal mumbo jumbo, and spiced with witty personal observations."

—ASSOCIATED PRESS

▲

"Well-produced and slickly written, the [Nolo] books are designed to take the mystery out of seemingly involved procedures, carefully avoiding legalese and leading the reader step-by-step through such everyday legal problems as filling out forms, making up contracts, and even how to behave in court."

—SAN FRANCISCO EXAMINER

▲

"...Nolo publications...guide people simply through the how, when, where and why of law."

—WASHINGTON POST

▲

"Increasingly, people who are not lawyers are performing tasks usually regarded as legal work... And consumers, using books like Nolo's, do routine legal work themselves."

—NEW YORK TIMES

▲

"...All of [Nolo's] books are easy-to-understand, are updated regularly, provide pull-out forms...and are often quite moving in their sense of compassion for the struggles of the lay reader."

—SAN FRANCISCO CHRONICLE

Affix
25¢
Stamp

NOLO PRESS
950 Parker St.
Berkeley, CA 94710